ARISTOTLE
SELECTIONS

ARISTOTLE
SELECTIONS

EDITED BY

W. D. ROSS

CHARLES SCRIBNER'S SONS
NEW YORK

5 7 9 11 13 15 17 19 F/P 20 18 16 14 12 10 8 6

Printed in the United States of America
ISBN 0-684-14699-1

INTRODUCTION

In any attempt to understand the mind of Aristotle, perhaps the most important thing of all to remember is that he was an Ionian, a member of that branch of the Greek race which was responsible for the origin of the philosophy of nature in the school of Miletus, and which was distinguished from other branches by a devouring curiosity about the facts of nature and their explanation. A new (or almost new) note had been introduced into Greek philosophy by two men of a different origin, Socrates and Plato, the only Athenians among all the great philosophers of Greece: the note of interest in the life and destiny of man rather than in the explanation of natural fact. Aristotle's philosophy may be regarded as due to the fusion of these two influences. But he was from first to last an Ionian, an observer of the facts of nature, a man for whom no problem was too detailed to whet his curiosity. This has its bad side. He sometimes fails to see the wood for the trees. He dwells so much on the minutiae of controversy that his general *Weltanschauung* on some important points remains obscure in spite of the great volume of his works that has come down to us. But it makes him a most effective complement to Plato. Each to some extent supplies the deficiencies of the other. Plato's rich imagination, the unifying tendency of his mind, which led him to great generalizations that fire the mind of his readers, his discontent with things as they are and his flight from 'things here'; the facts of the sensible world, to 'things yonder', the world of pure Forms, his revolutionary views about political and social life, are balanced by Aristotle's absorbed interest in the 'given' in all its forms, his appeal to the 'observed facts', his acceptance of existing institutions like the family and private property which for all their fallibility he yet perceives to correspond to permanent needs of human nature. And it is perhaps not going too far to say that this broad difference is at bottom racial.

The second influence that must be reckoned with is a more particular one. He was the son of a physician, and a member of a family which claimed descent from Asclepius and in which the practice of medicine was hereditary. It is not unlikely that as a boy he helped his father in dissections, and it seems certain that he practised dissection in later life. Thus the racial tendency to minute observation was reinforced by a family bias. And it is worth noting that it was just in medical science that the most minute and most comprehensive observations had been and were being made by Hippocrates and the members of his school. Though Aristotle himself does not seem to have followed up the study of this branch of science, yet it is the Hippocratean writings that gave a model for his observations on animals.

The third great influence on his thought is that of Plato. He was for some nineteen years a member of Plato's school, and to Plato's influence every page of Aristotle's philosophical writings bears witness. While he expresses a growing dissatisfaction with Plato's otherworldliness, it would be true to say that almost every one of his leading ideas is the modification of one inherited from Plato. His 'universals' are Plato's Ideas shorn of their separateness and asserted to exist only 'in' things, not 'over' or 'apart from' them. The main lines of his classification of the faculties of the soul are taken from Plato, though he carries the analysis much further and has perhaps more sense of the continuity between different faculties. Plato opposes reason broadly to perception. So does Aristotle, but he points out that perception is of the individual as characterized by general qualities, and that reason apprehends general qualities as present in individual things. His ethics, with its insistence on a basis in unreflective habituation to do good acts *and* on a later reflection on the reasons for doing them, is in both respects Platonic. A careful commentator can point to Platonic origins for a very great proportion of the things Aristotle says. Yet it would be a vast mistake to describe Aristotle as a mere borrower or as a mere exponent of a watered-down and vulgarized Platonism. He constantly brings into a system suggestions which in Plato remain isolated. Plato had reached the conceptions of 'substance', 'quality', 'quantity', and 'relation'; but the attempt to form an exhaustive list of categories seems (in spite of some recent endeavours to show the contrary) to be an original idea. And, more broadly, Plato's view of the world, which is primarily interested in 'being', is transformed into something very different by a constant dwelling on the problems of 'becoming'.

There is a wide-spread tendency to contrast Plato the mathematician with Aristotle the biologist; to describe Aristotle as incompetent in mathematical questions and to assign to biology a large part in the determination of his general system. On the first of these two questions the truth seems to be that Aristotle was a competent mathematician, abreast of the knowledge of his day, but that he did not make new additions to it, and that pretty much the same is true of Plato. Some of Aristotle's mathematical allusions (e.g. in his account of justice) are difficult to follow, but this is simply due to the fact that there, more than in most places, we have mere lecturenotes which would be expanded in delivery and made clearer by blackboard demonstrations. The mathematics there involved is so simple compared with that which he uses in other passages (e.g. in his account of the rainbow) that it would be absurd to suppose he did not understand it. The things I would mention as indicating very considerable mathematical power are his discussions of the infinite and of the continuous; they are, so far as we know, really pioneer discussions for which nothing but Zeno's paradoxes had prepared the way; and he criticizes Zeno with great ability. The difference between Plato and Aristotle with regard to mathematics is that Plato was properly impressed with the great future of the study, more so than Aristotle seems to have been, and that he was more interested in the *philosophy* of mathematics. Plato's latest thought seems indeed to have been very largely occupied with the nature of number and with its significance as the basis of everything in the universe. This, however, was not a new thing; Plato was carrying on the Pythagorean tradition. And for myself I have little doubt that he perpetuated some of the Pythagorean crudities. Aristotle complains that 'the men of the present day'—the Platonists—have turned philosophy into mathematics. It is very hard to arrive at a just decision on the merits of this controversy. In the books in which he enters most fully into it, the last two of the *Metaphysics,* Aristotle is dealing with three distinct views, those of Plato, Speusippus, and Xenocrates. But from motives of delicacy in criticizing men who were or had been his friends he hardly ever mentions them by name. For the most part he refers to the theories by description; and it is by no means easy to sort out the references and assign them respectively to the three thinkers. And for these theories we have very little evidence except

what we gather from Aristotle himself. The recon-
struction of Plato's thought is thus extremely uncertain,
and it is accordingly difficult to know how far Aristotle's
criticisms are justified. His attitude towards all these
theories is in the main critical, but he is careful to point
out good features in each, though very likely not *all*
their good features. I should not like to say that he
never goes wrong in his criticism of them, but I believe
his main line of argument to be correct. He is strongly
opposed to what he calls elsewhere the 'transition to
another class of things', the attempt to reduce the irre-
ducible. He sees clearly that the point is a different
thing from the mere arithmetical unit, and that no number of points will make a line, no number of lines a
plane, no number of planes a solid. He is therefore
opposed to any attempt to derive material things from
mere numbers or to identify the material element of
things, as Plato had done, with space. He insists that
there must be matter which has spatial characteristics
but is something more than they.

Let us turn to Aristotle's biology. One more often
sees vague references to the influence of biology on his
system than attempts to exhibit it in detail, and it is
worth while to make such an attempt. How far, for
instance, is his insistence on the distinction between
potentiality and actuality due to his study of the phenomena of growth and development. Not in any special
way, I think. He is just as likely to illustrate the distinction by the presence of the statue potentially in the
block of marble, or by the transmutation of the four
elements, as by biological facts. It seems to be due to
a more general feature of his thought, his close absorp-
tion in observed facts, of whatever nature they may be.
He finds change everywhere, and he finds that he cannot
explain change by the notion of actual being alone, but

must bring in the notion of the A which is just not B but on the point of becoming so. I should regard his interest in biology and his metaphysics of potentiality and actuality as results of the same cause rather than the first as the cause of the second. Again, take his doctrine of fixed genera and indivisible species. He holds that it is not an arbitrary matter which of the general terms applicable to a thing we treat as standing for the species to which it belongs. There is one *infima species* to which the thing essentially belongs; its other attributes are logically subsidiary—properties or accidents. Here I think biology did greatly affect his thought. There is no dictum that he more often repeats than 'it takes a man to produce a man'. True, it needs no profound research to discover this. But it is an instance of a fact to which biological studies were constantly directing his attention—the fact of the apparent (and real, so long as we do not take geological periods of time into account) fixity of animal species. This fact greatly impressed him. It is in the long run his main argument for the presence of teleology in nature. 'How careful of the type she seems' is one of his leading thoughts about nature. But here again it was not only biology that led his thoughts in this direction. For in mathematics—in the division of number, for instance, into odd and even, or of triangle into equilateral, isosceles, and scalene—he had evidence, and much more secure evidence, of rigid classifications inherent in the nature of things. In fact, if he had let his biological studies influence his general thought more, he would have been led away from his doctrine of natural kinds. For he is fully conscious of the difficulty of classification in biology, of the fact that animals may be classified either into hot-blooded and cold-blooded, or according to their mode of reproduction, or in various other ways between which convenience is the main reason for our choice. He is aware too of the existence of intermediate species not belonging distinctly to any one of the superior genera.

Another direction in which he was influenced by biology was his political thought. There is an interesting passage of the *Politics* in which he envisages a classification of constitutions less crude than the customary one into rule by one, by few, or by many; a classification which takes account of the various forms assumed in different states by the organs of the body politic, as biological classification takes account of the forms assumed by the bodily organs. And it is not fanciful to see in the fourth and sixth books of the *Politics* an attempt to achieve for states the precise description of their types which he does for animals in the *Historia Animalium*. Yet here again it would perhaps be true to describe his biology and his political researches as products of the same observational habit of mind, rather than the one as the cause of the other.

Aristotle is much more successful in his biology than in his physics, his chemistry, and his astronomy. But it was not because he thought different methods were appropriate in biology from those appropriate in the other sciences. In both alike his object is to study the phenomena as carefully as possible and to put forward only such theories as will 'save' them. His mind is as much set as Bacon's was on putting observation before theory, and on making the theory fit the facts rather than the facts the theory. But in the physical sciences, more than in biology, he was under the sway of a body of existing beliefs which it did not occur to him to doubt, any more than it did to any of his contemporaries. And he was hampered far more in the one study than in the other by the lack of precise instruments of observation, of measurement, and of weighing. It is only at a comparatively late period in the development of the biological sciences that these instruments become necessary if further advance is to be made; and Aristotle was thus able to do much to advance the early study of these sciences. In the more abstract physical sciences everything seems to depend from the start on precise quantitative data; in the absence of these, theory is bound to go far astray and always has done so; if we do not get the quantities right we get nothing right. In the more concrete sciences, which take account of the secondary qualities, much good work can be done in the observation of these long before quantitative exactness is reached, though at a later stage such exactness is a necessary condition of further progress. Before Aristotle's time, the Hippocratean school had made much more valuable researches into the symptoms, if not into the cure, of disease, than any that had been made in physics or in chemistry. Of the physical sciences astronomy alone had made considerable progress; and there the Greeks had inherited the labours of the Chaldaeans and were able to apply to good effect their own wonderful mathematical genius. Thus, in the main, Aristotle's success in biology and his failure in physics and chemistry reflect the general position of affairs in his time, as well as the inherent character of the sciences themselves.

Aristotle's was an essentially tidy mind. He loved to define, and he loved to classify. Both these tendencies have their merits and their defects. In philosophy at any rate, and to some extent in science, we do not get far unless we train ourselves to use our terms strictly, and to define them when they are definable. But it is a mistake to think that our main work is then over. Aristotle, to do him justice, did not make this mistake. His mistake was rather the opposite one, of supposing that definition was a comparatively easy preliminary task, and that the main work of science lies in deducing conclusions from definitions, whereas the truth is that it is often only after prolonged study of our terms that we are able to make their meaning precise, and that even then we can deduce little or nothing from our definitions.   In his logic Aristotle lays it down that science should start with axioms, definitions, and hypotheses of the existence of the fundamental objects of the science.   There is, I suppose, no science but mathematics in which this will take us very far.   It was certainly not by this method that he reached the success he did in biology.   But probably he did not think of biology as a science.   By a science he meant just a body of research in which this method *does* work, i.e. a mathematical science, and he never, I think, applies the name science quite deliberately to anything else.   Biology, psychology, ethics, politics, were rather inquiries than sciences.   He expressly disclaims for his results in ethics, for instance, such certainty as he claims for the results of science proper.   His results will, he thinks, at best be true 'for the most part'. He says definitely that mathematical exactness is not to be looked for here; and I suppose he would have said the same of biology.

His love of classification has probably had more fruitful results.   To it we owe his doctrine of the categories, which as regards its main members, substance, quality, and relation, remains the foundation of our attempts to inventorize the contents of the universe.   To it we owe his classification of the sciences themselves (if we use 'science' in a sense less strict than that assigned to it in his logic).   In a dialogue of Plato we are apt to find— and this is part of its charm—metaphysics and ethics, psychology and politics, all present together.   And that method has its justification.   All things do belong together, and the last word cannot be said about anything till we have the synoptic vision which will make us spectators of all time and all existence. But meantime our progress is aided by a sorting out of our problems into their main groups, and a separate consideration of these groups. This is what Aristotle was the first human being to do with any thoroughness; and to him we owe not only the names of many of our sciences but to a large extent the general lines of division between them. To him again we owe a much more elaborate attempt to classify the faculties of the soul than any that existed before him. Faculty psychologies have been much attacked, and they are open to attack when they think that by assigning a function to a named faculty they have explained it. Aristotle is not, I think, open to this objection. He reasons correctly that if the soul has a certain class of activities, it must have a power to perform these activities, and he makes great use of the faculties as a means of classification of and ready reference to the phenomena. But he does not, or does not as a rule, think that he has achieved his task in so doing. He still brings an unwearied curiosity to the solution of particular problems. Indeed, whatever may be thought of his success in solving problems, few people have ever either descried so many, or seen so clearly which are the most important.

The attempt to trace the development of Aristotle's thought through his works is still in its infancy. The application of stylistic tests for determining the order of the works, which has been so fruitful in the case of Plato, has hardly been tried in the case of Aristotle, though Rudolph Eucken, who afterwards became so famous in another sphere, supplied a valuable contribution to this by his early studies of Aristotle's use of prepositions and of particles. It may however be questioned whether this method is likely ever to throw so much light on the Aristotelian as it has on the Platonic corpus. The general impression made by Aristotle's style is that it varies much less from first to last than Plato's does. Nor are Aristotle's allusions to historical events likely to yield very decisive results. They are, apart from the *Politics,* very few; and in works unpublished in the author's lifetime we have always to take account of the possibility of allusions having been inserted by the author into works written long before. The main line of inquiry must take the form of a speculation as to the changes of interest and of doctrine which are psychologically most probable. Valuable work in this direction was done by Mr. T. Case in his *Encyclopaedia Britannica* article, in which he pointed out that the works in which Aristotle is most Platonic are likely to have been the earliest. This had long been assumed in the case of the *Topics,* of which the whole central part (Bks. II-VII. 2) moves almost entirely within the Platonic circle of ideas, and betrays no knowledge of the syllogism. Mr. Case points out that the *De Interpretatione,* which one scholar had described as the latest of Aristotle's works, must be an early work, since the analysis of the judgment in it is much more primitive than that in the *Prior Analytics* and more akin to that in Plato's *Sophistes.* The *Eudemian Ethics,* which most modern scholars had treated as later than Aristotle, he successfully shows to be a genuine work of the master, and an early one, standing in a closer relation to Plato than the *Nicomachean Ethics* does. The question has been examined more systematically by Prof. Werner Jaeger, the first scholar to select the *development* of Aristotle's thought as the subject of a long and elaborate book. While details of his theory are open to doubt, his main conclusions are not, I think, likely to be upset, and he has thrown a flood of light on the whole Aristotelian question. His general conclusion is that we can trace in

Aristotle a steady progress from the exposition of a
broad *Weltanschauung*, Platonic in its general character,
and a pre-occupation with the super-sensible world, to
the splitting up of the world of knowledge into definite
spheres and the pursuit of intensive research into the observable facts in these spheres, notably in those of biology and of comparative politics. We must also take
account of the fact established, as I think, by Prof.
D'Arcy Thompson, that the biological works (at least
the *History of Animals*) must have been begun early,
during Aristotle's residence in the Troad and in Lesbos.
The general order of the works which we can deduce
from these considerations is that Aristotle began by writing dialogues on the Platonic model, but that in the latest
of these (notably in the *De Philosophia)* his protest
against Plato's 'separation' of the Forms and numbers
from sensible things began to be felt. The dialogues
belong in the main to the time of his membership of
the Platonic Academy (366-347). To the period of his
stay in the Troad, in Lesbos, and in Macedonia (347-
335 or 334) belongs the earliest form of those extant
works which are largely Platonic in character—the *Organon,* the *Physics,* the *De Caelo,* the *De Generatione
et Corruptione,* the third book of the *De Anima,* the
Eudemian Ethics, the Platonic parts of the *Metaphysics*
and the *Politics,* and the *Historia Animalium.* To his
second Athenian period (335 or 334-322) belong the rest
of his works of research—the *Meteorologica,* the bulk
of the works on psychology and biology, the collection
of constitutions, and the other great historical researches
which we know little more than by name. To this
period also belong the *Nicomachean Ethics,* the *Rhetoric,* and the completion and working up of the extant
works begun in the middle period. It would seem safe
to assume that Aristotle's general development is likely

to have been away from the Platonism which as a young
man he accepted and inculcated in his earliest dialogues.
Now Plato's thought is mainly metaphysical and ethical,
and these are the subjects to which Aristotle's training
in the Platonic school would first direct his attention.   It
is these that occupy his thoughts chiefly in the dialogues.
In the latest dialogues we find him already beginning to
break with Platonic metaphysics, but much less completely than in most of his extant works.   It is likely
that this tendency ran pretty continuously through his
life.   In the *Categories* he still expresses a qualified
Platonism.   Plato had made Forms or essences the real
substances; sensible things belonged for him to the
world of the half-real.   In the *Categories* individual
things are for Aristotle the primary substances; but he
still recognizes species and genera as secondary substances.   In the *Metaphysics* he expresses himself more
strongly by saying that species and genera are not,
strictly speaking, substances at all.   And within the
Metaphysics we can note a further change.   In Bk. Z.
Aristotle's analysis of sensible substance is into form
and matter, where 'form' is his restatement of the
Platonic Forms, and 'matter' is his restatement of
Plato's 'space' or 'receptacle of generation'.   But in
Θ he tends to supplement this analysis of a sensible
thing as it is at a moment by an analysis of its history
in successive stages of potentiality and actuality.
Again, Λ differs from ZHΘ by the recognition of a
third element, alongside of form and matter, viz. privation; and this too involves the treatment of sensible
things as undergoing change rather than as they are
at a moment.   Now this is also the analysis offered in
the *Physics*.   In another respect too Λ has affinities
with the *Physics* and seems definitely to presuppose it.
The brief argument in Λ leading up to the doctrine of

the First Mover is a résumé of the elaborate argument in *Physics* V-VIII. I am inclined to think, therefore, that Λ represents a later phase of Aristotle's thought than ZHΘ, and that in the interval the *Physics,* either in its present or in an earlier form, was composed. I would add two further points which to my mind confirm the view that Λ represents the culmination of his metaphysical thought. (1) The first is that this is, more perhaps than any other book, that in which he emphasizes the primary reality of the individual thing. He says here of the universal, more boldly than he speaks of it anywhere else, that it does not exist, and this would naturally represent the latest point in the progress of his thought, if we assume that this was steadily away from Platonism to what I may call Ionicism. And (2) while the discussions of ZHΘ seem to be a natural development out of Plato's idealism, the discussion of the infinite and the continuous, elaborated in is *Physics* and presupposed by Λ, is an achievement for which Plato does not prepare the way and which must have been the fruit of Aristotle's maturity.

Besides metaphysics, the other great subject to which Aristotle's early Platonic training drew his attention was ethics. What sort of development of his thought can we trace here? The sequence is provided by the lost *Protrepticus,* and (as I think) by the *Magna Moralia,* the *Eudemian Ethics,* and the *Nicomachean Ethics.* At first Aristotle seems to have adopted Plato's ascetic view of the relation between soul and body, and of the unimportance of external goods as a condition of happiness. On Plato's death the ascetic view was carried on and stated in an extreme form by Speusippus, but Xenocrates taught that happiness, while depending primarily on virtue, required also bodily and external goods. This tolerant view, substantially identical with that of Aristotle, was not improbably worked out by the two men when they were together at Assos. Both in the *Magna Moralia,* in the *Eudemian Ethics,* and in *Nicomachean Ethics* VII, Aristotle expresses as against Speusippus the view that pleasure is not a mere movement or disturbance of the soul, but an activity. It is only in *Nicomachean Ethics* X, that we find what must be a later refinement on that view, the doctrine that pleasure is not activity but the feeling that accompanies activity. This distinction, so plainly true, was not likely to have been abandoned once it had been reached, and I therefore regard this book as the culminating point of Aristotle's ethics; and this alone is enough to date the final form of the *Nicomachean Ethics* as later than the *Magna Moralia* and the *Eudemian Ethics.* And further, since *Metaphysics* Λ describes God's activity as *being* pleasure, *Nicomachean Ethics* X seems to be later than Λ.

What other traces of development can be found in the three extant ethical works? The final part of the *Eudemian Ethics* is a discussion of two things, good fortune and 'gentlemanliness'. It finds the proper limit of the bodily goods included under good fortune to lie in that desire and possession of them which will conduce to the contemplation of God. This is a more definitely theological and therefore, I think, a more Platonic conclusion than the ideal of the contemplative life of science and philosophy which we find in the *Nicomachean Ethics.* And the limit of 'gentlemanliness' is similarly stated to be the service and contemplation of God and the control of desire by reason. This again is more theological than the conclusion of the *Nicomachean Ethics.* Again, the *Eudemian Ethics* describes the ideal condition of the soul as that in which reason as little as possible 'perceives' the desiring element of the soul. This is more ascetic and Platonic than the ideal of the *Nicomachean*

Ethics, in which the life of moral action (which involves desire) is a factor, though a subordinate one. The ideal of 'gentlemanliness' is itself a somewhat old-fashioned Greek ideal which we find in Herodotus, Thucydides, Xenophon, and Plato. The substitution for this of the contemplative life seems pretty plainly a later and more individual view of Aristotle's own.

The other main point in which Aristotle's progress in ethical thought can be traced is in the doctrine of φρονησις. Plato draws no distinction between φρονησις and σοφια ; they are both simply names for wisdom. The *Eudemian Ethics* starts from the position of Plato's *Philebus.* There Plato asks whether the good is φρονησ ι or pleasure. Similarly the *Eudemian Ethics* asks whether it is φρονησις pleasure, or virtue. In this work φρονησις first appears as a name for speculative philosophy. Then it is connected with the practical philosphy of Socrates and co-ordinated with politics and economics. Finally it is inserted among the moral virtues and treated as a mean between cunning and simplicity. Furthur, it does not occur in the division of virtues into moral and intellectual, nor in the definition of virtue. Contrast with this the clear-cut and consistent doctrine of the *Nicomachean Ethics,* in which it is treated throughout as an intellectual virtue, but as that theoretical virtue which is concerned only with what we ought to do, and as the intellectual basis of moral excellence. Here we can see Aristotle moving away from the Platonic doctrine that there is one knowledge of universal good which is at the same time metaphysics and moral insight.

I suppose the development of these metaphysical and ethical views to have been going on pretty much through Aristotle's life from the age of about thirty onwards. But meantime other interests which had less of a starting-point in Plato seem to have sprung up. His residence in Lesbos seems to have aroused the interest in the observation of living things, which was already latent in his Ionic nature. He now began the composition of the *History of Animals,* and on this followed the more theoretical biological works, and, I suppose, the *De Anima* and the *Parva Naturalia.* The instinct of observation, comparison, and classification which found its first expression here was probably extended to the sphere of political life, and to this we owe the development of his political thought. The chronological order of the books of the *Politics* is highly problematic. But it seems to be fairly safe to regard Books I-III as its earliest part. Bk. I starts with a criticism of the sophistic doctrine that the state exists only by convention, and of the Platonic doctrine that the state differs only in size from other communities. It has, that is to say, very definite *points d'appui* in earlier thought. Bk. II similarly starts with a criticism of Plato's views in the *Republic* and the *Laws.* Bk. III is a discussion, Platonic and indeed Socratic in spirit, of such questions as 'what is a state?', 'what is a citizen?', 'is the good man the same as the good citizen?'; and continues with a classification of constitutions based on that in Plato's *Politicus.* Bks. IV-VI are a study, for which there is far less preparation in earlier thought and which is very much in the vein of Aristotle's biological researches, of the detailed structure of the various kinds of state; Bk. IV, it has been aptly said, is Aristotle's morphology, and Bk. V his pathology, of the state. We see Aristotle gradually passing from a study of broad philosophical problems about the state such as we find in Plato to a more historical and scientific study of it. Further, the mass of detailed observation of different constitutions in these middle books not improbably presupposes the descrip-

tion of 158 constitutions which Aristotle and his pupils
are known to have carried out, and for this a considerable time must be allowed. Bks. VII and VIII form
a puzzling problem. Occupied as they are with the
study of the ideal constitution, they seem to Jaeger to
be plainly early, and he places them before Bks. IV-
VI in date. On the other hand, von Arnim has pointed
out that it is natural to suppose that the detailed study
of the six constitutions, begun in Bk. III, would be continued in the next book, as it actually is in Bk. IV,
whereas the study of the ideal state in Bks. VII and
VIII, which hardly gets beyond the topic of education,
would interrupt most seriously the study of the six constitutions. He points out also that the somewhat democratic constitution of Bks. VII and VIII, in which all
the citizens in turn are ruled and rule, is very different
from the aristocratic and Platonic ideal adumbrated in
Bk. III. On the whole I think he is right in treating
Bks. VII and VIII as being the latest part of the *Politics* and representing the limit, in this case not a very
extreme one, of Aristotle's reaction from Plato.

Where, in all this development, does Aristotle's logic,
the most definitive of all his additions to knowledge, come
in? For reasons in part already given I am inclined
to date the *Categories* early. The doctrine of the Categories is so omnipresent in his extant works that it is
natural to suppose he must have written it down early
in his career, and in the first nine chapters, at any rate,
there is nothing that looks unlike an early work. The
purely linguistic beginning, with the distinction of ambiguous from unambiguous terms and of words from
sentences, seems to me indicative of an early origin. So
is the recognition of genera and species as substances,
in contrast with the later description of them as
elements in the substance of individual things.

Jæger argues that Aristotle must have gone far in his discussion of logical inquiries before he ventured on the criticism of Platonic theories in the early dialogue *Eudemus,* but of this I cannot feel convinced. He had undoubtedly thought about logical questions, but I see little trace of systematic logical doctrine, such as we find in all the parts of the *Organon.* Fairly early, however, if it is by Aristotle at all, the *Categories* must have been. The *De interpretatione* is even more unmistakably early. It starts with Plato's simple analysis of the sentence into the noun and the verb, and the examples of the proposition given in the early chapters are two-word propositions such as 'man is', 'man walks'. But later he introduces another type of proposition, 'man is just', etc., and makes what must be called a first attempt to disentangle the copula from the predicate. Propositions of this type are described as those in which 'the *is* is a third element asserted in addition', 'a third noun—or verb—added to the other two'. *Man* and *just* are the 'underlying things', and *is* is an 'addition'. "Aristotle is aware of the distinction between the existential and the copulative *is*. But he has as yet no very clear idea of their relation. He sees that the analysis of the proposition into noun and verb is not *always* sufficient. But he makes no attempt to analyse *all* propositions into subject, predicate, and copula. He sees that the copula is not an element of the proposition on all fours with its subject and predicate. But he does not point out that it is simply the expression of the act of asserting a connexion, in distinction from the elements of reality whose connexion is asserted. In the *Prior Analytics,* which represents Aristotle's maturer thought, the copula appears completely disengaged from the predicate. When propositions are considered as premisses of syllogism, which is the point of view of the

Prior Analytics, it becomes necessary to isolate in *every* proposition a predicate which may become the subject of another proposition; and Aristotle accordingly formulates all propositions there in the form 'A is B' (or 'B belongs to A'.)" [1]

The bulk of the *Topics* again is early. If you consider the vast part which dialectical discussion plays in the age of the sophists and in the pages of Plato, it would seem natural to expect that Aristotle's thought would be drawn pretty early to the study of it. Further, the main part of the work constantly uses methods of argument, and instances, that were common form in the Academy. The doctrine of the syllogism, which (we must remember) is just as applicable to dialectical as to scientific reasoning, is entirely absent. The whole mode of thought strikes one as immature in comparison with the *Analytics.* And above all, once Aristotle had discovered how really to prove things, it is hard to believe that he would have devoted so much time to showing how it is possible to reason in an ingenious but essentially futile fashion about them.

How Aristotle reached the most original of all his discoveries, the reduction of reasoning to the syllogistic form, I do not pretend to know. Those who read Maier's volumes will find there various possible starting-points in earlier thought. Between the starting-points, however, and the doctrine itself there is a great gulf, and nothing other than one of the flashes of insight of which only genius is capable will explain his arrival at the doctrine. For the working out of the doctrine into its details, a working out which, apart from the treatment of probable inference, is formally almost perfect, a considerable time must be allowed. On this supervened the *Posterior Analytics,* in which the doctrine of the

[1] Cf. Ross's *Aristotle,* pp. 27-28.

syllogism is presupposed and much that requires a deeper analysis is added. While the *Prior Analytics* is pure logic, in the *Posterior Analytics* metaphysical considerations come in as well; and in view of many points of contact I would hazard a guess that this work belongs to about the same time as Metaphysics Z.

The above account is almost entirely conjectural; very few of my suggestions as to relative date and to development can be demonstrated, and some are not unlikely to be disproved. But it may be of some help to students to have before them even a conjectural account of the direction in which the mind of the author they are studying is moving.

The present selection begins (§§ 1-13) with Logic, which Aristotle regarded as a necessary preliminary to the study of any of the sciences (§§ 4, 20). Here special attention should be paid to the doctrine of the categories, in which terms are classified with reference to the kinds of things they stand for, and to the doctrine of the predicables, in which predicates are classified with reference to their relation to their subjects. Both of these doctrines are fundamental in Aristotle's whole teaching and have played a great part in the history of philosophy; and the distinctions of substance, quality, quantity, relation, and of genus, differentia, property, accident have entered into the common vocabulary of educated men. The Selections give only the basis of Aristotle's formal logic (§§ 5-7), but illustrate rather more fully the more philosophical logic of the *Posterior Analytics*. The last chapter of this work (§ 13) connects well with the first chapter of the *Metaphysics* (§ 14). In the section on metaphysics (§§ 14-37) I have incorporated certain parts of the *Physics* which lead up to the argument of *Metaphysics*. §§ 38-48 illustrate the general principles of Aristotle's natural philosophy. §§ 49-52 illustrate his powers of observation, which in the region of animal life were quite extraordinary. Some of his leading ideas on biology are indicated in §§ 53–61, and on psychology in §§ 62–68. His ethical system is exhibited fairly fully in §§ 69–89, and on this naturally follows the section on political philosophy (§§ 90–100). § 101 illustrates well his knowledge of human nature, and §§ 102–103 give some of the essential parts of his analysis of poetry, and in particular of tragedy.

The use of these Selections will be much facilitated if the student will read with them some book which gives a general account of Aristotle's doctrine, such as Prof. A. E. Taylor's *Aristotle* (Jacks, London, 1919), or Prof. J. L. Stocks's *Aristotelianism* (Harraps, London, and Longmans, New York, 1925). Those who wish for a fuller treatment may be referred to my *Aristotle* (2nd ed., Methuens, London, and Scribners, New York, 1930), and to Mr. G. R. G. Mure's *Aristotle* (Benns, London, 1932).

W. D. Ross.

CONTENTS

PAGE

ARISTOTLE
SELECTIONS

SELECTIONS FROM ARISTOTLE

1. Things are said to be named 'equivocally' when, though they have a common name, the definition corresponding with the name differs for each. Thus, a real man and a figure in a picture can both lay claim to the name 'animal'; yet these are equivocally so named, for, though they have a common name, the definition corresponding with the name differs for each. For should any one define in what sense each is an animal, his definition in the one case will be appropriate to that case only.

On the other hand, things are said to be named 'univocally' which have both the name and the definition answering to the name in common. A man and an ox are both 'animal', and these are univocally so named, inasmuch as not only the name, but also the definition, is the same in both cases: for if a man should state in what sense each is an animal, the statement in the one case would be identical with that in the other.

Things are said to be named 'derivatively', which derive their name from some other name, but differ from it in termination. Thus the grammarian derives his name from the word 'grammar', and the courageous man from the word 'courage'.

Forms of speech are either simple or composite. Examples of the latter are such expressions as 'the man runs', 'the man wins'; of the former 'man', 'ox', 'runs', 'wins'.

Of things themselves some are predicable of a subject, and are never present in a subject. Thus 'man' is predicable of the individual man, and is never present in a subject.

1

By being 'present in a subject' I do not mean present as parts are present in a whole, but being incapable of existence apart from the said subject.

Some things, again, are present in a subject, but are never predicable of a subject. For instance, a certain point of grammatical knowledge is present in the mind, but is not predicable of any subject; or again, a certain whiteness may be present in the body (for colour requires a material basis), yet it is never predicable of anything.

Other things, again, are both predicable of a subject and present in a subject. Thus while knowledge is present in the human mind, it is predicable of grammar.

There is, lastly, a class of things which are neither present in a subject nor predicable of a subject, such as the individual man or the individual horse. But, to speak more generally, that which is individual and has the character of a unit is never predicable of a subject. Yet in some cases there is nothing to prevent such being present in a subject. Thus a certain point of grammatical knowledge is present in a subject.

When one thing is predicated of another, all that which is predicable of the predicate will be predicable also of the subject. Thus, 'man' is predicated of the individual man; but 'animal' is predicated of 'man'; it will, therefore, be predicable of the individual man also: for the individual man is both 'man' and 'animal'.

If genera are different and co-ordinate, their differentiae are themselves different in kind. Take as an instance the genus 'animal' and the genus 'knowledge'. 'With feet', 'two-footed', 'winged', 'aquatic', are differentiæ of 'animal'; the species of knowledge are not distinguished by the same differentiæ. One species of knowledge does not differ from another in being 'two-footed'.

But where one genus is subordinate to another, there is nothing to prevent their having the same differentiæ for the greater class is predicated of the lesser, so that all the differentiæ of the predicate will be differentiæ also of the subject.

Expressions which are in no way composite signify substance, quantity, quality, relation, place, time, position, state, action, or affection. To sketch my meaning roughly, examples of substance are 'man' or 'the horse', of quantity, such terms as 'two cubits long' or 'three cubits long', of quality, such attributes as 'white', 'grammatical'. 'Double', 'half', 'greater', fall under the category of relation; 'in the market place,' 'in the Lyceum', under that of place; 'yesterday', 'last year', under that of time. 'Lying', 'sitting', are terms indicating position, 'shod', 'armed', state; 'to lance', 'to cauterize', action; 'to be lanced', 'to be cauterized', affection.

No one of these terms, in and by itself, involves an affirmation; it is by the combination of such terms that positive or negative statements arise. For every assertion must, as is admitted, be either true or false, whereas expressions which are not in any way composite, such as 'man', 'white', 'runs', 'wins', cannot be either true or false.

Substance, in the truest and primary and most definite sense of the word, is that which is neither predicable of a subject nor present in a subject; for instance, the individual man or horse. But in a secondary sense those things are called substances within which, as species, the primary substances are included; also those which, as genera, include the species. For instance, the individual man is included in the species 'man', and the genus to which the species belongs is 'animal'; these, therefore—that is to say, the species 'man' and the genus 'animal'—are termed secondary substances.

It is plain from what has been said that both the name and the definition of the predicate must be predicable of the subject. For instance, 'man' is predicated of the individual man. Now in this case the name of the species 'man' is applied to the individual, for we use the term 'man' in describing the individual; and the definition of 'man' will also be predicated of the individual man, for the individual man is both man and animal. Thus, both the name and the definition of the species are predicable of the individual.

With regard, on the other hand, to those things which are present in a subject, it is generally the case that neither their name nor their definition is predicable of that in which they are present. Though, however, the definition is never predicable, there is nothing in certain cases to prevent the name being used. For instance, 'white' being present in a body is predicated of that in which it is present, for a body is called white: the definition, however, of the colour 'white' is never predicable of the body.

Everything except primary substances is either predicable of a primary substance or present in a primary substance. This becomes evident by reference to particular instances which occur. 'Animal' is predicated of the species 'man', therefore of the individual man, for if there were no individual man of whom it could be predicated, it could not be predicated of the species 'man' at all. Again, colour is present in body, therefore in individual bodies, for if there were no individual body in which it was present, it could not be present in body at all. Thus everything except primary substances is either predicated of primary substances, or is present in them, and if these last did not exist, it would be impossible for anything else to exist.

Of secondary substances, the species is more truly substance than the genus, being more nearly related to primary substance. For if any one should render an account of what a primary substance is, he would render a more instructive account, and one more proper to the subject, by stating the species than by stating the genus. Thus, he would give a more instructive account of an individual man by stating that he was man than by stating that he was animal, for the former description is peculiar to the individual in a greater degree, while the latter is too general. Again, the man who gives an account of the nature of an individual tree will give a more instructive account by mentioning the species 'tree' than by mentioning the genus 'plant'.

Moreover, primary substances are most properly called substances in virtue of the fact that they are the entities which underlie everything else, and that everything else is either predicated of them or present in them. Now the same relation which subsists between primary substance and everything else subsists also between the species and the genus: for the species is to the genus as subject is to predicate, since the genus is predicated of the species, whereas the species cannot be predicated of the genus. . . .

All substance appears to signify that which is individual. In the case of primary substance this is indisputably true, for the thing is a unit. In the case of secondary substances, when we speak, for instance, of 'man' or 'animal', our form of speech gives the impression that we are here also indicating that which is individual, but the impression is not strictly true; for a secondary substance is not an individual, but a class with a certain qualification; for it is not one and single as a primary substance is; the words 'man', 'animal', are predicable of more than one subject.

Yet species and genus do not merely indicate quality, like the term 'white'; 'white' indicates quality and nothing further, but species and genus determine the quality with reference to a substance: they signify substance qualitatively differentiated. The determinate qualification covers a larger field in the case of the genus than in that of the species: he who uses the word 'animal' is herein using a word of wider extension than he who uses the word 'man'.

Another mark of substance is that it has no contrary. What could be the contrary of any primary substance, such as the individual man or animal? It has none. Nor can the species or the genus have a contrary. Yet this characteristic is not peculiar to substance, but is true of many other things, such as quantity. There is nothing that forms the contrary of 'two cubits long' or of 'three cubits long', or of 'ten', or of any such term. A man may contend that 'much' is the contrary of 'little', or 'great' of 'small', but of definite quantitative terms no contrary exists.

Substance, again, does not appear to admit of variation of degree. I do not mean by this that one substance cannot be more or less truly substance than another, for it has already been stated that this is the case; but that no single substance admits of varying degrees within itself. For instance, one particular substance, 'man', cannot be more or less man either than himself at some other time or than some other man. One man cannot be more man than another, as that which is white may be more or less white than some other white object, or as that which is beautiful may be more or less beautiful than some other beautiful object. The same quality, moreover, is said to subsist in a thing in varying degrees at different times. A body, being white, is said to be whiter at one time than it was before, or, being warm, is said to be warmer or less warm than at some other time. But substance is not said to be more or less that which it is: a man is not more truly a man at one time than he was before, nor is anything, if it is substance, more or less what it is. Substance, then, does not admit of variation of degree.

The most distinctive mark of substance appears to be that, while remaining numerically one and the same, it is capable of admitting contrary qualities. From among things other than substance, we should find ourselves unable to bring forward any which possessed this mark. Thus, one and the same colour cannot be white and black. Nor can the same one action be good and bad: this law holds good with everything that is not substance. But one and the selfsame substance, while retaining its identity, is yet capable of admitting contrary qualities. The same individual person is at one time white, at another black, at one time warm, at another cold, at one time good, at another bad.

2. Spoken words are the symbols of mental experience and written words are the symbols of spoken words. Just as all men have not the same writing, so all men have not the same speech sounds, but the mental experiences, which these directly symbolize, are the same for all, as also are those things of which our experiences are the images. This matter has, however, been discussed in my treatise about the soul, for it belongs to an investigation distinct from that which lies before us.

As there are in the mind thoughts which do not involve truth or falsity, and also those which must be either true or false, so it is in speech. For truth and falsity imply combination and separation. Nouns and verbs, provided nothing is added, are like thoughts without combination or separation; 'man' and 'white', as isolated terms, are not yet either true or false. In proof of this, consider the word 'goat-stag'. It has significance, but there is no truth or falsity about it, unless 'is' or 'is not' is added, either in the present or in some other tense.

By a noun we mean a sound significant by convention, which has no reference to time, and of which no part is significant apart from the rest. In the noun 'Fair-steed', the part 'steed' has no significance in and by itself, as in the phrase 'fair steed'. Yet there is a difference between simple and composite nouns; for in the former the part is in no way significant, in the latter it contributes to the meaning of the whole, although it has not an independent meaning. Thus in the word 'pirate-boat' the word 'boat' has no meaning except as part of the whole word.

The limitation 'by convention' was introduced because nothing is by nature a noun or name—it is only so when it becomes a symbol; inarticulate sounds, such as those which brutes produce, are significant, yet none of these constitutes a noun.

The expression 'not-man' is not a noun. There is indeed no recognized term by which we may denote such an expression, for it is not a sentence or a denial. Let it then be called an indefinite noun.

3. Every sentence has meaning, not as being the natural means by which a physical faculty is realized, but, as we have said, by convention. Yet every sentence is not a proposition; only such are propositions as have in them either truth or falsity. Thus a prayer is a sentence, but is neither true nor false.

Let us therefore dismiss all other types of sentence but the proposition, for this last concerns our present inquiry, whereas the investigation of the others belongs rather to the study of rhetoric or of poetry.

The first class of simple propositions is the simple affirmation, the next, the simple denial; all others are only one by conjunction.

Every proposition must contain a verb or the tense of a verb. The phrase which defines the species 'man', if no verb in present, past, or future time be added, is not a proposition. It may be asked how the expression 'a footed animal with two feet' can be called single; for it is not the circumstance that the words follow in unbroken succession that effects the unity. This inquiry, however, finds its place in an investigation foreign to that before us.

We call those propositions single which indicate a single fact, or the conjunction of the parts of which results in unity: those propositions, on the other hand, are separate and many in number, which indicate many facts, or whose parts have no conjunction.

Let us, moreover, consent to call a noun or a verb an expression only, and not a proposition, since it is not possible for a man to speak in this way when he is expressing something, in such a way as to make a statement, whether his utterance is an answer to a question or an act of his own initiation.

To return: of propositions one kind is simple, i.e. that which asserts or denies something of something, the other composite, i.e. that which is compounded of simple propositions. A simple proposition is a statement, with meaning, as to the presence of something in a subject or its absence, in the present, past, or future, according to the divisions of time.

An affirmation is a positive assertion of something about something, a denial a negative assertion.

Now it is possible both to affirm and to deny the presence of something which is present or of something which is not, and since these same affirmations and denials are possible with reference to those times which lie outside the present, it would be possible to contradict any affirmation or denial. Thus it is plain that every affirmation has an opposite denial, and similarly every denial an opposite affirmation.

We will call such a pair of propositions a pair of contradictories. Those positive and negative propositions are said to be contradictory which have the same subject and predicate. The identity of subject and of predicate must not be 'equivocal'. Indeed there are definitive qualifications besides this, which we make to meet the casuistries of sophists.

Some things are universal, others individual. By the term 'universal' I mean that which is of such a nature as to be predicated of many subjects, by 'individual' that which is not thus predicated. Thus 'man' is a universal, 'Callias' an individual.

Our propositions necessarily sometimes concern a universal subject, sometimes an individual.

If, then, a man states a positive and a negative proposition of universal character with regard to a universal, these two propositions are 'contrary'. By the expression 'a proposition of universal character with regard to a universal', such propositions as 'every man is white', 'no man is white' are meant. When, on the other hand, the positive and negative propositions, though they have regard to a universal, are yet not of universal character, they will not be contrary, albeit the meaning intended is sometimes contrary. As instances of propositions made with regard to a universal, but not of universal character, we may take the propositions 'man is white', 'man is not white'. 'Man' is a universal, but the proposition is not made as of universal character; for the word 'every' does not make the subject a universal, but rather gives the proposition a universal character. If, however, both predicate and subject are distributed, the proposition thus constituted is contrary to truth; no affirmation will, under such circumstances, be true. The proposition 'every man is every animal' is an example of this type.

An affirmation is opposed to a denial in the sense which I denote by the term 'contradictory', when, while the subject remains the same, the affirmation is of universal character and the denial is not. The affirmation 'every man is white' is the *contradictory* of the denial 'not every man is white', or again, the proposition 'no man is white' is the *contradictory* of the proposition 'some men are white'. But propositions are opposed as *contraries* when both the affirmation and the denial are universal, as in the sentences 'every man is white', 'no man is white', 'every man is just', 'no man is just'.

4. The proposal of our treatise is to find a line of inquiry whereby we shall be able to reason from opinions that are generally accepted about every problem propounded to us, and also shall ourselves, when standing up to an argument, avoid saying anything that will obstruct us. First, then, we must say, What is Reasoning? and what its varieties? in order to grasp dialectical reasoning: for this is the object of our search in the treatise before us.

Now reasoning is an argument in which, certain things being laid down, something other than these necessarily comes about through them. (*a*) It is a 'demonstration', when the premisses from which the reasoning starts are true and primary, or are such that our knowledge of them has originally come through premisses which are primary and true: (*b*) Reasoning, on the other hand, is 'dialectical', if it starts from opinions that are generally accepted. Things are 'true' and 'primary' which are believed on the strength not of anything else but of themselves: for in regard to the first principles of science it is improper to ask any further for the why and wherefore of them; each of the first principles should command belief in and by itself. On the other hand, those opinions are 'generally accepted' which are accepted by every one or by the majority or by the philosophers—i.e. by all, or by the majority, or by the most notable and illustrious of them. Again (*c*), Reasoning is 'contentious' if it starts from opinions that seem to be generally accepted, but are not really such, or again if it merely seems to reason from opinions that are or seem to be generally accepted. For not every opinion that seems to be generally accepted actually is generally accepted. For in none of the opinions which we call generally accepted is the illusion entirely on the surface, as happens in the case of the principles of contentious arguments; for the nature of the fallacy in them is obvious immediately, and as a rule even to persons with little power of comprehension. So then, of the contentious reasonings mentioned, the former really deserves to be called 'reasoning' as well, but the other should be called 'contentious reasoning', but not 'reasoning', since it appears to reason, but does not really do so.

Further (*d*), besides all the reasonings we have mentioned there are the mis-reasonings that start from the premisses peculiar to the special sciences, as happens (for example) in the case of geometry and her sister sciences. For this form of reasoning appears to differ from the reasonings mentioned above; the man who draws a false figure reasons from things that are neither true and primary, nor yet generally accepted. For he does not fall within the definition; he does not assume opinions that are received either by every one or by the majority or by philosophers—that is to say, by all, or by most, or by the most illustrious of them—but he conducts his reasoning upon assumptions which, though appropriate to the science in question, are not true; for he effects his mis-reasoning either by describing the semicircles wrongly or by drawing certain lines in a way in which they could not be drawn.

The foregoing must stand for an outline survey of the species of reasoning. In general, in regard both to all that we have already discussed and to those which we shall discuss later, we may remark that that amount of distinction between them may serve, because it is not our purpose to give the exact definition of any of them; we merely want to describe them in outline: we consider it quite enough from the point of view of the line of inquiry before us to be able to recognize each of them in some sort of way.

Next in order after the foregoing, we must say for how many and for what purposes the treatise is useful. They are three—intellectual training, casual encounters, and the philosophical sciences. That it is useful as a training is obvious on the face of it. The possession of a plan of inquiry will enable us more easily to argue about the subject proposed. For purposes of casual encounters, it is useful because when we have counted up the opinions held by most people, we shall meet them on the ground not of other people's convictions but of their own, while we shift the ground of any argument that they appear to us to state unsoundly.

For the study of the philosophical sciences it is useful, because the ability to raise searching difficulties on both sides of a subject will make us detect more easily the truth and error about the several points that arise. It has a further use in relation to the ultimate bases of the principles used in the several sciences. For it is impossible to discuss them at all from the principles proper to the particular science in hand, seeing that the principles are the *prius* of everything else: it is through the opinions generally held on the particular points that these have to be discussed, and this task belongs properly, or most appropriately, to dialectic: for dialectic is a process of criticism wherein lies the path to the principles of all inquiries.

We shall be in perfect possession of the way to proceed when we are in a position like that which we occupy in regard to rhetoric and medicine and faculties of that kind: this means the doing of that which we choose by the means that are available. For it is not every method that the rhetorician will employ to persuade, or the doctor to heal: still, if he omits none of the available means, we shall say that his grasp of the science is adequate.

First, then, we must see of what parts our inquiry consists. Now if we were to grasp (*a*) with reference to how many, and what kind of things, arguments take place, and with what materials they start, and (*b*) how we are to become well supplied with these, we should have sufficiently won our goal. Now the materials with which arguments start are equal in number, and are identical, with the subjects on which reasonings take place. For arguments start with 'propositions,' while the subjects on which reasonings take place are 'problems'. Now every proposition and every problem indicates either a genus or a peculiarity or an accident—for the differentia too, applying as it does to a class (or genus) should be ranked together with the genus. Since, however, of what is peculiar to anything part signifies its essence, while part does not, let us divide the 'peculiar' into both the aforesaid parts, and call that part which indicates the essence a 'definition', while of the remainder let us adopt the terminology which is generally current about these things, and speak of it as a 'property'. What we have said, then, makes it clear that according to our present division, the elements turn out to be four, all told, namely either property or definition or genus or accident. Do not let any one suppose us to mean that each of these enunciated by itself constitutes a proposition or problem, but only that it is from these that both problems and propositions are formed. The difference between a problem and a proposition is a difference in the turn of the phrase. For if it be put in this way, ' "An animal that walks on two feet" is the definition of man, is it not?' or ' "Animal" is the genus of man, is it not?' the result is a proposition: but if thus, 'Is "an animal that walks on two feet" a definition of man or no?' the result is a problem. Similarly too in other cases. Naturally, then, problems and propositions are equal in number: for out of every proposition you will make a problem if you change the turn of the phrase.

We must now say what are 'definition', 'property', 'genus', and 'accident'. A 'definition' is a phrase signifying a thing's essence. It is rendered in the form either of a phrase in lieu of a term, or of a phrase in lieu of another phrase; for it is sometimes possible to define the meaning of a phrase as well. People whose rendering consists of a term only, try it as they may, clearly do not render the definition of the thing in question, because a definition is always a phrase of a certain kind. One may, however, use the word 'definitory' also of such a remark as 'The "becoming" is "beautiful"', and likewise also of the question, 'Are sensation and knowledge the same or different?', for argument about definitions is mostly concerned with questions of sameness and difference. In a word we may call 'definitory' everything that falls under the same branch of inquiry as definitions; and that all the above-mentioned examples are of this character is clear on the face of them. For if we are able to argue that two things are the same or are different, we shall be well supplied by the same turn of argument with lines of attack upon their definitions as well: for when we have shown that they are not the same we shall have demolished the definition. Observe, please, that the converse of this last statement will not hold: for to show that they are the same is not enough to establish a definition. To show, however, that they are not the same is enough of itself to overthrow it.

A 'property' is a predicate which does not indicate the essence of a thing, but yet belongs to that thing alone, and is predicated convertibly of it. Thus it is a property of man to be capable of learning grammar: for if A be a man, then he is capable of learning grammar, and if he be capable of learning grammar, he is a man. For no one calls anything a 'property' which may possibly belong to something else, e.g. 'sleep' in the case of man, even though at a certain time it may happen to belong to him alone. That is to say, if any such thing were actually to be called a property, it will be called not a 'property' absolutely, but a 'temporary' or a 'relative' property: for 'being on the right hand side' is a temporary property, while 'two-footed' is in point of fact ascribed as a property in certain relations; e.g. it is a property of Man relatively to a horse and a dog. That nothing which may belong to anything else than A is a convertible predicate of A is clear: for it does not necessarily follow that if something is asleep it is a man.

A 'genus' is what is predicated in the category of essence of a number of things exhibiting differences in kind. We should treat as predicates in the category of essence all such things as it would be appropriate to mention in reply to the question, 'What is the object before you?'; as, for example, in the case of man, if asked that question, it is appropriate to say 'He is an animal'. The question, 'Is one thing in the same genus as another or in a different one?' is also a 'generic' question; for a question of that kind as well falls under the same branch of inquiry as the genus: for having argued that 'animal' is the genus of man, and likewise also of ox, we shall have argued that they are in the same genus; whereas if we show that it is the genus of the one but not of the other, we shall have argued that these things are not in the same genus.

An 'accident' is (1) something which, though it is none of the foregoing—i.e. neither a definition nor a property nor a genus—yet belongs to the thing: (2) something which may possibly either belong or not belong to any one and the self-same thing, as (e.g.) the 'sitting posture' may belong or not belong to some self-same thing. Likewise also 'whiteness', for there is nothing to prevent the same thing being at one time white, and at another not white. Of the definitions of accident the second is the better: for if he adopts the first, any one is bound, if he is to understand it, to know already what 'definition' and 'genus' and 'property' are, whereas the second is sufficient of itself to tell us the essential meaning of the term in question. To Accident are to be attached also all comparisons of things together, when expressed in language that is drawn in any kind of way from what happens (*accidit*) to be true of them; such as, for example, the question, 'Is the honourable or the expedient preferable?' and 'Is the life of Virtue or the life of self-indulgence the pleasanter?' and any other problem which may happen to be phrased in terms like these. For in all such cases the question is 'to which of the two does the predicate in question happen (*accidit*) to belong more closely?' It is clear on the face of it that there is nothing to prevent an accident from becoming a temporary or a relative property. Thus the sitting posture is an accident, but will be a temporary property, whenever a man is the only person sitting, while if he be not the only one sitting, it is still a property relatively to those who are not sitting. So then, there is nothing to prevent an accident from becoming both a relative and a temporary property; but a property absolutely it will never be.

5. A premiss is a sentence affirming or denying one thing of another. This is either universal or particular or indefinite. By universal I mean the statement that something belongs to all or none of something else; by particular that it belongs to some or not to some or not to all; by indefinite that it does or does not belong, without any mark to show whether it is universal or particular, e.g. 'contraries are subjects of the same science', or 'pleasure is not good'. The demonstrative premiss differs from the dialectical, because the demonstrative premiss is the assertion of one of two contradictory statements (the demonstrator does not ask for his premiss, but lays it down), whereas the dialectical premiss depends on the adversary's choice between two contradictories. But this will make no difference to the

production of a syllogism in either case; for both the demonstrator and the dialectician argue syllogistically after stating that something does or does not belong to something else. Therefore a syllogistic premiss without qualification will be an affirmation or denial of something concerning something else in the way we have described; it will be demonstrative, if it is true and obtained through the first principles of its science; while a dialectical premiss is the giving of a choice between two contradictories, when a man is proceeding by question, but when he is syllogizing it is the assertion of that which is apparent and generally admitted, as has been said in the *Topics*. The nature then of a premiss and the difference between syllogistic, demonstrative, and dialectical premisses, may be taken as sufficiently defined by us in relation to our present need, but will be stated accurately in the sequel.

I call that a term into which the premiss is resolved, i.e. both the predicate and that of which it is predicated, 'being' being added and 'not being' removed, or vice versa.

A syllogism is discourse in which, certain things being stated, something other than what is stated follows of necessity from their being so. I mean by the last phrase that they produce the consequence, and by this, that no further term is required from without in order to make the consequence necessary.

I call that a perfect syllogism which needs nothing other than what has been stated to make plain what necessarily follows; a syllogism is imperfect, if it needs either one or more propositions, which are indeed the necessary consequences of the terms set down, but have not been expressly stated as premisses.

That one term should be included in another as in a whole is the same as for the other to be predicated of all of the first. And we say that one term is predicated of all of another, whenever no instance of the subject can be found of which the other term cannot be asserted: 'to be predicated of none' must be understood in the same way.

Every premiss states that something either is or must be or may be the attribute of something else; of premisses of these three kinds some are affirmative, others negative, in respect of each of the three modes of attribution; again some affirmative and negative premisses are universal, others particular, others indefinite. It is necessary then that in universal attribution the terms of the negative premiss should be convertible, e.g. if no pleasure is good, then no good will be pleasure; the terms of the affirmative must be convertible, not however universally, but in part, e.g. if every pleasure is good, some good must be pleasure; the particular affirmative must convert in part (for if some pleasure is good, then some good will be pleasure); but the particular negative need not convert, for if some animal is not man, it does not follow that some man is not animal.

6. Whenever three terms are so related to one another that the last is contained in the middle as in a whole, and the middle is either contained in, or excluded from, the first as in or from a whole, the extremes must be related by a perfect syllogism. I call that term middle which is itself contained in another and contains another in itself: in position also this comes in the middle. By extremes I mean both that term which is itself contained in another and that in which another is contained. . . .

Whenever the same thing belongs to all of one subject, and to none of another, or to all of each subject

or to none of either, I call such a figure the second;
by middle term in it I mean that which is predicated of
both subjects, by extremes the terms of which this is
said, by major extreme that which lies near the middle,
by minor that which is further away from the middle.
The middle term stands outside the extremes, and is
first in position. A syllogism cannot be perfect anyhow in this figure, but it may be valid whether the
terms are related universally or not. . . .

But if one term belongs to all, and another to none,
of a third, or if both belong to all, or to none, of it,
I call such a figure the third; by middle term in it I
mean that of which both the predicates are predicated,
by extremes I mean the predicates, by the major extreme that which is further from the middle, by the
minor that which is nearer to it. The middle term
stands outside the extremes, and is last in position. A
syllogism cannot be perfect in this figure either, but
it may be valid whether the terms are related universally or not to the middle term.

7. We must now state that not only dialectical and
demonstrative syllogisms are formed by means of the
aforesaid figures, but also rhetorical syllogisms and in
general any form of persuasion, however it may be
presented. For every belief comes either through syllogism or from induction.

Now induction, or rather the syllogism which springs
out of induction, consists in establishing syllogistically
a relation between one extreme and the middle by means
of the other extreme, e.g. if B is the middle term between A and C, it consists in proving through C that
A belongs to B. For this is the manner in which we
make inductions. For example let A stand for long-
lived, B for bileless, and C for the particular long-lived

animals, e.g. man, horse, mule. *A* then belongs to the whole of *C*: for whatever is bileless is long-lived. But *B* also ('not possessing bile') belongs to all *C*. If then *C* is convertible with *B*, and the middle term is not wider in extension, it is necessary that *A* should belong to *B*. For it has already been proved that if two things belong to the same thing, and the extreme is convertible with one of them, then the other predicate will belong to the predicate that is converted. But we must apprehend *C* as made up of all the particulars. For induction proceeds through an enumeration of all the cases.

Such is the syllogism which establishes the first and immediate premiss: for where there is a middle term the syllogism proceeds through the middle term; when there is no middle term, through induction. And in a way induction is opposed to syllogism: for the latter proves the major term to belong to the third term by means of the middle, the former proves the major to belong to the middle by means of the third. In the order of nature, syllogism through the middle term is prior and better known, but syllogism through induction is clearer to *us*.

We have an 'example' when the major term is proved to belong to the middle by means of a term which resembles the third. It ought to be known both that the middle belongs to the third term, and that the first belongs to that which resembles the third. For example let *A* be evil, *B* making war against neighbours, *C* Athenians against Thebans, *D* Thebans against Phocians. If then we wish to prove that to fight with the Thebans is an evil, we must assume that to fight against neighbours is an evil. Evidence of this is obtained from similar cases, e.g. that the war against the Phocians was an evil to the Thebans. Since then to fight against neighbours is an evil, and to fight against the Thebans is to fight against neighbours, it is clear that to fight against the Thebans is an evil. Now it is clear that B belongs to C and to D (for both are cases of making war upon one's neighbours) and that A belongs to D (for the war against the Phocians did not turn out well for the Thebans): but that A belongs to B will be proved through D. Similarly if the belief in the relation of the middle term to the extreme should be produced by several similar cases. Clearly then to argue by example is neither like reasoning from part to whole, nor like reasoning from whole to part, but rather reasoning from part to part, when both particulars are subordinate to the same term, and one of them is known. It differs from induction, because induction starting from all the particular cases proves (as we saw) that the major term belongs to the middle, and does not apply the syllogistic conclusion to the minor term, whereas argument by example does make this application and does not draw its proof from all the particular cases.

START

8. All instruction given or received by way of argument proceeds from pre-existent knowledge. This becomes evident upon a survey of all the species of such instruction. The mathematical sciences and all other speculative disciplines are acquired in this way, and so are the two forms of dialectical reasoning, syllogistic and inductive; for each of these latter makes use of old knowledge to impart new, the syllogism assuming an audience that accepts its premises, induction exhibiting the universal as implicit in the clearly known particular. Again, the persuasion exerted by rhetorical arguments is in principle the same, since they use either example, a kind of induction, or enthymeme, a form of syllogism.

The pre-existent knowledge required is of two kinds.

In some cases admission of the fact must be assumed, in others comprehension of the meaning of the term used, and sometimes both assumptions are essential. Thus, we assume that every predicate can be either truly affirmed or truly denied of any subject, and that 'triangle' means so and so; as regards 'unit' we have to make the double assumption of the meaning of the word and the existence of the thing. The reason is that these several objects are not equally obvious to us. Recognition of a truth may in some cases contain as factors both previous knowledge and also knowledge acquired simultaneously with that recognition—knowledge, this latter, of the particulars actually falling under the universal and therein already virtually known. For example, the student knew beforehand that the angles of every triangle are equal to two right angles; but it was only at the actual moment at which he was being led on to recognize this as true in the instance before him that he came to know 'this figure inscribed in the semicircle' to be a triangle. For some things (viz. the singulars finally reached which are not predicable of anything else as subject) are only learnt in this way, i.e. there is here no recognition through a middle of a minor term as subject to a major. Before he was led on to recognition or before he actually drew a conclusion, we should perhaps say that in a manner he knew, in a manner not.

If he did not in an unqualified sense of the term *know* the existence of this triangle, how could he *know* without qualification that its angles were equal to two right angles? No: clearly he *knows* not without qualification but only in the sense that he *knows* universally. If this distinction is not drawn, we are faced with the dilemma in the *Meno*: either a man will learn nothing or what he already knows; for we cannot accept the solution which some people offer. A man is asked, 'Do you, or do you not, know that every pair is even?' He says he does know it. The questioner then produces a particular pair, of the existence, and so *a fortiori* of the evenness, of which he was unaware. The solution which some people offer is to assert that they do not know that every pair is even, but only that everything which they know to be a pair is even: yet what they know to be even is that of which they have demonstrated evenness, i.e. what they made the subject of their premiss, viz. not merely every triangle or number which they know to be such, but any and every number or triangle without reservation. For no premiss is ever couched in the form 'every number which you know to be such', or 'every rectilinear figure which you know to be such': the predicate is always construed as applicable to any and every instance of the thing. On the other hand, I imagine there is nothing to prevent a man in one sense knowing what he is learning, in another not knowing it. The strange thing would be, not if in some sense he knew what he was learning, but if he were to know it in that precise sense and manner in which he was learning it.

We suppose ourselves to possess unqualified scientific knowledge of a thing, as opposed to knowing it in the accidental way in which the sophist knows, when we think that we know the cause on which the fact depends, as the cause of that fact and of no other, and, further, that the fact could not be other than it is. Now that scientific knowing is something of this sort is evident—witness both those who falsely claim it and those who actually possess it, since the former merely imagine themselves to be, while the latter are also actually, in the condition described. Consequently the

proper object of unqualified scientific knowledge is
something which cannot be other than it is.

There may be another manner of knowing as well
—that will be discussed later. What I now assert is
that at all events we do know by demonstration. By
demonstration I mean a syllogism productive of scientific knowledge, a syllogism, that is, the grasp of which
is *eo ipso* such knowledge. Assuming then that my
thesis as to the nature of scientific knowing is correct,
the premisses of demonstrated knowledge must be true,
primary, immediate, better known than and prior to
the conclusion, which is further related to them as
effect to cause. Unless these conditions are satisfied,
the basic truths will not be 'appropriate' to the conclusion. Syllogism there may indeed be without these
conditions, but such syllogism, not being productive of
scientific knowledge, will not be demonstration. The
premisses must be true: for that which is non-existent
cannot be known—we cannot know, e.g., that the diagonal of a square is commensurate with its side. The
premisses must be primary and indemonstrable; otherwise they will require demonstration in order to be
known, since to have knowledge, if it be not accidental
knowledge, of things which are demonstrable, means precisely to have a demonstration of them. The premisses
must be the causes of the conclusion, better known than
it, and prior to it; its causes, since we possess scientific
knowledge of a thing only when we know its cause;
prior, in order to be causes; antecedently known, this
antecedent knowledge being not our mere understanding of the meaning, but knowledge of the fact as well.
Now 'prior' and 'better known' are ambiguous terms,
for there is a difference between what is prior and
better known in the order of being and what is prior and
better known to man. I mean that objects nearer to

sense are prior and better known to man; objects without qualification prior and better known are those further from sense. Now the most universal causes are furthest from sense and particular causes are nearest to sense, and they are thus exactly opposed to one another. In saying that the premisses of demonstrated knowledge must be primary, I mean that they must be the 'appropriate' basic truths, for I identify primary premiss and basic truth.

A 'basic truth' in a demonstration is an immediate proposition. An immediate proposition is one which has no other proposition prior to it. A proposition is either part of an enunciation, i.e. it predicates a single attribute of a single subject. If a proposition is dialectical, it assumes either part indifferently; if it is demonstrative, it lays down one part to the definite exclusion of the other because that part is true. The term 'enunciation' denotes either part of a contradiction indifferently. A contradiction is an opposition which of its own nature excludes a middle. The part of a contradiction which conjoins a predicate with a subject is an affirmation; the part disjoining them is a negation. I call an immediate basic truth of syllogism a 'thesis' when, though it is not susceptible of proof by the teacher, yet ignorance of it does not constitute a total bar to progress on the part of the pupil: one which the pupil must know if he is to learn anything whatever is an axiom. I call it an axiom because there are such truths and we give them the name of axioms *par excellence.* If a thesis assumes one part or the other of an enunciation, i.e. asserts either the existence or the non-existence of a subject, it is a hypothesis; if it does not so assert, it is a definition. Definition *is* a 'thesis' or a 'laying something down', since the arithmetician lays it down that to be a unit is to be quantitatively indivisible; but it is not a hypothesis, for to define what a unit is is not the same as to affirm its existence.

Now since the required ground of our knowledge—i.e. of our conviction—of a fact is the possession of such a syllogism as we call demonstration, and the ground of the syllogism is the facts constituting its premisses, we must not only know the primary premisses—some if not all of them—beforehand, but know them better than the conclusion: for the cause of an attribute's inherence in a subject always itself inheres in the subject more firmly than that attribute, e.g. the cause of our loving anything is dearer to us than the object of our love. So since the primary premisses are the cause of our knowledge—i.e. of our conviction—it follows that we know them better—that is, are more convinced of them —than their consequences, precisely because our knowledge of the latter is the effect of our knowledge of the premisses. Now a man cannot believe in anything more than in the things he knows, unless he has either actual knowledge of it or something better than actual knowledge. But we are faced with this paradox if a student whose belief rests on demonstration has not prior knowledge; a man must believe in some, if not in all, of the basic truths more than in the conclusion. Moreover, if a man sets out to acquire the scientific knowledge that comes through demonstration, he must not only have a better knowledge of the basic truths and a firmer conviction of them than of the connexion which is being demonstrated: more than this, nothing must be more certain or better known to him than these basic truths in their character as contradicting the fundamental premisses which lead to the opposed and erroneous conclusion. For indeed the conviction of pure science must be unshakable.

Some hold that, owing to the necessity of knowing

the primary premisses, there is no scientific knowledge. Others think there is, but that all truths are demonstrable. Neither doctrine is either true or a necessary deduction from the premisses. The first school, assuming that there is no way of knowing other than by demonstration, maintain that an infinite regress is involved, on the ground that if behind the prior stands no primary, we could not know the posterior through the prior (wherein they are right, for one cannot traverse an infinite series): if on the other hand—they say—the series terminates and there are primary premisses, yet these are unknowable because incapable of demonstration, which according to them is the only form of knowledge. And since thus one cannot know the primary premisses, knowledge of the conclusions which follow from them is not pure scientific knowledge nor properly knowing at all, but rests on the mere supposition that the premisses are true. The other party agrees, with them as regards knowing, holding that it is only possible by demonstration, but they see no difficulty in holding that all truths are demonstrated, on the ground that demonstration may be circular and reciprocal.

Our own doctrine is that not all knowledge is demonstrative: on the contrary, knowledge of the immediate premisses is independent of demonstration. (The necessity of this is obvious; for since we must know the prior premisses from which the demonstration is drawn, and since the regress must end in immediate truths, those truths must be indemonstrable.) Such, then, is our doctrine, and in addition we maintain that besides scientific knowledge there is its originative source which enables us to recognize the definitions.

9. It is no less evident that the peculiar basic truths of each inhering attribute are indemonstrable; for basic

truths from which they might be deduced would be basic truths of all that is, and the science to which they belonged would possess universal sovereignty. This is so because he knows better whose knowledge is deduced from higher causes, for his knowledge is from prior premisses when it derives from causes themselves uncaused: hence, if he knows better than others or best of all, his knowledge would be science in a higher or the highest degree. But, as things are, demonstration is not transferable to another genus, with such exceptions as we have mentioned of the application of geometrical demonstrations to theorems in mechanics or optics, or of arithmetical demonstrations to those of harmonics.

It is hard to be sure whether one knows or not; for it is hard to be sure whether one's knowledge is based on the basic truths appropriate to each attribute—the differentia of true knowledge. We think we have scientific knowledge if we have reasoned from true and primary premisses. But that is not so: the conclusion must be homogeneous with the basic facts of the science.

I call the basic truths of every genus those elements in it the existence of which cannot be proved. As regards both these primary truths and the attributes dependent on them the meaning of the name is assumed. The fact of their existence as regards the primary truths must be assumed; but it has to be proved of the remainder, the attributes. Thus we assume the meaning alike of unity, straight, and triangular; but while as regards unity and magnitude we assume also the fact of their existence, in the case of the remainder proof is required.

Of the basic truths used in the demonstrative sciences some are peculiar to each science, and some are common, but common only in the sense of analogous, being of use only in so far as they fall within the genus constituting the province of the science in question.

Peculiar truths are, e.g., the definitions of line and straight; common truths are such as 'take equals from equals and equals remain'. Only so much of these common truths is required as falls within the genus in question: for a truth of this kind will have the same force even if not used generally but applied by the geometer only to magnitudes, or by the arithmetician only to numbers. Also peculiar to a science are the subjects the existence as well as the meaning of which it assumes, and the essential attributes of which it investigates, e.g. in arithmetic units, in geometry points and lines.

10. Scientific knowledge is not possible through the act of perception. Even if perception as a faculty is of 'the such' and not merely of a 'this somewhat', yet one must at any rate actually perceive a 'this somewhat', and at a definite present place and time: but that which is commensurately universal and true in all cases one cannot perceive, since it is not 'this' and it is not 'now'; if it were, it would not be commensurately universal —the term we apply to what is always and everywhere. Seeing, therefore, that demonstrations are commensurately universal and universals imperceptible, we clearly cannot obtain scientific knowledge by the act of perception: nay, it is obvious that even if it were possible to perceive that a triangle has its angles equal to two right angles, we should still be looking for a demonstration—we should not (as some say) possess knowledge of it; for perception must be of a particular, whereas scientific knowledge involves the recognition of the commensurate universal. So if we were on the moon, and saw the earth shutting out the sun's light, we should

not know the cause of the eclipse: we should perceive
the present fact of the eclipse, but not the reasoned
fact at all, since the act of perception is not of the
commensurate universal.

11. The kinds of questions we ask are as many as the
kinds of things which we know. They are in fact four:
—(1) whether the connexion of an attribute with a
thing is a fact, (2) what is the reason of the connexion,
(3) whether a thing exists, (4) what is the nature of
the thing. Thus, when our question concerns a complex of thing and attribute and we ask whether the
thing is thus or otherwise qualified—whether, e.g., the
sun suffers eclipse or not—then we are asking as to
the fact of a connexion. That our inquiry ceases with
the discovery that the sun does suffer eclipse is an indication of this; and if we know from the start that the
sun suffers eclipse, we do not inquire whether it does
so or not. On the other hand, when we know the fact
we ask the reason; as, for example, when we know that
the sun is being eclipsed and that an earthquake is in
progress, it is the reason of eclipse or earthquake into
which we inquire.

Where a complex is concerned, then, those are the two
questions we ask; but for some objects of inquiry we
have a different kind of question to ask, such as whether
there is or is not a centaur or a God. (By 'is or is not'
I mean 'is or is not, without further qualification'; as
opposed to 'is or is not (e.g.) white'.) On the other
hand, when we have ascertained the thing's existence,
we inquire as to its nature, asking, for instance, 'what,
then, is God?' or 'what is man?'.

These, then, are the four kinds of questions we ask,
and it is in the answers to these questions that our
knowledge consists.

Now when we ask whether a connexion is a fact, or whether a thing without qualification *is,* we are really asking whether the connexion or the thing has a 'middle'; and when we have ascertained either that the connexion is a fact or that the thing *is*—i.e. ascertained either the partial or the unqualified being of the thing—and are proceeding to ask the reason of the connexion or the nature of the thing, then we are asking what the 'middle' is.

(By distinguishing the fact of the connexion and the existence of the thing as respectively the partial and the unqualified being of the thing, I mean that if we ask 'does the moon suffer eclipse?', or 'does the moon wax?', the question concerns a part of the thing's being; for what we are asking in such questions is whether a thing is this or that, i.e. has or has not this or that attribute: whereas, if we ask whether the moon or night exists, the question concerns the unqualified being of a thing.)

We conclude that in all our inquiries we are asking either whether there is a 'middle' or what the 'middle' is: for the 'middle' here is precisely the cause, and it is the cause that we seek in all our inquiries. Thus, 'Does the moon suffer eclipse?' means 'Is there or is there not a cause producing eclipse of the moon?', and when we have learnt that there is, our next question is, 'What, then, is this cause?'; for the cause through which a thing *is*—not *is this or that,* i.e. has this or that attribute, but without qualification *is*—and the cause through which it is—not *is* without qualification, but *is this or that* as having some essential attribute or some accident—are both alike the 'middle'. By that which *is* without qualification I mean the subject, e.g. moon or earth or sun or triangle; by that which a subject *is* (in the partial sense) I mean a property, e.g. eclipse.

equality or inequality, interposition or non-interposition. For in all these examples it is clear that the nature of the thing and the reason of the fact are identical: the question 'What is eclipse?' and its answer 'The privation of the moon's light by the interposition of the earth' are identical with the question 'What is the reason of eclipse?' or 'Why does the moon suffer eclipse?' and the reply 'Because of the failure of light through the earth's shutting it out'. Again, for 'What is a concord? A commensurate numerical ratio of a high and a low note', we may substitute 'What reason makes a high and a low note concordant? Their relation according to a commensurate numerical ratio.' 'Are the high and the low note concordant?' is equivalent to 'Is their ratio commensurate?'; and when we find that it is commensurate, we ask 'What, then, is their ratio?'.

Cases in which the 'middle' is sensible show that the object of our inquiry is always the 'middle': we inquire, because we have not perceived it, whether there is or is not a 'middle' causing e.g. an eclipse. On the other hand, if we were on the moon we should not be inquiring either as to the fact or the reason, but both fact and reason would be obvious simultaneously. For the act of perception would have enabled us to know the universal too; since, the present fact of an eclipse being evident, perception would then at the same time give us the present fact of the earth's screening the sun's light, and from this would arise the universal.

Thus, as we maintain, to know a thing's nature is to know the reason why it is; and this is equally true of things in so far as they are said without qualification to *be* as opposed to being possessed of some attribute, and in so far as they are said to be possessed of some attribute such as equal to two right angles, or greater or less.

12. Since definition is said to be the statement of a thing's nature, obviously one kind of definition will be a statement of the meaning of the name, or of an equivalent nominal formula. A definition in this sense tells you, e.g., the meaning of the phrase 'triangular character'. When we are aware that triangle exists, we inquire the reason why it exists. But it is difficult thus to learn the definition of things the existence of which we do not genuinely know—the cause of this difficulty being, as we said before, that we only know accidentally whether or not the thing exists. Moreover, a statement may be a unity in either of two ways, by conjunction, like the *Iliad*, or because it exhibits a single predicate as inhering not accidentally in a single subject.

That then is one way of defining definition. Another kind of definition is a formula exhibiting the cause of a thing's existence. Thus the former signifies without proving, but the latter will clearly be a *quasi*-demonstration of essential nature, differing from demonstration in the arrangement of its terms. For there is a difference between stating why it thunders, and stating what is the essential nature of thunder; since the first statement will be 'Because fire is quenched in the clouds', while the statement of what the nature of thunder is will be 'The noise of fire being quenched in the clouds'. Thus the same statement takes a different form: in one form it is continuous demonstration, in the other definition.

13. As to the basic premisses, how they become known and what is the developed state of knowledge of them is made clear by raising some preliminary problems.

We have already said that scientific knowledge through demonstration is impossible unless a man knows the primary immediate premisses. But there are questions which might be raised in respect of the apprehension of these immediate premisses: one might not only ask whether it is of the same kind as the apprehension of the conclusions, but also whether there is or is not scientific knowledge of both; or scientific knowledge of the latter, and of the former a different kind of knowledge; and, further, whether the developed states of knowledge are not innate but come to be in us, or are innate but at first unnoticed. Now it is strange if we possess them from birth; for it means that we possess apprehensions more accurate than demonstration and fail to notice them. If on the other hand we acquire them and do not previously possess them, how could we apprehend and learn without a basis of preexistent knowledge? For that is impossible, as we used to find in the case of demonstration. So it emerges that neither can we possess them from birth, nor can they come to be in us if we are without knowledge of them to the extent of having no such developed state at all. Therefore we must possess a capacity of some sort, but not such as to rank higher in accuracy than these developed states. And this at least is an obvious characteristic of all animals, for they possess a congenital discriminative capacity which is called sense-perception. But though sense-perception is innate in all animals, in some the sense-impression comes to persist, in others it does not. So animals in which this persistence does not come to be have either no knowledge at all outside the act of perceiving, or no knowledge of objects of which no impression persists; animals in which it does come into being have perception and can continue to retain the sense-impression in the soul: and when such persistence is frequently repeated a further distinction at once arises between those which out of the persistence of such sense-impressions develop a power of systematizing them and those which do not. So out of sense-perception comes to be what we call memory, and out of frequently repeated memories of the same thing develops experience; for a number of memories constitute a single experience. From experience again—i.e. from the universal now stabilized in its entirety within the soul, the one beside the many which is a single identity within them all—originate the skill of the craftsman and the knowledge of the man of science, skill in the sphere of coming to be and science in the sphere of being.

We conclude that these states of knowledge are neither innate in a determinate form, nor developed from other higher states of knowledge, but from sense-perception. It is like a rout in battle stopped by first one man making a stand and then another, until the original formation has been restored. The soul is so constituted as to be capable of this process.

Let us now restate the account given already, though with insufficient clearness. When one of a number of logically indiscriminable particulars has made a stand, the earliest universal is present in the soul: for though the act of sense-perception is of the particular, its content is universal—is man, for example, not the man Callias. A fresh stand is made among these rudimentary universals, and the process does not cease until the indivisible concepts, the true universals, are established: e.g. such and such a species of animal is a step towards the genus animal, which by the same process is a step towards a further generalization.

Thus it is clear that we must get to know the primary premisses by induction; for the method by which even sense-perception implants the universal is inductive. Now of the thinking states by which we grasp truth, some are unfailingly true, others admit of error—opinion, for instance, and calculation, whereas scientific

knowing and intuition are always true: further, no other
kind of thought except intuition is more accurate than
scientific knowledge, whereas primary premises are
more knowable than demonstrations, and all scientific
knowledge is discursive. From these considerations it
follows that there will be no scientific knowledge of
the primary premises, and since except intuition nothing can be truer than scientific knowledge, it will be
intuition that apprehends the primary premises—a result which also follows from the fact that demonstration
cannot be the originative source of demonstration, nor,
consequently, scientific knowledge of scientific knowledge. If, therefore, it is the only other kind of true
thinking except scientific knowing, intuition will be
the originative source of scientific knowledge. And
the originative source of science grasps the original
basic premiss, while science as a whole is similarly
related as originative source to the whole body of fact.

14. All men by nature desire to know. An indication
of this is the delight we take in our senses; for even
apart from their usefulness they are loved for themselves; and above all others the sense of sight. For not
only with a view to action, but even when we are not
going to do anything, we prefer sight to almost everything else. The reason is that this, most of all the senses,
makes us know and brings to light many differences
between things.

By nature animals are born with the faculty of sensation, and from sensation memory is produced in some
of them, though not in others. And therefore the
former are more intelligent and apt at learning than
those which cannot remember; those which are incapable of hearing sounds are intelligent though they cannot
be taught, e.g. the bee, and any other race of animals

that may be like it; and those which besides memory have this sense of hearing can be taught.

The animals other than man live by appearances and memories, and have but little of connected experience; but the human race lives also by art and reasonings. And from memory experience is produced in men; for many memories of the same thing produce finally the capacity for a single experience. Experience is almost identified with science and art, but really science and art come to men *through* experience; for 'experience made art', as Polus says, and rightly, 'but inexperience luck'. And art arises, when from many notions gained by experience one universal judgement about a class of objects is produced. For to have a judgement that when Callias was ill of this disease this did him good, and similarly in the case of Socrates and in many individual cases, is a matter of experience; but to judge that it has done good to all persons of a certain constitution, marked off in one class, when they were ill of this disease, e.g. to phlegmatic or bilious people when burning with fever,—this is a matter of art.

[handwritten marginalia: DEFINITION OF ART / ANOTHER WORD FOR INDUCTION]

With a view to action experience seems in no respect inferior to art, and we even see men of experience succeeding more than those who have theory without experience. The reason is that experience is knowledge of individuals, art of universals, and actions and productions are all concerned with the individual; for the physician does not cure *man*, except in an incidental way, but Callias or Socrates or some other called by some such individual name, who happens to be a man. If, then, a man has the theory without the experience, and knows the universal but does not know the individual included in this, he will often fail to cure; for it is the individual that is to be cured. But yet we think that *knowledge* and *understanding* belong to art

rather than to experience, and we suppose artists to
be wiser than men of experience (which implies that
Wisdom depends in all cases rather on knowledge);
and this because the former know the cause, but the
latter do not. For men of experience know that the
thing is so, but do not know why, while the others
know the 'why' and the cause. Hence we think that
the master-workers in each craft are more honourable
and know in a truer sense and are wiser than the manual
workers, because they know the causes of the things
that are done (we think the manual workers are like
certain lifeless things which act indeed, but act without
knowing what they do, as fire burns,—but while the
lifeless things perform each of their functions by a
natural tendency, the labourers perform them through
habit); thus we view them as being wiser not in virtue
of being able to act, but of having the theory for themselves and knowing the causes. And in general it is
a sign of the man who knows, that he can teach, and
therefore we think art more truly knowledge than experience is; for artists can teach, and men of mere
experience cannot.

Again, we do not regard any of the senses as Wisdom; yet surely these give the most authoritative knowledge of particulars. But they do not tell us the 'why'
of anything—e.g. why fire is hot; they only say that
it is hot.

At first he who invented any art that went beyond
the common perceptions of man was naturally admired
by men, not only because there was something useful
in the inventions, but because he was thought wise and
superior to the rest. But as more arts were invented,
and some were directed to the necessities of life, others
to its recreation, the inventors of the latter were naturally always regarded as wiser than the inventors of

the former, because their branches of knowledge did
not aim at utility.   Hence when all such inventions
were already established, the sciences which do not aim
at giving pleasure or at the necessities of life were
discovered, and first in the places where men first
began to have leisure.   This is why the mathematical
arts were founded in Egypt; for there the priestly caste
was allowed to be at leisure.

We have said in the *Ethics* what the difference is
between art and science and the other kindred faculties;
but the point of our present discussion is this, that all
men suppose what is called Wisdom to deal with the
first causes and the principles of things.   This is why,
as has been said before, the man of experience is thought
to be wiser than the possessors of any perception whatever, the artist wiser than the man of experience, the
master-worker than the mechanic, and the theoretical
kinds of knowledge to be more of the nature of Wisdom
than the productive.   Clearly then Wisdom is knowledge about certain causes and principles.

Since we are seeking this knowledge, we must inquire
of what kind are the causes and the principles, the
knowledge of which is Wisdom.   If we were to take
the notions we have about the wise man, this might perhaps make the answer more evident.   We suppose first,
then, that the wise man knows all things, as far as
possible, although he has not knowledge of each of
them in detail; secondly, that he who can learn things
that are difficult, and not easy for man to know, is wise
(sense-perception is common to all, and therefore easy
and no mark of Wisdom); again, he who is more exact
and more capable of teaching the causes is wiser, in
every branch of knowledge; and of the sciences, also,
that which is desirable on its own account and for the
sake of knowing it is more of the nature of Wisdom

than that which is desirable on account of its results, and the superior science is more of the nature of Wisdom than the ancillary; for the wise man must not be ordered but must order, and he must not obey another, but the less wise must obey *him*.

Such and so many are the notions, then, which we have about Wisdom and the wise. Now of these characteristics that of knowing all things must belong to him who has in the highest degree universal knowledge; for he knows in a sense all the subordinate objects. And these things, the most universal, are on the whole the hardest for men to know; for they are furthest from the senses. And the most exact of the sciences are those which deal most with first principles; for those which involve fewer principles are more exact than those which involve additional principles, e.g. arithmetic than geometry. But the science which investigates causes is also the more communicable, for the people who teach are those who tell the causes of each thing. And understanding and knowledge pursued for their own sake are found most in the knowledge of that which is most knowable; for he who chooses to know for the sake of knowing will choose most readily that which is most truly knowledge, and such is the knowledge of that which is most knowable; and the first principles and the causes are most knowable; for by reason of these, and from these, all other things are known, but these are not known by means of the things subordinate to them. And the science which knows to what end each thing must be done is the most authoritative of the sciences, and more authoritative than any ancillary science; and this end is the good in each class, and in general the supreme good in the whole of nature. Judged by all the tests we have mentioned, then, the name in question ['Wisdom'] falls to the same science;

this must be a science that investigates the first principles and causes; for the good, i.e. the end and aim, is one of the causes.

That it is not a science of production is clear even from the history of the earliest philosophers. For it is owing to their wonder that men both now begin and at first began to philosophize; they wondered originally at the obvious difficulties, then advanced little by little and stated difficulties about the greater matters, e.g. about the phenomena of the moon and those of the sun, and about the stars and about the genesis of the universe. And a man who is puzzled and wonders thinks himself ignorant (whence even the lover of myth is in a sense a lover of Wisdom, for the myth is composed of wonders); therefore since they philosophized in order to escape from ignorance, evidently they were pursuing science in order to know, and not for any utilitarian end. And this is confirmed by the facts; for it was when almost all the necessities of life and the things that make for comfort and recreation were present, that such knowledge began to be sought. Evidently then we do not seek it for the sake of any other advantage; but as the man is free, we say, who exists for himself and not for another, so we pursue this as the only free science, for it alone exists for itself.

Hence the possession of it might be justly regarded as beyond human power; for in many ways human nature is in bondage, so that according to Simonides 'God alone can have this privilege', and it is unfitting that man should not be content to seek the knowledge that is suited to him. If, then, there is something in what the poets say, and jealousy is natural to the divine power, it would probably occur in this case above all, and all who excelled in this knowledge would be unfortunate. But the divine power cannot be jealous (nay, according to the proverb, 'bards tell many a lie'), nor should any science be thought more honourable than one of this sort. For the most divine science is also most honourable; and this science alone is, in two ways, most divine. For the science which it would be most meet for God to have is a divine science, and so is any science that deals with divine objects; and this science alone has both these qualities; for (1) God is thought to be among the causes of all things and to be a first principle, and (2) such a science either God alone can have, or God above all others. All the sciences, indeed, are more necessary than this, but none is better.

Yet the acquisition of it must in a sense end in something which is the opposite of our original inquiries. For all men begin, as we said, by wondering that the matter is so (as those who have not yet perceived the explanation marvel at automatic marionettes)—whether the object of their wonder be the solstices or the incommensurability of the diagonal of a square with the side; for it seems wonderful to all men that there is a thing which cannot be measured even by the smallest unit. But we must end in the contrary and, according to the proverb, the better state, as is the case in these instances when men learn the cause; for there is nothing which would surprise a geometer so much as if the diagonal turned out to be commensurable.

We have stated, then, what is the nature of the science we are searching for, and what is the mark which our search and our whole investigation must reach.

Evidently we have to acquire knowledge of the original causes (for we say we know each thing only when we think we recognize its first cause), and causes are spoken of in four senses. In one of these we mean the substance, i.e. the essence (for the 'why' is reducible finally to the formula, and the ultimate 'why' is a cause and principle); in another the matter or substratum, in a third the source of the change, and in a fourth the cause opposed to this, the purpose and the good (for this is the end of all generation and change).

15. The supporters of the ideal theory were led to it because they were persuaded of the truth of the Heraclitean doctrine that all sensible things are ever passing away, so that if knowledge or thought is to have an object, there must be some other and permanent entities, apart from those which are sensible; for there can be no knowledge of things which are in a state of flux. Socrates occupied himself with the excellences of character, and in connection with them became the first to raise the problem of universal definitions—for in the realm of physics the problem was only touched on by Democritus, who defined, after a fashion, the hot and the cold; while the Pythagoreans had before this treated of a few things, whose definitions they connected with numbers—e.g. opportunity, justice, or marriage. But it was natural that Socrates should seek the essence. For he was seeking to syllogize, and the essence is the starting-point of syllogisms. For there was as yet none of the dialectical power which enables people even without knowledge of the essence to speculate about contraries and inquire whether the same science deals with contraries. For two things may be fairly ascribed to Socrates—inductive arguments and universal definition, both of which are concerned with the starting-point of science. But Socrates did not make the universals or the definitions exist apart; his successors, however, gave them separate existence, and this was the kind of thing they called Ideas.

Therefore it followed for them, almost by the same

argument, that there must be Ideas of all things that
are spoken of universally, and it was almost as if a man
wished to count certain things, and while they were
few thought he would not be able to count them, but
made them more and then counted them; for the Forms
are almost more numerous than the groups of sensible
things, yet it was in seeking the causes of sensible things
that they proceeded from these to the Forms. For to
each set of substances there answers a Form which has
the same name and exists apart from the substances,
and so also in the other categories there is one character
common to many individuals, whether these be sensible
or eternal.

Again, of the ways in which it is proved that the
Forms exist, none is convincing; for from some no inference necessarily follows, and from some it follows
that there are Forms even of things of which the Platonists think there are no Forms.

For according to the arguments from the sciences
there will be Forms of all things of which there are
sciences, and according to the argument that there is
one attribute common to many things there will be
Forms even of negations, and according to the argument
that thought has an object when the individual object
has perished, there will be Forms of perishable things;
for we can have an image of these. Again, of the most
accurate arguments, some lead to Ideas of relations,
of which the Platonists say there is no independent
class, and others involve the difficulty of the 'third
man'. And in general the arguments for the Forms
destroy that for whose existence the assertors of Forms
are more anxious than for the existence of the Ideas;
for it follows that not the dyad but number is first,
and the relative is prior to the absolute—and besides
this there are all the other points on which certain peo-

ple, by following out the opinions held about the Forms, have come into conflict with the principles of the theory.

Again, according to the assumption on which the belief in the Ideas rests, there will be Forms not only of substances but also of many other things; for the concept is single, not only in the case of substances, but also in that of non-substances, and there are sciences of other things than substance; and a thousand other such conclusions also follow. But according to the necessities of the case and the opinions about the Forms, if they can be shared in there must be Ideas of substances only. For they are not shared in incidentally, but each Form must be shared in as something not predicated of a subject. (E.g. if a thing shares in 'the double itself', it shares also in 'eternal', but incidentally; for 'the double' happens to be eternal.) Therefore the Forms will be substance. And the same names indicate substance in this and in the ideal world (or what will be the meaning of saying that there is something apart from the particulars—the one over many?). And if the Ideas and the things that share in them have the same Form, there will be something common: for why should '2' be one and the same in all the perishable 2's, or in the 2's which are many but eternal, and not the same in the '2 itself' as in the individual 2? But if they have not the same Form, they will have only the name in common, and it is as if one were to call both Callias and a piece of wood 'man', without observing any community between them.

But if we are to suppose that in other respects the common formulæ apply to the Forms, e.g., that 'plane figure' and the other parts of the formula apply to the circle-in-itself, but the name of that of which it is the Form is to be added, we must inquire whether this is not absolutely meaningless. For to what will this be added? To 'centre' or to 'plane' or to all the parts of the formula? For all the elements in the essence are Ideas, e.g. 'animal' and 'two-footed'. Further, the added notion must be an Idea, just as 'plane' must be a definite entity which will be present as genus in all its species.

Above all one might discuss the question what on earth the Forms contribute to sensible things, either to those that are eternal or to those which come into being and cease to be; for they cause neither movement nor any change in them. But again they help in no wise towards the *knowledge* of other things (for they are not even the substance of these, else they would have been in them), nor towards their being, at least if they are not *in* the individuals which share in them; though in that sense white might be thought to cause the whiteness of the white thing in which it is mixed. But this argument, which was used first by Anaxagoras, and later by Eudoxus in his discussion of difficulties and by certain others, is too easily upset; for it is easy to collect many insuperable objections to such a view.

But further all other things cannot come from the Forms in any of the ways that are usually suggested. And to say that they are patterns and the other things share in them is to use empty words and poetical metaphors. For what is it that works, looking to the Ideas? And any thing can both be and come into being without being copied from something else, so that, whether Socrates exists or not, a man like Socrates might come to be. And evidently this might be so even if Socrates were eternal. And according to the Platonic principles there will be several patterns of the same thing, and therefore several Forms, e.g. 'animal' and 'two-footed', and also 'man-himself', will be Forms of man. Again, the Forms are patterns not only of sensible things, but of things-in-themselves also, e.g. the genus is the pattern of the species of the genus; therefore the same thing will be pattern and copy.

Again, it might be thought impossible that substance and that whose substance it is should exist apart; how, therefore, could the Ideas, being substances of things, exist apart? *WE NEED FORMAL CAUSE & AN EFFICIENT CAUSE*

In the *Phaedo* it is stated in this way—that the Forms are causes both of being and of becoming. Yet though the Forms exist, still things do not come into being, unless there is something to move them; and many other things come into being (e.g. a house or a ring), of which they say there are no Forms. Clearly therefore even the things of which they say there are Ideas can both be and come into being owing to such causes as produce the things just mentioned, and not owing to the Forms. But regarding the Ideas it is possible, both in this way and by more abstract and more accurate arguments, to collect many objections like those we have considered.

YOU CANNOT RUN TO INFINITY

16. Evidently there is a first principle, and the causes of things are neither an infinite series nor infinitely various in kind. For (1), on the one hand, one thing cannot proceed from another, as from matter, *ad infinitum,* e.g. flesh from earth, earth from air, air from fire, and so on without stopping; nor on the other hand can the efficient causes form an endless series, man for instance being acted on by air, air by the sun, the sun by Strife, and so on without limit. Similarly the final causes cannot go on *ad infinitum,*—walking for the sake of health, this for the sake of happiness, happiness for the sake of something else, and so one thing always for the sake of another. And the case of the formal cause is similar. For in the case of an intermediate, which has a

last term and a prior term outside it, the prior must be
the cause of the later terms. For if we had to say which
of the three is the cause, we should say the first; surely
not the last, for the final term is the cause of none; nor
even the intermediate, for it is the cause only of one.
It makes no difference whether there is one intermediate
or more, nor whether they are infinite or finite in number. But of series which are infinite in this way, and
of the infinite in general, all the parts down to that
now present are alike intermediates; so that if there
is no first there is no cause at all.

Nor can there be an infinite process downwards, with
a beginning in the upper direction, so that water should
proceed from fire, earth from water, and so always
some other kind should be produced. For one thing
comes *from* another in two ways (if we exclude the
sense in which 'from' means 'after', as we say 'from the
Isthmian games come the Olympian'), (*a*) as the man
comes from the boy, by the boy's changing, or (*b*) as air
comes from water. By 'as the man comes from the
boy' we mean 'as that which has come to be from that
which is coming to be, or as that which is finished
from that which is being achieved' (for as becoming is
between being and not being, so that which is becoming
is always between that which is and that which is not;
and the learner is a man of science in the making, and
this is what is meant when we say that *from* a learner
a man of science is being made); on the other hand,
coming from another thing as water comes from air
implies the destruction of the other thing. This is why
changes of the former kind are not reversible,—the boy
does not come from the man (for that which comes to
be does not come to be *from* the process of coming
to be, but exists *after* the process of coming to be; for
it is thus that the day comes from the morning—in the

sense that it comes after the morning; and therefore the morning cannot come from the day); but changes of the other kind are reversible. But in both cases it is impossible that the number of terms should be infinite. For terms of the former kind being intermediates must have an end, and terms of the latter kind change into *one another;* for the destruction of either is the generation of the other.

At the same time it is impossible that the first cause, being eternal, should be destroyed; for while the process of becoming is not infinite in the upward direction, a first cause by whose destruction something came to be could not be eternal.

Further, the *final cause* is an end, and that sort of end which is not for the sake of something else, but for whose sake everything else is; so that if there is to be a last term of this sort, the process will not be infinite; but if there is no such term there will be no final cause. But those who maintain the infinite series destroy the Good without knowing it. Yet no one would try to do anything if he were not going to come to a limit. Nor would there be reason in the world; the reasonable man, at least, always acts for a purpose; and this is a limit, for the end is a limit.

But the *formal cause,* also, cannot be reduced always to another definition which is fuller in expression. For the original definition is always more of a definition, and not the later one; and in a series in which the first term is not correct, the next is not so either.—Further, those who speak thus destroy science; for it is not possible to have this till one comes to the indivisible concepts. And knowledge becomes impossible; for how can one think things that are infinite in this way? For this is not like the case of the line, to whose divisibility there is no stop, but which we cannot think if we do not make a stop; so that one who is tracing the infinitely divisible line cannot be counting the possibilities of section.

But further, the *matter* in a changeable thing must be cognized.

Again, nothing infinite can exist; and if it could, at least being infinite is not infinite.

But (2) if the *kinds* of causes had been infinite in number, then also knowledge would have been impossible; for we think we know, only when we have ascertained all the causes, but that which is infinite by addition cannot be gone through in a finite time.

17. The effect which lecturers produce on a hearer depends on his habits; for we demand the language we are accustomed to, and that which is different from this seems not in keeping but somewhat unintelligible and foreign because of its unwontedness. For the customary is more intelligible. The force of habit is shown by the laws, in whose case, with regard to the legendary and childish elements in them, habit has more influence than our knowledge about them. Some people do not listen to a speaker unless he speaks mathematically, others unless he gives instances, while others expect him to cite a poet as witness. And some want to have everything done accurately, while others are annoyed by accuracy, either because they cannot follow the connexion of thought or because they regard it as pettifoggery. For accuracy has something of this character, so that as in trade so in argument some people think it mean. Therefore one must be already trained to know how to take each sort of argument, since it is absurd to seek at the same time knowledge and the way of attaining knowledge; and neither is easy to get.

18. There is a science which investigates being as being and the attributes which belong to this in virtue of its own nature. Now this is not the same as any of the so-called special sciences; for none of these others deals generally with being as being. They cut off a part of being and investigate the attributes of this part—this is what the mathematical sciences for instance do. Now since we are seeking the first principles and the highest causes, clearly there must be some thing to which these belong in virtue of its own nature. If then our predecessors who sought the elements of existing things were seeking these same principles, it is necessary that the elements must be elements of being not by accident but just because it *is* being. Therefore it is of being as being that we also must grasp the first causes.

There are many senses in which a thing may be said to 'be', but they are related to one central point, one definite kind of thing, and have not merely the *epithet* 'being' in common. Everything which is healthy is related to health, one thing in the sense that it preserves health, another in the sense that it produces it, another in the sense that it is a symptom of health, another because it is capable of it. And that which is medical is relative to the medical art, one thing in the sense that it possesses it, another in the sense that it is naturally adapted to it, another in the sense that it is a function of the medical art. And we shall find other words used similarly to these. So, too, there are many senses in which a thing is said to be, but all refer to one starting-point; some things are said to be because they are substances, others because they are affections of substance, others because they are a process towards substance, or destructions or privations or qualities of substance, or productive or generative of substance, or of things which are relative to substance, or negations of some of these things or of substance itself. It is for this reason that we say even of non-being that it *is* non-being. As, then, there is one science which deals with all healthy things, the same applies in the other cases also. For not only in the case of things which have one common notion does the investigation belong to one science, but also in the case of things which are related to one common nature; for even these in a sense have one common notion. It is clear then that it is the work of one science also to study all things that are, *qua* being.—But everywhere science deals chiefly with that which is primary, and on which the other things depend, and in virtue of which they get their names. If, then, this is substance, it is of substances that the philosopher must grasp the principles and the causes.

19. It is the function of the philosopher to be able to investigate all things. For if it is not the function of the philosopher, who is it who will inquire whether Socrates and Socrates seated are the same thing, or whether one thing has one contrary, or what contrariety is, or how many meanings it has? And similarly with all other such questions. Since, then, these are essential modifications of unity *qua* unity and of being *qua* being, not *qua* numbers or lines or fire, it is clear that it belongs to this science to investigate both the essence of these concepts and their properties. And those who study these properties err not by leaving the sphere of philosophy, but by forgetting that substance, of which they have no correct idea, is prior to these other things. For number *qua* number has peculiar attributes, such as oddness and evenness, commensurability and equality excess and defect, and these belong to numbers either in themselves or in relation to one another. And simi

larly the solid and the motionless and that which is in motion and the weightless and that which has weight have other peculiar properties. So too certain properties are peculiar to being as such, and it is about these that the philosopher has to investigate the truth.—An indication of this may be mentioned:—dialecticians and sophists assume the same guise as the philosopher, for sophistic is philosophy which exists only in semblance, and dialecticians embrace all things in their dialectic, and being is common to all things; but evidently their dialectic embraces these subjects because these are proper to philosophy.—For sophistic and dialectic turn on the same class of things as philosophy, but this differs from dialectic in the nature of the faculty required and from sophistic in respect of the purpose of the philosophic life. Dialectic is merely critical where philosophy claims to know, and sophistic is what appears to be philosophy but is not.

20. The attempts of some who discuss the terms on which truth should be accepted, are due to a want of training in logic; for they should know these things already when they come to a special study, and not be inquiring into them while they are pursuing it.—Evidently then the philosopher, who is studying the nature of all substance, must inquire also into the principles of syllogism.

But he who knows best about each genus must be able to state the most certain principles of his subject, so that he whose subject is being *qua* being must be able to state the most certain principles of all things. This is the philosopher, and the most certain principle of all is that regarding which it is impossible to be mistaken; for such a principle must be both the best known (for all men may be mistaken about things which they

do not know), and non-hypothetical. For a principle
which every one must have who knows anything about
being, is not a hypothesis; and that which every one
must know who knows anything, he must already have
when he comes to a special study. Evidently then such
a principle is the most certain of all; which principle
this is, we proceed to say. It is, that the same attribute
cannot at the same time belong and not belong to the
same subject in the same respect; we must presuppose,
in face of dialectical objections, any further qualifications which might be added. This, then, is the most
certain of all principles, since it answers to the definition given above. For it is impossible for any one to
believe the same thing to be and not to be, as some think
Heraclitus says; for what a man says he does not necessarily believe. If it is impossible that contrary attributes
should belong at the same time to the same subject (the
usual qualifications must be presupposed in this premise
too), and if an opinion which contradicts another is
contrary to it, obviously it is impossible for the same
man at the same time to believe the same thing to be
and not to be; for if a man were mistaken in this point
he would have contrary opinions at the same time. It
is for this reason that all who are carrying out a demonstration reduce it to this as an ultimate belief; for this
is naturally the starting-point even for all the other
axioms.

21. 'Cause' means (1) that from which (as immanent
material) a thing comes into being, e.g. the bronze of
the statue and the silver of the saucer, and the classes
which include these. (2) The form or pattern, i.e.
the formula of the essence, and the classes which include this (e.g. the ratio 2 : 1 and number in general are
causes of the octave) and the parts of the formula. (3)

That from which the change or the freedom from change
first begins, e.g. the adviser is a cause of the action,
and the father a cause of the child, and in general the
maker a cause of the thing made and the change-pro-
ducing of the changing.   (4) The end, i.e. that for
the sake of which a thing is, e.g. health is the cause
of walking.   For why does one walk? We say 'that
one may be healthy', and in speaking thus we think we
have given the cause.   The same is true of all the
means that intervene before the end, when something
else has put the process in motion (as e.g. thinning
or purging or drugs or instruments intervene before
health is reached); for all these are for the sake of
the end, though they differ from one another in that
some are instruments and others are actions.

These, then, are practically all the senses in which
causes are spoken of, and as they are spoken of in
several senses it follows that there are several causes
of the same thing, and in no accidental sense, e.g. both
the art of sculpture and the bronze are causes of the
statue not in virtue of anything else but *qua* statue;
not, however, in the same way, but the one as matter
and the other as source of the movement.   And things
can be causes of one another, e.g. exercise of good condition, and the latter of exercise; not, however, in the
same way, but the one as end and the other as source
of movement.—Again, the same thing is sometimes a
cause of contraries; for that which when present causes
a particular thing, we sometimes charge, when absent,
with the contrary, e.g. we impute the shipwreck to the
absence of the steersman, whose presence was the cause
of safety; and both—the presence and the privation
—are causes as sources of movement.

All the causes now mentioned fall under four senses
which are the most obvious.   For the letters are the

causes of syllables, and the material is the cause of manufactured things, and fire and earth and all such things are the causes of bodies, and the parts are causes of the whole, and the hypotheses are causes of the conclusion, in the sense that they are that out of which these respectively are made; but of these some are cause as *substratum* (e.g. the parts), others as *essence* (the whole, the synthesis, and the form). The semen, the physician, the adviser, and in general the agent, are all *sources of change* or of rest. The remainder are causes as the *end* and the good of the other things; for that, for the sake of which other things are, is naturally the best and the end of the other things; let us take it as making no difference whether we call it good or apparent good.

These, then, are the causes, and this is the number of their kinds, but the *varieties* of causes are many in number, though when summarized these also are comparatively few. Causes are spoken of in many senses, and even of those which are of the same kind some are causes in a prior and others in a posterior sense, e.g. both 'the physician' and 'the professional man' are causes of health, and 'the ratio 2 :1' and 'number' are causes of the octave, and the classes that include any particular cause are always causes of the particular effect. Again, there are accidental causes and the classes which include these, e.g. while in one sense 'the sculptor' causes the statue, in another sense 'Polyclitus' causes it, because the sculptor happens to be Polyclitus; and the classes that include the accidental cause are also causes, e.g. 'man'—or in general 'animal'—is the cause of the statue, because Polyclitus is a man, and a man is an animal. Of accidental causes also some are more remote or nearer than others, as, for instance, if 'the white' and 'the musical' were called causes of the statue, and not only 'Polyclitus' or 'man'. But besides all these varieties of causes, whether proper or accidental, some are called causes as being able to act, others as acting, e.g. the cause of the house's being built is the builder, or the builder when building.—The same variety of language will be found with regard to the effects of causes, e.g. a thing may be called the cause of this statue or of a statue or in general of an image, and of this bronze or of bronze or of matter in general; and similarly in the case of accidental effects. Again, both accidental and proper causes may be spoken of in combination, e.g. we may say not 'Polyclitus' nor 'the sculptor', but 'Polyclitus the sculptor'.

Yet all these are but six in number, while each is spoken of in two ways: for (1) they are causes either as the individual, or as the class that includes the individual, or as the accidental, or as the class that includes the accidental, and these either as combined, or as taken simply; and (2) all may be taken as acting or as having a capacity. But they differ inasmuch as the acting causes and the individuals exist, or do not exist, simultaneously with the things of which they are causes, e.g. this particular man who is curing, with this particular man who is recovering health, and this particular builder with this particular thing that is being built; but the potential causes are not always in this case; for the house does not perish at the same time as the builder.

22. Things are said to 'be' (1) in an accidental sense, (2) by their own nature.

(1) In an accidental sense, e.g., we say 'the just is musical', and 'the man is musical' and 'the musical is a man', just as we say 'the musical builds', because the builder happens to be musical or the musical hap-

pens to be a builder; for here 'one thing is another'
means 'one is an accident of another'. So in the cases
we have mentioned; for when we say 'the man is musical' and 'the musical is a man', or 'the white is musical'
or 'the musical is white', the last two mean that both
attributes are accidents of the same thing, which *is;*
the first that the attribute is an accident of that which
is; while 'the musical is a man' means that 'musical' is
an accident of man. In this sense, too, the not-white is
said to *be,* because that of which it is an accident *is.*
Thus when one thing is said in an accidental sense to
be another, this is either because both belong to the
same thing, and this *is,* or because that to which the
attribute belongs *is,* or because the subject which has
as an attribute that of which it is itself predicated,
itself *is.*

(2) The kinds of essential being are those that are
indicated by the figures of predication; for the senses
of 'being' are just as many as these figures. Since
some predicates indicate what the subject is, others its
quality, others quantity, others relation, others activity
or passivity, others its 'where', others its 'when', 'being'
has a meaning answering to each of these. For there
is no difference between 'the man is recovering' and
'the man recovers', nor between 'the man is walking'
or 'cutting' and 'the man walks' or 'cuts'; and similarly
in all other cases.

(3) 'Being' and 'is' mean that a statement is true,
'not being' that it is not true but false,—and this alike
in affirmation and negation; e.g. 'Socrates *is* musical'
means that this is true, or 'Socrates *is* not-white' means
that this is true; but 'the diagonal of the square *is not*
commensurate with the side' means that it is false to
say it is.

(4) Again, 'being' and 'that which is', in these cases

we have mentioned, sometimes mean being potentially, and sometimes being actually. For we say both of that which sees potentially and of that which sees actually, that it is 'seeing', and both of that which can use knowledge and of that which is using it, that it knows, and both of that to which rest is already present and of that which can rest, that it rests. And similarly in the case of substances we say the Hermes is in the stone, and the half of the line is in the line, and we say of that which is not yet ripe that it is corn. *When a thing is potential and when it is not yet potential* must be explained elsewhere.

23. Since natural science, like other sciences, confines itself to one class of beings, i.e. to that sort of substance which has the principle of its movement and rest present in itself, evidently it is neither practical nor productive. For the principle of production is in the producer—it is either reason or art or some potency, while the principle of action is in the doer—viz. will, for that which is done and that which is willed are the same. Therefore, if all thought is either practical or productive or theoretical, physics must be a theoretical science, but it will theorize about such being as admits of being moved, and only about that kind of substance which in respect of its definition is for the most part not separable from matter. Now, we must not fail to notice the nature of the essence and of its definition, for, without this, inquiry is but idle. Of things defined, i.e. of essences, some are like 'snub', and some like 'concave'. And these differ because 'snub' is bound up with matter (for what is snub is a concave *nose*), while concavity is independent of perceptible matter. If then all natural things are analogous to the snub in their nature—e.g. nose, eye, face, flesh, bone, and, in

general, animal; leaf, root, bark, and, in general, plant
(for none of these can be defined without reference
to movement—they always have matter), it is clear
how we must seek and define the 'what' in the case
of natural objects, and also why it belongs to the student of nature to study soul to some extent, i.e. so much
of it as is not independent of matter.

That physics, then, is a theoretical science, is plain
from these considerations. Mathematics also is theoretical; but whether its objects are immovable and separable
from matter, is not at present clear; it is clear, however,
that it *considers some* mathematical objects *qua* immovable and *qua* separable from matter. But if there
is something which is eternal and immovable and separable, clearly the knowledge of it belongs to a theoretical
science,—not, however, to physics (for physics deals
with certain movable things) nor to mathematics, but
to a science prior to both. For physics deals with
things which are inseparable from matter but not immovable, and some parts of mathematics deal with
things which are immovable, but probably not separable, but embodied in matter; while the first science
deals with things which are both separable and immovable. Now all causes must be eternal, but especially these; for they are the causes of so much of the
divine as appears to us. There must, then, be three
theoretical philosophies, mathematics, physics, and
what we may call theology, since it is obvious that if
the divine is present anywhere, it is present in things
of this sort. And the highest science must deal with
the highest genus, so that the theoretical sciences are
superior to the other sciences, and this to the other
theoretical sciences. One might indeed raise the question whether first philosophy is universal, or deals with
one genus, i.e. some one kind of being; for not even the

mathematical sciences are all alike in this respect,—
geometry and astronomy deal with a certain particular
kind of thing, while universal mathematics applies alike
to all. We answer that if there is no substance other
than those which are formed by nature, natural science
will be the first science; but if there is an immovable
substance, the science of this must be prior and must
be first philosophy, and universal in this way, because it
is first.

24. There are several senses in which a thing may be
said to 'be', as we pointed out previously in our book
on the various senses of words; for in one sense the
'being' meant is 'what a thing is' or the individual thing,
and in another sense it means that a thing is of a certain quality or quantity or has some such predicate asserted of it. While 'being' has all these senses, obviously that which 'is' primarily is the 'what', which
indicates the substance of the thing. For when we say
of what quality a thing is, we say that it is good or
beautiful, but not that it is three cubits long or that
it is a man; but when we say *what* it is, we do not
say 'white' or 'hot' or 'three cubits long', but 'man' or
'God'. And all other things are said to be because
they are, some of them, quantities of that which *is*
in this primary sense, others qualities of it, others
affections of it, and others some other determination
of it. And so one might raise the question whether
walking and being healthy and sitting are, each of them,
existent or non-existent, and similarly in any other
case of this sort; for none of them is either self-subsistent or capable of being separated from substance,
but rather, if anything, it is that which walks or is
seated or is healthy that is an existent thing. Now
these are seen to be more real because there is some-

thing definite which underlies them; and this is the substance or individual, which is implied in such a predicate; for 'good' or 'sitting' apart from that which sits
or is good has no meaning. Clearly then it is in virtue
of this category that each of the others *is*. Therefore
that which is primarily and *is* simply (not 'is something') must be substance.

Now there are several senses in which a thing is said
to be first; but substance is first in every sense—(1) in
formula, (2) in order of knowledge, (3) in time. For
(3) of the other categories none can exist independently,
but only substance. And (1) in formula also this is
first; for in the formula of each term the formula of
its substance must be present. And (2) we think we
know each thing most fully, when we know what it is,
e.g. what man is or what fire is, rather than when we
know its quality, its quantity, or where it is; since we
know each of these predicates also, only when we know
what the quantity or the quality *is*.

And indeed the question which was raised of old and
is raised now and always, and is always the subject of
doubt, viz. what being is, is just the question, what is
substance? For it is this that some assert to be one,
others more than one, and that some assert to be limited in number, others unlimited. And so we also must
consider chiefly and primarily and almost exclusively
what that is which *is* in this sense.

Substance is thought to belong most obviously to
bodies; and so we say that both animals and plants
and their parts are substances, and so are natural bodies
such as fire and water and earth and everything of the
sort, and all things that are parts of these or composed
of these (either of parts or of the whole bodies), e.g.
the heaven and its parts, stars and moon and sun. But
whether these alone are substances, or there are also

others, or only some of these, or some of these and some other things are substances, or none of these but only some other things, must be considered. Some think the limits of body, i.e. surface, line, point, and unit, are substances, and more so than body or the solid.

Further, some do not think there is anything substantial besides sensible things, but others think there are eternal substances which are more in number and more real, e.g. Plato posited two kinds of substance—the Forms and the objects of mathematics—as well as a third kind, viz. the substance of sensible bodies. And Speusippus made still more kinds of substance, beginning with the One, and making principles for each kind of substance, one for numbers, another for spatial magnitudes, and then another for the soul; and in this way he multiplies the kinds of substance. And some say Forms and numbers have the same nature, and other things come after them, e.g. lines and planes, until we come to the substance of the material universe and to sensible bodies.

Regarding these matters, then, we must inquire which of the common statements are right and which are not right, and what things are substances, and whether there are or are not any besides sensible substances, and how sensible substances exist, and whether there is a separable substance (and if so why and how) or there is no substance separable from sensible substances; and we must first sketch the nature of substance.

The word 'substance' is applied, if not in more senses, still at least to four main objects; for both the essence and the universal and the genus are thought to be the substance of each thing, and fourthly the substratum. Now the substratum is that of which the others are predicated, while it is itself not predicated of anything else. And so we must first determine the

nature of this; for that which underlies a thing primarily is thought to be in the truest sense its substance.
And in one sense matter is said to be of the nature of
substratum, in another, shape, and in a third sense,
the compound of these. By the matter I mean, for instance, the bronze, by the shape the plan of its form,
and by the compound of these (the concrete thing) the
statue. Therefore if the form is prior to the matter
and more real, the compound of both will be prior also
for the same reason.

We have now outlined the nature of substance, showing that it is that which is not predicated of a subject,
but of which all else is predicated. But we must not
merely state the matter thus; for this is not enough.
The statement itself is obscure, and further, on this
view, *matter* becomes substance. For if this is not
substance, it is beyond our power to say what else is.
When all else is taken away evidently nothing but
matter remains. For of the other elements some are
affections, products, and potencies of bodies, while
length, breadth, and depth are quantities and not substances. For a quantity is not a substance; but the substance is rather that to which these belong primarily.
But when length and breadth and depth are taken away
we see nothing left except that which is bounded by
these, whatever it be; so that to those who consider
the question thus matter alone must seem to be substance. By matter I mean that which in itself is neither
a particular thing nor of a certain quantity nor assigned
to any other of the categories by which being is determined. For there is something of which each of
these is predicated, so that its being is different from
that of each of the predicates; for the predicates other
than substance are predicated of substance, while substance is predicated of matter. Therefore the ultimate

substratum is of itself neither a particular thing nor of a particular quantity nor otherwise positively characterized; nor yet negatively, for negations also will belong to it only by accident.

If we adopt this point of view, then, it follows that matter is substance. But this is impossible; for both separability and individuality are thought to belong chiefly to substance. And so form and the compound of form and matter would be thought to be substance, rather than matter. The substance compounded of both, i.e. of matter and shape, may be dismissed; for it is posterior and its nature is obvious. And matter also is in a sense manifest. But we must inquire into the third kind of substance; for this is the most difficult.

It is agreed that there are some substances among sensible things, so that we must look first among these. For it is an advantage to advance to that which is more intelligible. For learning proceeds for all in this way —through that which is less intelligible by nature to that which is more intelligible; and just as in conduct our work is to start from what is good for each and make what is good in itself good for each, so it is our work to start from what is more intelligible to oneself and make what is intelligible by nature intelligible to oneself. Now what is intelligible and primary for particular sets of people is often intelligible to a very small extent, and has little or nothing of reality. But yet one must start from that which is barely intelligible but intelligible to oneself, and try to understand what is intelligible in itself, passing, as has been said, by way of those very things which one understands.

Since at the start we distinguished the various marks by which we determine substance, and one of these was thought to be the essence, we must investigate this. And first let us make some abstract linguistic remarks about it. The essence of each thing is what it is said to be *propter se*. For being you is not being musical; for you are not by your very nature musical. What, then, you are by your very nature is your essence.

But not the whole of this is the essence of a thing; not that which it is *propter se* as a surface is *propter se* white, because being a surface is not *identical* with being white. But again the combination of both—'being a white surface'—is not the essence of surface. Why? Because 'surface' itself is repeated. The formula, therefore, in which the term itself is not present but its meaning is expressed, this is the formula of the essence of each thing. Therefore if to be a white surface is to be a smooth surface, to be white and to be smooth are one and the same.

But since there are compounds of substance with the other categories (for there is a substrate for each category, e.g. for quality, quantity, time, place, and motion), we must inquire whether there is a formula of the essence of each of them, i.e. whether to these compounds also there belongs an essence, e.g. to white man the essence of white man. Let the compound be denoted by 'X'. What is the essence of X? But, it may be said, this also is not a *propter se* expression. We reply that there are just two ways in which a predicate may fail to be true of a subject *propter se*, and one of these results from the addition, and the other from the omission, of a determinant. *One* kind of predicate is not *propter se* because the term that is being defined is combined with another determinant, e.g. if in defining the essence of white one were to state the formula of white *man; another* because in the subject another determinant is combined with that which is expressed in the formula, e.g. if X meant white man, and one were to define X as white; white man is white indeed, but its essence is not to be white. But is being-X an essence at all? Probably not. For the essence is an individual type; but when an attribute is asserted of an alien subject, the complex is not an individual type, e.g. white man is not an individual type, since individuality belongs only to substances. Therefore there is an essence only of those things whose formula is a definition. But we have a definition not where we have a word and a formula identical in meaning (for in that case all formulae or sets of words would be definitions; for there will be some name for any set of words whatever, so that even the *Iliad* would be a definition), but where there is a formula of something primary; and primary things are those which do not imply the predication of one element in them of another, alien element. Nothing, then, which is not a species of a genus will have an *essence*—only species will have it, for in these the subject is not thought to participate in the attribute and to have it as an affection, nor to have it by accident; but for everything else as well, if it has a name, there will be a *formula of its meaning*—viz. that this attribute belongs to this subject; or instead of a simple formula we shall be able to give a more accurate one; but there will be no definition nor essence.

But after all, 'definition,' like 'what a thing is,' has several meanings; 'what a thing is' in one sense means substance and the individual, in another one or other of the predicands, quantity, quality, and the like. For as 'is' is predicable of all things, not however in the same sense, but of one sort of thing primarily and of others in a secondary way, so too the 'what' belongs in the full sense to substance, but in a limited sense to the other categories. For even of a quality we might ask what it is, so that a quality also is a 'what',—not in the full sense, however, but just as, in the case of that which is not, some say, emphasizing the linguistic form, that that which is not *is*—not *is* simply, but *is* non-existent.

Now we must inquire how we should express ourselves on each point, but still more how the facts actually stand. And so now also since it is evident what language we use, essence will belong, just as the 'what' does, primarily and in the simple sense to substance, and in a secondary way to the other categories also,—not essence in the full sense, but the essence of a quality or of a quantity. For it must be either by an equivocation that we say these *are,* or by making qualifications and abstractions (in the way in which that which is not known may be said to be known),—the truth being that we use the word neither ambiguously nor in the same sense, but just as we apply the word 'medical' when there is a *reference* to one and the same thing, not *meaning* one and the same thing, nor yet speaking ambiguously; for a patient and an operation and an instrument are called medical neither by an ambiguity nor with a single meaning, but with reference to a common end. But it does not matter in which of the two ways one likes to describe the facts; this is evident, that definition and essence in the primary and simple sense belong to substances.

[25.] Of things that come to be some come to be by nature, some by art, some spontaneously. Now everything that comes to be comes to be by the agency of something and from something and comes to be something. And the something which I say it comes to be may be found in any category; it may come to be either a 'this' or of some size or of some quality or somewhere.

Now natural comings to be are the comings to be of those things which come to be by nature; and that out of which they come to be is what we call matter; and that by which they come to be is something which exists naturally; and the something which they come to be is a man or a plant or one of the things of this kind, which we say are substances if anything is. All things produced either by nature or by art have matter; for each of them is capable both of being and of not being, and this capacity is the matter in each. And, in general, both that from which they are produced is nature, and the type according to which they are produced is nature (for that which is produced, e.g. a plant or an animal, has a nature), and so is that by which they are produced—the so-called 'formal' nature, which is specifically the same as the nature of the thing produced (though it is in another individual); for man begets man.

Thus, then, are natural products produced; all other productions are called 'makings'. And all makings proceed either from art or from a potency or from thought. Some of them happen also spontaneously or by luck just as natural products sometimes do; for there also the same things sometimes are produced without seed as well as from seed. Concerning these cases, then, we must inquire later, but from art proceed the things of which the form is in the soul of the artist. (By form I mean the essence of each thing and its primary substance.) I say 'form' and not 'form or privation', for even contraries have in a sense the same form; for the substance of a privation is the opposite substance, e.g. health is the substance of disease; for it is by its absence that disease exists; and health is the formula and the knowledge in the soul. The healthy subject, then, is produced as the result of the following train of thought; since *this* is health, if the subject is to be healthy *this* must first be present, e.g. a uniform state of body, and if this is to be present, there must be heat; and the physician goes on thinking thus until he reduces the matter to a final step which he himself can take. Then the process from this point onward, i.e. the process towards health, is called a 'making'. Therefore it follows that in a sense health comes from health and house from house, that with matter from that without matter; < 'from health' and 'from house', > for the medical art and the building art are the form of health and of the house; and < 'from that without matter', > for I call the essence substance without matter. . . .

Since anything which is produced is produced by something (and this I call the starting-point of the production), and from something (and let this be taken to be not the privation but the matter; for the meanings we attach to these have already been distinguished), and since something is produced (and this is either a sphere or a circle or whatever else it may chance to be), just as we do not make the substratum—the bronze, so we do not make the sphere, except incidentally, because the bronze sphere is a sphere and we make the former. For to make a 'this' is to make a 'this' out of the general substratum. I mean that to make the bronze round is not to make the round or the sphere, but something else, i.e. to produce this form in something else as a medium. For if we make the form, we must make it out of something else; for this was assumed. E.g. we make a bronze sphere; and that in the sense that out of this, which is bronze, we make this other, which is a sphere. If, then, we make the sphere itself, clearly we must make it in the same way, and the processes of making will regress to infinity. Obviously then the form also, or whatever we ought to call the shape of the sensible thing, is not produced, nor does production relate to it,—i.e. the essence is

not produced; for this is that which is made to be in
something else by art or by nature or by some potency.
But that there is a *bronze sphere,* this we make. For
we make it out of bronze and the sphere; we bring
the form into this particular matter, and the result is
a bronze sphere. But if the essence of sphere in general is produced, something must be produced out of
something. For the product will always have to be
divisible, and one part must be this and another that,
I mean the one must be matter and the other form.
If then a sphere is 'the figure whose circumference
is at all points equidistant from the centre', part of this
will be the medium in which the thing made will be, and
part will be in that medium, and the whole will be the
thing produced, which corresponds to the bronze sphere.
It is obvious then from what has been said that the thing,
in the sense of form or substance, is not produced, but
the concrete thing which gets its name from this is
produced, and that in everything which comes to be
matter is present, and one part of the thing is matter
and the other form.

Is there then a sphere apart from the individual
spheres or a house apart from the bricks? Rather we
may say that no individual would ever have been coming to be, if this had been so. The 'form' however
means the 'such', and is not a 'this'—a definite thing;
but the artist makes, or the father generates, a 'such'
out of a 'this'; and when it has been generated, it is
a 'this such'. And the whole 'this', Callias or Socrates,
is analogous to 'this bronze sphere', but man and animal
to 'bronze sphere' in general. Obviously then the
cause which consists of the Forms (taken in the sense
in which some maintain the existence of the Forms, i.e.
if they are something apart from the individuals) is
useless with regard both to comings-to-be and to sub-

stances; and the Forms need not, for this reason at
least, be self-subsistent substances. In some cases it
is even obvious that the producer is of the same kind
as the produced (not, however, the same nor one in
number, but in form), e.g. in the case of natural products (for man produces man), unless something happens contrary to nature, e.g. the production of a mule
by a horse. And even these cases are similar; for
that which would be found to be common to horse and
ass, the genus next above them, has not received a name,
but it would doubtless be both, as the mule is both.
Obviously, therefore, it is quite unnecessary to set up
a Form as a pattern (for we should have looked for
Forms in these cases if in any; for these are substances
if anything is so); the begetter is adequate to the making of the product and to the causing of the form in
the matter. And when we have the whole, such and
such a form in this flesh and in these bones, this is
Callias or Socrates; and they are different in virtue
of their matter (for that is different), but the same
in form; for their form is indivisible.

26. Now let us treat first of definition, in so far as we
have not treated of it in the *Analytics;* for the problem
stated in them is useful for our inquiries concerning
substance. I mean this problem:—wherein consists
the unity of that, the formula of which we call a definition, as for instance in the case of man, 'two-footed
animal'; for let this be the formula of man. Why,
then, is this one, and not many, viz. 'animal' *and* 'two-
footed'? For in the case of 'man' and 'white' there is
a plurality when one term does not belong to the other,
but a unity when it does belong and the subject, man,
has a certain attribute; for then a unity is produced
and we have 'the white man'. In the present case, on

the other hand—that of 'animal' and 'two-footed'—one does not share in the other; the genus is not thought to share in its differentiae; for then the same thing would share in contraries; for the differentiae by which the genus is divided are contrary. And even if the genus does share in them, the same argument applies, since the differentiae present in man are many, e.g. endowed with feet, two-footed, featherless. Why are these one and not many? Not because they are present in one thing; for on this principle a unity can be made out of any set of attributes. But surely all the attributes in the definition *must* be one; for the definition is a single formula and a formula of substance, so that it must be a formula of some one thing; for substance means a 'one' and a 'this', as we maintain.

We must first inquire about definitions arising out of divisions. There is nothing in the definition except the first-named genus and the differentia. The other genera are the first genus and along with this the differentiae that are taken with it, e.g. the first may be 'animal', the next 'animal which is two-footed', and again 'animal which is two-footed and featherless', and similarly if the definition includes more terms. And in general it makes no difference whether it includes many or few terms,—nor, therefore, whether it includes few or simply two; and of the two the one is differentia and the other genus, e.g. in 'two-footed animal' 'animal' is genus, and the other is differentia. If then the genus absolutely does not exist apart from the species which it as genus includes, or if it exists but exists as matter (for the voice is genus and matter, but its differentiae make the kinds, i.e. the letters, out of it), clearly the definition is the formula which comprises the differentiae.

But it is also necessary in division to take the differentia of the differentia; e.g. 'endowed with feet' is a

differentia of 'animal'; again we must know the differentia of 'animal endowed with feet' *qua* endowed
with feet.   Therefore we must not say, if we are to
speak rightly, that of that which is endowed with feet
one part has feathers and one is featherless; if we say
this we say it through incapacity; we must divide it *qua*
cloven-footed or not-cloven; for these are differentiae
in the foot; cloven-footedness is a form of footedness.
And we always want to go on so till we come to the
species that contain no differences.   And then there
will be as many kinds of foot as there are differentiae,
and the kinds of animals endowed with feet will be
equal in number to the differentiae.   If then this is so,
clearly the *last* differentia will be the substance of the
thing and its definition, since it is not right to state
the same things more than once in our definitions; for
it is superfluous.   And this does happen; for when we
say 'animal which is endowed with feet, and two-footed'
we have said nothing other than 'animal having feet,
having two feet'; and if we divide this by the proper
division, we shall be saying the same thing many times
—as many times as there are differentiae.

If then a differentia of a differentia be taken at each
step, one differentia—the last—will be the form and the
substance; but if we divide according to accidental qualities, e.g. if we were to divide that which is endowed
with feet into the white and the black, there will be
as many differentiae as there are processes of division.
Therefore it is plain that the definition is the formula
which contains the differentiae, or, according to the
right method, the last of these.   This would be evident, if we were to change the order of such definitions,
e.g. that of man, saying 'animal which is two-footed
and endowed with feet'; for 'endowed with feet' is
superfluous when 'two-footed' has been said.   But order

is no part of the substance; for how are we to think the one element posterior and the other prior? Regarding the definitions, then, which arise out of divisions, let this much be taken as stated in the first place as to their nature.

Let us again return to the subject of our inquiry, which is substance. As the substrate and the essence and the compound of these are called substance, so also is the universal. About two of these we have spoken; about the essence and about the substrate, of which we have said that it underlies in two senses, either being an individual thing—which is the way in which an animal underlies its attributes—, or as the matter underlies the complete reality. The universal also is thought by some to be in the fullest sense a cause, and a principle; therefore let us attack the discussion of this point also. For it seems impossible that any universal term should be the name of a substance. For primary substance is that kind of substance which is peculiar to an individual, which does not belong to anything else; but the universal is common, since that is called universal which naturally belongs to more than one thing. Of which individual then will this be the substance? Either of all or of none. But it cannot be the substance of all; and if it is to be the substance of one, this one will be the others also; for things whose substance is one and whose essence is one are themselves also one.

Further, substance means that which is not predicable of a subject, but the universal is predicable of some subject always.

But perhaps the universal, while it cannot be substance in the way in which the essence is so, can be present in this, e.g. 'animal' can be present in 'man' and 'horse'. Then clearly there is a formula of the universal. And it makes no difference even if there is not a formula of everything that is in the substance; for none the less the universal will be the substance of something. 'Man' is the substance of the individual man in whom it is present; therefore the same will happen again; for a substance, e.g. 'animal', must be the substance of that in which it is present as something peculiar to it. And further it is impossible and absurd that the individual, i.e. the substance, if it consists of parts, should not consist of substances nor of what is individual, but of quality; for that which is not substance, i.e. the quality, will then be prior to substance and to the individual. Which is impossible; for neither in formula nor in time nor in knowledge can the affections be prior to the substance; for then they would be separable from it. Further, in Socrates there will be a substance in a substance, so that he will be the substance of two things. And in general it follows, if man and such things are substances, that none of the elements in their formulae is the substance of anything, nor does it exist apart from the species or in anything else; I mean, for instance, that no 'animal' exists apart from the particular animals, nor does any other of the elements present in formulae exist apart.

If, then, we view the matter from these standpoints, it is plain that no universal attribute is a substance, and this is plain also from the fact that no common predicate indicates a 'this', but rather a 'such'. If not, many difficulties follow and especially the 'third man'.

The conclusion is evident also (1) from the following consideration—that a substance cannot consist of substances present in it actually (for things that are thus actually two are never actually one, though if they are *potentially* two, they can be one, e.g. the double line consists of two halves—potentially; for the *actualization* of the halves divides them from one another; therefore if the substance is one, it will not consist of substances present in it); and (2) according to the argument which Democritus states rightly; he says one thing cannot come from two nor two from one; for he identifies his indivisible magnitudes with substances. It is clear therefore that the same will hold good of number, if number is a synthesis of units, as is said by some; for 'two' is either not one, or there is no unit present in it actually.

27. Evidently even of the things that are thought to be substances, most are only potencies,—e.g. the parts of animals (for none of them exists separately; and when they *are* separated, then they too exist, all of them, merely as matter) and earth and fire and air; for none of them is one, but they are like a heap before it is fused by heat and some one thing is made out of the bits. One might suppose especially that the parts of living things and the corresponding parts of the soul are both, i.e. exist in complete reality as well as in potency, because they have sources of movement in something in their flexures; for which reason some animals live when divided. Yet all the parts must exist only potentially, when they are one and continuous by nature,—not by force or even by growing together, for such a phenomenon is an abnormality.

28. To return to the difficulty which has been stated with respect to definitions and numbers, what is the cause of the unity of each of them? In the case of all things which have several parts and in which the whole is not, as it were, a mere heap, but the totality is something besides the parts, there is a cause of unity; for as regards material things contact is the cause in some

cases, and in others viscidity or some other such quality. And a definition is a set of words which is one not by being connected together, like the *Iliad,* but by dealing with one object.—What then is it that makes man one; why is he one and not many, e.g. animal+ biped, especially if there are, as some say, an ideal animal and an ideal biped? Why are not those Ideas the ideal man, so that men would exist by participation not in man, nor in one Idea, but in two, animal and biped? And in general man would be not one but more than one thing, animal and biped.

Clearly, then, if people proceed thus in their usual manner of definition and speech, they cannot explain and solve the difficulty. But if, as we say, one element is matter and another is form, and one is potentially and the other actually, the question will no longer be thought a difficulty. For this difficulty is the same as would arise if 'round bronze' were the definition of X; for this symbol would be a sign of the definitory formula, so that the question is, what is the cause of the unity of 'round' and 'bronze'? The difficulty disappears, because the one is matter, the other form. What then is the cause of this—the reason why that which was potentially is actually,—what except, in the case of things which are generated, the agent? For there is no other reason why the potential sphere becomes actually a sphere, but this was the essence of either. Of matter some is the object of reason, some of sense, and part of the formula is always matter and part is actuality, e.g. the circle is (1) a figure which (2) is plane. But of the things which have no matter, either for reason or for sense, each is by its nature essentially a kind of unity, as it is essentially a kind of being—individual substance, quality, or quantity. And so neither 'existent' nor 'one' is present in definitions, and an essence

is by its very nature a kind of unity as it is a kind
of being. This is why none of these has any reason
outside itself for being one, nor for being a kind of
being; for each is by its nature a kind of being and a
kind of unity, not as being in the genus 'being' or 'one'
nor in the sense that being and unity can exist apart
from particulars.

Owing to the difficulty about unity some speak of 'participation', and raise the question, what is the cause
of participation and what is it to participate; and others
speak of 'communion', as Lycophron says knowledge
is a communion of knowing with the soul; and others
say life is a 'composition' or 'connexion' of soul with
body. Yet the same account applies to all cases; for
being healthy will be either a communion or a connexion
or a composition of soul and health, and the fact that
the bronze is a triangle will be a composition of bronze
and triangle, and the fact that a thing is white will be
a composition of surface and whiteness.—The reason
is that people look for a unifying formula, and a difference, between potency and complete reality. But, as
has been said, the proximate matter and the form are
one and the same thing, the one potentially, the other
actually. Therefore to ask the cause of their being one
is like asking the cause of unity in general; for each
thing is a unity, and the potential and the actual are
somehow one. Therefore there is no other cause here
unless there is something which caused the movement
from potency into actuality. And all things which
have *no* matter are *without qualification* essentially
unities.

29. Since we have treated of the kind of potency which
is related to movement, let us discuss actuality, its genus
and its differentia. In the course of our analysis it will

also become clear, with regard to the potential, that we not only ascribe potency to that whose nature it is to move something else, or to be moved by something else, either without qualification or in some particular way, but also use the word in another sense, in the pursuit of which we have discussed these previous senses. Actuality means the existence of the thing, not in the way which we express by 'potentially'; we say that potentially, for instance, a statue of Hermes is in the block of wood and the half-line is in the whole, because it might be separated out, and we call even the man who is not studying a man of science, if he is capable of actually studying a particular problem. Our meaning can be seen in the particular cases by induction, and we must not seek a definition of everything but be content to grasp the analogy,—that as that which is building is to that which is capable of building, so is the waking to the sleeping, and that which is seeing to that which has its eyes shut but has sight, and that which is shaped out of the matter to the matter, and that which has been wrought up to the unwrought. Let actuality be defined by one member of this antithesis, and 'the potential' by the other. But all things are not said in the *same sense* to exist actually, but only by analogy—as A is in B or to B, C is in D or to D; for some are as movement to potency, and the others as determinate substance to some sort of matter.

The infinite and the void and all similar things are said to exist potentially and actually in a different sense from that in which many other things are said so to exist, e.g. that which sees or walks or is seen. For of the latter class these predicates can at some time be truly asserted without qualification; for the seen is so called sometimes because it is being seen, sometimes because it is capable of being seen. But the infinite does not exist potentially in the sense that it will ever actually have separate existence; its separateness is only in knowledge. For the fact that division never ceases to be possible gives the result that this actuality exists potentially, but not that it exists separately.

30. The infinite is either that which is incapable of being traversed because it is not its nature to be traversed (this corresponds to the sense in which the voice is 'invisible'), or that which admits only of incomplete traverse or scarcely admits of traverse, or that which, though it naturally admits of traverse, is not traversed or limited; further, a thing may be infinite in respect of addition or of subtraction or of both. The infinite cannot be a separate, independent thing. For if it is neither a spatial magnitude nor a plurality, but infinity itself is its substance and not an accident, it will be indivisible; for the divisible is either magnitude or plurality. But if indivisible, it is not infinite, except as the voice is invisible; but people do not mean this, nor are we examining this sort of infinite, but the infinite as untraversable. Further, how can an infinite exist by itself, unless number and magnitude also exist by themselves,—since infinity is an attribute of these? Further, if the infinite is an accident of something else, it cannot be *qua* infinite an element in things, as the invisible is not an element in speech, though the voice is invisible. And evidently the infinite cannot exist actually. For then any part of it that might be taken would be infinite; for 'to be infinite' and 'the infinite' are the same, if the infinite is substance and not predicated of a subject. Therefore it is either indivisible, or if it is secable, it is divisible into ever divisible parts; but the same thing cannot be many infinites, yet as a part of air is air, so a part of the infinite would be

infinite, if the infinite is a substance and a principle.
Therefore it must be insecable and indivisible. But the
actually infinite cannot be indivisible; for it must be
a quantity. Therefore infinity belongs to a subject
incidentally. But if so, as we have said, it cannot be
it that is a principle, but rather that of which it is an
accident—the air or the even number.

This inquiry is universal; but that the infinite is not
among sensible things, is evident from the following
argument. If the definition of a body is 'that which
is bounded by planes', there cannot be an infinite body
either sensible or intelligible; nor a separate and infinite
number, for number or that which has a number can
be completely enumerated. The truth is evident from
the following concrete argument. The infinite can
neither be composite nor simple. For (1) it cannot be
a composite body, since the elements are limited in multitude. For the contraries must be equal and no *one*
of them must be infinite; for if one of the two bodies
falls at all short of the other in potency, the finite will
be destroyed by the infinite. And that *each* should be
infinite is impossible. For body is that which has extension in all directions, and the infinite is the bound-
lessly extended, so that the infinite body will be infinite
in every direction. Nor (2) can the infinite body be
one and simple—neither, as some say, something which
is apart from the elements, from which they generate
these (for there is no such body apart from the elements; for everything can be resolved into that of which
it consists, but no such product of analysis is observed
except the simple bodies), nor fire nor any other of the
elements. For apart from the question how any of
them could be infinite, the All, even if it is finite, cannot either be or become one of them, as Heraclitus says
all things sometime become fire. The same argument

applies to the One, which the natural philosophers posit besides the elements. For everything changes from the contrary, e.g. from hot to cold.

Further, every sensible body is somewhere, and whole and part have the same proper place, e.g. the whole earth and part of the earth. Therefore if (1) the infinite body is homogeneous, it will be unmovable or it will be always moving. But the latter is impossible; for why should it rather move down than up or anywhere else? E.g. if there is a clod which is part of an infinite body, where will this move or rest? The proper place of the body which is homogeneous with it is infinite. Will the clod occupy the whole place, then? And how? < This is impossible. > What then is its rest or its movement? It will either rest everywhere, and then it cannot move; or it will move everywhere, and then it cannot be still. But (2) if the infinite body has unlike parts, the proper places of the parts are unlike also, and, firstly, the body of the All is not one except by contact, and, secondly, the parts will be either finite or infinite in variety of kind. *Finite* they cannot be; for then those of one kind will be infinite in quantity and those of another will not (if the All is infinite), e.g. fire or water would be infinite, but such an infinite part would be destruction to its contrary. But if the parts are *infinite* and simple, their places also are infinite and the elements will be infinite; and if this is impossible, and the places are finite, the All also must be limited.

In general, there cannot be an infinite body and also a proper place for all bodies, if every sensible body has either weight or lightness. For it must move either towards the middle or upwards, and the infinite—either the whole or the half—cannot do either; for how will you divide it? Or how will part of the infinite be up and part down, or part extreme and part middle? Further, every sensible body is in a place, and there are six kinds of place, but these cannot exist in an infinite body. In general, if there cannot be an infinite place, there cannot be an infinite body; <and there cannot be an infinite place >, for that which is in a place is somewhere, and this means either up or down or in one of the other directions, and each of these is a limit.

The infinite is not the same in the sense that it is one thing whether exhibited in distance or in movement or in time, but the posterior among these is called infinite in virtue of its relation to the prior, i.e. a movement is called infinite in virtue of the distance covered by the spatial movement or alteration or growth, and a time is called infinite because of the movement which occupies it.

31. That which changes changes either from positive into positive, or from negative into negative, or from positive into negative, or from negative into positive. (By positive I mean that which is expressed by an affirmative term.) Therefore there must be three changes; for that from negative into negative is not change; for the terms are neither contraries nor contradictories, because there is no opposition. The change from the negative into the positive which is its contradictory is generation—absolute change absolute generation, and partial change partial generation; and the change from positive to negative is destruction—absolute change absolute destruction, and partial change partial destruction. If, then, 'that which is not' has several senses, and movement can attach neither to that which implies putting together or separating, nor to that which implies potency and is opposed to that which is in the full sense (true, the not-white or not-good *can* be moved

incidentally, for the not-white might be a man; but that which is not a particular thing at all can in no wise be moved), that which is not cannot be moved, and if this is so, generation cannot be movement; for that which is not *is* generated. For even if we admit to the fullest that its generation is accidental, yet it is true to say that 'not-being' is predicable of that which is generated absolutely. (Similarly *rest* cannot belong to that which is not.) These difficulties, then, follow, and also this, that everything that is moved is in a place, but that which is not is not in a place; for then it would be somewhere. Nor is destruction movement; for the contrary of movement is movement or rest, but the contrary of destruction is generation. Since every movement is a change, and the kinds of change are the three named above, and of these those in the way of generation and destruction are not movements, and these are the changes from a thing to its contradictory, only the change from positive into positive can be movement. And the subjects are either contrary or intermediate; for even privation must be regarded as contrary, and is expressed by a positive term, e.g. 'naked' or 'toothless' or 'black'.

If the categories are classified as substance, quality, place, acting or being acted on, relation, quantity, there must be three kinds of movement—of quality, of quantity, of place. There is no movement in respect of substance (because there is nothing contrary to substance), nor in respect of relation (for it is possible that if one of two things in relation changes, the relative term which was true of the other thing ceases to be true, though this other does not change at all,—so that their movement is accidental, nor of agent and patient, nor of mover and moved, because there is no movement of movement nor generation of generation, nor, in general, change of change. . . .

Since, then motion can belong neither to being nor to relation nor to agent and patient, it remains that there can be motion only in respect of quality, quantity, and place; for in each of these we have a pair of contraries. Motion in respect of quality let us call alteration, a general name that is used to include both contraries; and by quality I do not mean here a property of substance (in that sense that which constitutes a specific distinction is a quality) but a passive quality in virtue of which a thing is said to be acted on or to be incapable of being acted on. Motion in respect of quantity has no name that includes both contraries, but it is called increase or decrease according as one or the other is designated; that is to say motion in the direction of complete magnitude is increase, motion in the contrary direction is decrease. Motion in respect of these has no name either general or particular; but we may designate it by the general name of locomotion.

32. Things which are in one place (in the strictest sense) are *together in place,* and things which are in different places are *apart.* Things whose extremes are together *touch.* That at which the changing thing, if it changes continuously according to its nature, naturally arrives before it arrives at the extreme into which it is changing, is *between.* That which is most distant in a straight line is *contrary in place.* That is *successive* which is after the beginning (the order being determined by position or form or in some other way) and has nothing of the same class between it and that which it succeeds, e.g. lines succeed a line, units a unit, or one house another house. (There is nothing to prevent a thing of some *other* class from being between.) For the

successive succeeds something and is something later; 'one' does not succeed 'two', nor the first day of the month the second. That which, being successive, touches, is *contiguous*. Since all change is between opposites, and these are either contraries or contradictories, and there is no middle term for contradictories, clearly that which is *between* is between contraries. The *continuous* is a species of the contiguous or of that which touches; two things are called continuous when the limits of each, with which they touch and are kept together, become one and the same, so that plainly the continuous is found in the things out of which a unity naturally arises in virtue of their contact. And plainly the successive is the first of these concepts; for the successive does not necessarily touch, but that which touches is successive. And if a thing is continuous, it touches, but if it touches, it is not necessarily continuous; and in things in which there is no touching, there is no organic unity. Therefore a point is not the same as a unit; for contact belongs to points, but not to units, which have only succession; and there is something between two of the former, but not between two of the latter. . . .

If the terms 'continuous', 'in contact', and 'in succession' as defined above—things being 'continuous' if their extremities are one, 'in contact' if their extremities are together, and 'in succession' if there is nothing of their own kind intermediate between them—nothing that is continuous can be composed of indivisibles; e.g. a line cannot be composed of points, the line being continuous and the point indivisible. For the extremities of two points can neither be *one* (since of an indivisible there can be no extremity as distinct from some other part) nor *together* (since that which has no parts can have no extremity, the extremity and the thing of which it is the extremity being distinct).

Moreover if that which is continuous is composed of points, these points must be either *continuous* or *in contact* with one another: and the same reasoning applies in the case of all indivisibles. Now for the reason given above they cannot be continuous; and one thing can be in contact with another only if whole is in contact with whole or part with part or part with whole. But since an indivisible has no parts, they must be in contact with one another as whole with whole. And if they are in contact with one another as whole with whole, they will not be continuous; for that which is continuous has distinct parts; and these parts into which it is divisible are different in this way, i.e. spatially separate.

Nor again can a point be *in succession* to a point or a moment to a moment in such a way that length can be composed of points or time of moments; for things are in succession if there is nothing of their own kind intermediate between them, whereas that which is intermediate between points is always a line and that which is intermediate between moments is always a period of time.

Again, if length and time could thus be composed of indivisibles, they could be divided into indivisibles, since each is divisible into the parts of which it is composed. But, as we saw, no continuous thing is divisible into things without parts. Nor can there be any thing of another kind intermediate between the points or between the moments; for if there could be any such thing it is clear that it must be either indivisible or divisible, and if it is divisible it must be divisible either into indivisibles or into divisibles that are infinitely divisible, in which case it is continuous.

Moreover it is plain that everything continuous is divisible into divisibles that are infinitely divisible; for if it were divisible into indivisibles, we should have an indivisible in contact with an indivisible, since the extremities of things that are continuous with one another are one, and such things are therefore in contact.

The same reasoning applies equally to magnitude, to time, and to motion; either all of these are composed of indivisibles and are divisible into indivisibles, or none. This may be made clear as follows. If a magnitude is composed of indivisibles, the motion over that magnitude must be composed of corresponding indivisible motions; e.g. if the magnitude ABC is composed of the indivisibles A, B, C, each corresponding part of the motion DEF of Z over ABC is indivisible. Therefore since where there is motion there must be something that is in motion, and where there is something in motion there must be motion, the actual state of motion will also be composed of indivisibles. So Z traverses A when its motion is D, B when its motion is E, and C similarly when its motion is F. Now a thing that is in motion from one place to another cannot at the moment when it was in motion both be in motion and at the same time have completed its motion at the place to which it was in motion; e.g. if a man is walking to Thebes he cannot be walking to Thebes and at the same time have completed his walk to Thebes; and, as we saw, Z traverses the partless section A in virtue of the presence of the motion D. Consequently, if Z actually passed through A *after* being in process of passing through, the motion must be divisible; for at the time when it was passing through, it neither was at rest nor had completed its passage but was in an intermediate state; while if it is passing through and has completed its passage *at the same moment,* then that which is walking will at the moment when it is walking have completed its walk and will be in the place to which it is walking, that is to say it will have completed its motion at the place to which it is in motion.

And if a thing is in motion over the whole ABC and its motion is the three D, E, and F, and if it is not in motion at all over the partless section A but has completed its motion over it, then the motion will consist not of motions but of starts, and it will be possible for a thing to have completed a motion without being in motion; for on this assumption it has completed its passage through A without passing through it. So it will be possible for a thing to have completed a walk without ever walking; for on this assumption it has completed a walk over a particular distance without walking over that distance. Since, then, everything must be either at rest or in motion, and Z is therefore at rest in each of the sections A, B, and C, it follows that a thing can be continuously at rest and at the same time in motion; for, as we saw, Z is in motion over the whole ABC and at rest in any part (and consequently in the whole) of it. Moreover if the indivisibles composing DEF are motions, it would be possible for a thing in spite of the presence in it of motion to be not in motion but at rest, while if they are not motions, it would be possible for motion to be composed of something other than motions.

And if length and motion are thus indivisible, it is neither more nor less necessary that time also be similarly indivisible, that is to say composed of indivisible moments; for if the whole distance is divisible and an equal velocity will cause a thing to pass through less of it in less time, the time must also be divisible, and conversely, if the time in which a thing is carried over the section A is divisible, this section A must also be divisible.

And since every magnitude is divisible into magnitudes—for we have shown that it is impossible for anything continuous to be composed of indivisible parts, and every magnitude is continuous—it necessarily follows that the quicker of two things traverses a greater magnitude in an equal time, an equal magnitude in less time, and a greater magnitude in less time, in conformity with the definition sometimes given of the 'quicker'. Suppose that A is quicker than B. Now since of two things that which changes sooner is quicker, in the time FG, in which A has changed from C to D, B will not yet have arrived at D but will be short of it; so that in an equal time the quicker will pass over a greater magnitude. More than this, it will pass over a greater magnitude in *less* time; for in the time in which A has arrived at D, B being the slower has arrived, let us say, at E. Then since A has occupied the whole time FG in arriving at D, it will have arrived at H in less time than this, say FK. Now the magnitude CH that A has passed over is greater than the magnitude CE, and the time FK is less than the whole time FG; so that the quicker will pass over a greater magnitude in less time. And from this it is also clear that the quicker will pass over an equal magnitude in less time than the slower. For since it passes over the greater magnitude in less time than the slower and (regarded by itself) passes over LM the greater in more time than LN the less, the time PR in which it passes over LM will be more than the time PS in which it passes over LN; so that, the time PR being less than the time PT in which the slower passes over LN, the time PS will also be less than the time PT; for it is less than the time PR, and that which is less than something else that is less than a thing, is also itself less than that thing. Hence it follows that the quicker will traverse an equal magnitude in less time than the

slower.   Again, since the motion of anything must always occupy either an equal time or less or more time
in comparison with that of another thing, and since,
whereas a thing is slower if its motion occupies more
time and of equal velocity if its motion occupies an
equal time, the quicker is neither of equal velocity nor
slower, it follows that the motion of the quicker can
occupy neither an equal time nor more time.   It can
only be, then, that it occupies less time, and thus we
get the necessary consequence that the quicker will pass
over an equal magnitude (as well as a greater) in less
time than the slower.

And since every motion is in time and a motion may
occupy any time, and the motion of everything that is
in motion may be either quicker or slower, both quicker
motion and slower motion may occupy any time; and
this being so, it necessarily follows that time also is
continuous.   By continuous I mean that which is divisible into divisibles that are infinitely divisible; and if
we take this as the definition of 'continuous', it follows
necessarily that time is continuous.   For since it has
been shown that the quicker will pass over an equal
magnitude in less time than the slower, suppose that
A is quicker and B slower, and that the slower has
traversed the magnitude CD in the time FG.   Now
it is clear that the quicker will traverse the same magnitude in less time than this; let us say in the time FH.
Again since the quicker has passed over the whole
CD in the time FH, the slower will in the same time
pass over CK, say, less than CD.   And since B, the
slower, has passed over CK in the time FH, the quicker
will pass over it in less time; so that the time FH
will again be divided.   And if this is divided the magnitude CK will also be divided just as CD was; and
again if the magnitude is divided, the time will also be

divided. And we can carry on this process for ever, taking the slower after the quicker and the quicker after the slower alternately, and using what has been demonstrated at each stage as a new point of departure; for the quicker will divide the time and the slower will divide the length. If, then, this alternation always holds good, and at every turn involves a division, it is evident that all time must be continuous. And at the same time it is clear that all magnitude is also continuous; for the divisions of which time and magnitude respectively are susceptible are the same and equal.

Moreover the current popular arguments make it plain that, if time is continuous, magnitude is continuous also, inasmuch as a thing passes over half a given magnitude in half the time taken to cover the whole; in fact without qualification it passes over a less magnitude in less time; for the divisions of time and of magnitude will be the same. And if either is infinite, so is the other, and the one is so in the same way as the other; i.e. if time is infinite in respect of its extremities, length is also infinite in respect of its extremities; if time is infinite in respect of divisibility, length is also infinite in respect of divisibility; and if time is infinite in both respects, magnitude is also infinite in both respects.

Hence Zeno's argument makes a false assumption in asserting that it is impossible for a thing to pass over or severally to come in contact with infinite things in a finite time. For there are two senses in which length and time and generally anything continuous are called 'infinite'; they are called so in respect either of divisibility or of their extremities. So while a thing in a finite time cannot come in contact with things quantitatively infinite, it can come in contact with things infinite in respect of divisibility; for in this sense the time itself is also infinite; and so we find that the time occupied by the passage over the infinite is not a finite but an infinite time, and the contact with the infinite is made by means of moments not finite but infinite in number.

The passage over the infinite, then, cannot occupy a finite time, and the passage over the finite cannot occupy an infinite time; if the time is infinite the magnitude must be infinite also, and if the magnitude is infinite, so also is the time. This may be shown as follows. Let AB be a finite magnitude, and let us suppose that it is traversed in infinite time C, and let a finite period CD of the time be taken. Now in this period the thing in motion will pass over a certain segment of the magnitude; let BE be the segment that it has thus passed over (this will be either an exact measure of AB or less or greater than an exact measure; it makes no difference which it is). Then, since a magnitude equal to BE will always be passed over in an equal time, and BE measures the whole magnitude, the whole time occupied in passing over AB will be finite; for it will be divisible into periods equal in number to the segments into which the magnitude is divisible. Moreover if it is the case that infinite time is not occupied in passing over every magnitude, but it is possible to pass over some magnitude, say BE, in a finite time, and if this BE measures the whole of which it is a part, and if an equal magnitude is passed over in an equal time, then it follows that the time like the magnitude is finite. That infinite time will not be occupied in passing over BE is evident if the time be taken as limited in one direction; for as the part will be passed over in less time than the whole, the time occupied in traversing this part must be finite, the limit in one direction being given. The same reasoning will also show the falsity of the assumption that infinite length can be traversed in a finite time. It is evident, then, from what has been said that neither a time nor a surface nor in fact anything continuous can be indivisible. . . .

Zeno's reasoning is fallacious, when he says that if everything when it occupies an equal space is at rest, and if that which is in locomotion is always occupying such a space at any moment, the flying arrow is therefore motionless. This is false, for time is not composed of indivisible moments any more than any magnitude is composed of indivisibles.

Zeno's arguments about motion, which cause so much disquietude to those who try to solve the problems that they present, are four in number. The first asserts the non-existence of motion on the ground that that which is in locomotion must arrive at the halfway stage before it arrives at the goal. This we have discussed above.

The second is the so-called 'Achilles', and it amounts to this, that in a race the quickest runner can never overtake the slowest, since the pursuer must first reach the point whence the pursued started, so that the slower must always hold a lead. This argument is the same in principle as that which depends on bisection, though it differs from it in that the spaces with which we successively have to deal are not divided into halves. The result of the argument is that the slower is not overtaken; but it proceeds along the same lines as the bisection-argument (for in both a division of the space in a certain way leads to the result that the goal is not reached, though the 'Achilles' goes further in that it affirms that even the quickest runner in legendary tradition must fail in his pursuit of the slowest), so that the solution must be the same. And

the axiom that that which holds a lead is never overtaken is false; it is not overtaken, it is true, while it
holds a lead; but it is overtaken nevertheless if it is
granted that it traverses the finite distance prescribed.
These, then, are two of his arguments.

The third is that already given above, to the effect
that the flying arrow is at rest, which result follows
from the assumption that time is composed of moments;
if this assumption is not granted, the conclusion will
not follow.

The fourth argument is that concerning the two rows
of bodies, each row being composed of an equal number
of bodies of equal size, passing each other on a race-
course as they proceed with equal velocity in opposite
directions, the one row originally occupying the space
between the goal and the middle point of the course and
the other that between the middle point and the starting-post. This, he thinks, involves the conclusion that
half a given time is equal to double that time. The
fallacy of the reasoning lies in the assumption that
a body occupies an equal time in passing with equal
velocity a body that is in motion and a body of equal
size that is not; which is false. For instance (so runs
the argument) let A, A . . . be the stationary bodies
of equal size, B, B . . . the bodies, equal in number
and in size to A, A . . . originally occupying the half
of the course from the starting-post to the middle of
the A's, and C, C . . . those originally occupying the
other half from the goal to the middle of the A's,
equal in number, size, and velocity to B, B. . . . Then
three consequences follow: First, as the B's and the
C's pass one another, the first B reaches the last C
at the same moment as the first C reaches the last B.
Secondly at this moment the first C has passed all the
A's, whereas the first B has passed only half the A's,

and has consequently occupied only half the time occupied by the first C, since each of the two occupies
an equal time in passing each A. Thirdly at the same
moment all the B's have passed all the C's; for the
first C and the first B will simultaneously reach the
opposite ends of the course, since (so says Zeno) the
time occupied by the first C in passing each of the B's
is equal to that occupied by it in passing each of the A's
because an equal time is occupied by both the first B and
the first C in passing all the A's. This is the argument,
but it presupposes the aforesaid fallacious assumption.

33. Motion, we say, is the actuality of the movable in
so far as it is movable. Each kind of motion, therefore,
necessarily involves the presence of the things that are
capable of that motion. In fact even apart from the
definition of motion everyone would admit that in each
kind of motion it is that which is capable of that motion that is in motion: thus it is that which is capable
of alteration that is altered and that which is capable
of local change that is in locomotion; and so there must
be something capable of being burned before there can
be a process of being burned and something capable
of burning before there can be a process of burning.
Moreover these things also must either have a beginning before which they had no being or they must be
eternal. Now if there is a becoming of every movable
thing, it follows that before the motion in question
another change or motion must take place in which that
which is capable of being moved or of causing motion
has its becoming. To suppose on the other hand that
these things were in being throughout all previous time
without there being any motion appears unreasonable
on a moment's thought, and still more unreasonable, we
shall find, on further consideration. For if we are to

say that while there are on the one hand things that are movable and on the other hand things that are motive, there is a time when there is a first movement and a first moved, and another time when there is no such thing but only something that is at rest, then this thing that is at rest must previously be in process of change; for there must have been some cause of its rest, rest being the privation of motion. Therefore before this first change there will be a previous change. . . .

The same reasoning will also serve to show the imperishability of motion; just as a becoming of motion would involve, as we saw, the existence of a process of change previous to the first, in the same way a perishing of motion would involve the existence of a process of change subsequent to the last; for when a thing ceases to be moved it does not therefore at the same time cease to be movable—e.g. the cessation of the process of being burned does not involve the cessation of the capacity of being burned, since a thing may be capable of being burned without being in process of being burned—nor when a thing ceases to be movement, does it therefore at the same time cease to be motive. Again, a thing that is perishable will have to perish after it has perished; and then that which has the property of causing it to perish will have to perish afterwards; for perishing also is a kind of change. If then the view we are criticizing involves these impossible consequences it is clear that motion is eternal and cannot have existed at one time and not at another.

34. Since there must always be motion without intermission there must necessarily be something eternal, a unity or it may be a plurality, that first imparts motion, and this first movent must be unmoved. Now

the question whether all things that are unmoved but impart motion are severally eternal is irrelevant to our present argument; but the following considerations will make it clear that there must necessarily be some such thing, which, while it has the capacity of moving something else, is itself unmoved and exempt from all change, which can affect it neither in an unqualified nor in accidental sense. Let us suppose, if any one likes, that in the case of certain things it is possible for them to be and not to be without any process of becoming and perishing; in fact it would seem to be necessary, if a thing that has not parts at one time is and at another is not, that any such thing should at one time be and at another time not be without undergoing any process of change. And let us further suppose it possible that some principles that are unmoved but capable of imparting motion, at one time are and at another are not. Even so, this cannot be true of all such principles, since there must clearly be something that causes things that move themselves, at one time to be and at another not to be. For since nothing that has not parts can be in motion, that which moves itself must as a whole have magnitude, though nothing that we have said makes this necessarily true of its movent. So the fact that some things become and others perish, and that this is so continuously, cannot be caused by any one of the things that, though they are unmoved, do not always exist; nor again can it be caused by some of them continually moving certain particular things and others moving other things. The eternity and continuity of the process cannot be caused either by any one of them singly or by the sum of them, because their causal relation must be eternal and necessary, whereas the sum of these movents is infinite and they do not all exist together.

It is clear then that though there may be countless instances of the perishing of some principles that are unmoved but impart motion, and though many things that move themselves perish and are succeeded by others that come into being, and though one thing that is unmoved moves one thing while another moves another; nevertheless there is something that comprehends them all and moreover influences each one of them, and this it is that is the cause of the fact that some things are and others are not, and of the continuous process of change; and this causes the motion of the other movents, while they are the causes of the motion of other things. Motion, then, being eternal, the first movent, if there is but one, will be eternal also; if there are more than one, there will be a plurality of such eternal movents. We ought however to suppose that there is one rather than many, and a finite rather than an infinite number. When the consequences of either assumption are the same, we should always assume that things are finite rather than infinite in number, since in things constituted by nature that which is finite and that which is better ought, if possible, to be present rather than the reverse; and here it is sufficient to assume only one movent, the first of unmoved things, which being eternal will be the principle of motion to everything else.

The following argument also makes it evident that the first movent must be something that is one and eternal. We have shown that there must always be motion. That being so, motion must also be continuous, because what is always is continuous, whereas what is merely successive is not continuous. But further, if motion is continuous, it is one; and it is one only if the movent and the moved that constitute it are each of them one, since in the event of a thing's being moved

now by one thing and now by another the whole motion
will not be continuous but successive.

35. We must consider whether it is or is not possible
that there should be a continuous motion, and, if it is
possible, which this motion is and which is the first or
primary motion; for it is plain that if there must always be motion, and a particular motion is primary
and continuous, then it is this motion that is imparted
by the first movent—and so is necessarily one and the
same and continuous and primary.

Now of the three kinds of motion that there are—
motion in respect of magnitude, motion in respect of
affection and motion in respect of place—it is this last,
which we call locomotion, that must be primary. This
may be shown as follows. It is impossible that there
should be increase without the previous occurrence of
alteration; for that which is increased, although in a
sense it is increased by what is like itself, is in a sense
increased by what is unlike itself: thus it is said that
contrary is nourishment to contrary; but growth is ef-
fected only by things becoming like to like. There
must be alteration in that there is this change from contrary to contrary. But the fact that a thing is altered
requires that there should be something that alters it,
something e.g. that makes the potentially hot into the
actually hot; so it is plain that the movent does not maintain a uniform relation to it but is at one time nearer to
and at another further from that which is altered; and
we cannot have this without locomotion. If, therefore, there must always be motion, there must also
always be locomotion as the primary motion, and if
there is a primary as distinguished from a secondary
form of locomotion, it must be the primary
form. . . .

It can now be shown plainly that rotation is the primary locomotion. Every locomotion is either rotatory or rectilinear or a compound of the two; and the two former must be prior to the last, since they are the elements of which the latter consists. Moreover rotatory locomotion is prior to rectilinear locomotion, because it is more simple and perfect, which may be shown as follows. The straight line traversed in rectilinear motion cannot be infinite; for there is no such thing as an infinite straight line; and even if there were it would not be traversed by anything in motion; for the impossible does not happen and it is impossible to traverse an infinite distance. On the other hand rectilinear motion on a finite straight line is if it turns back a composite motion, in fact two motions, while if it does not turn back it is imperfect and perishable; and in the order of nature, of thought, and of time alike the perfect is prior to the imperfect and the imperishable to the perishable. Again, a motion that admits of being eternal is prior to one that does not. Now rotatory motion can be eternal; but no other motion, whether locomotion or motion of any other kind, can be so, since in all of them rest must occur, and with the occurrence of rest the motion has perished.

36. There are three kinds of substance—the matter, which acquires individuality by being perceived (for all things that are characterized by contact and not by organic unity are matter and substratum); the nature (i.e. the individual character) that it moves towards, which is a positive state; and again, thirdly, the particular substance which is composed of these two, e.g. Socrates or Callias. Now in some cases the individual character does not exist apart from the composite substance, e.g. the form of house does not so exist, unless the art

of building exists apart (nor is there generation and destruction of these forms, but it is in another way that the house apart from its matter, and health, and all ideals of art, exist and do not exist); but if the individual character exists apart from the concrete thing, it is only in the case of natural objects. And so Plato was not far wrong when he said that there are as many Forms as there are kinds of natural things (if there are Forms at all),—though not of such things as fire, flesh, head; for all these are matter, and the last matter is the matter of that which is in the fullest sense substance. The moving causes exist as things preceding the effects, but causes in the sense of formulae are simultaneous with their effects. For when a man is healthy, then health also exists; and the shape of a bronze sphere exists at the same time as the bronze sphere. But we must examine whether any form also survives afterwards. For in some cases this may be so, e.g. the soul may be of this sort—not all soul but the reason; for doubtless it is impossible that *all* soul should survive. Evidently then there is no necessity, on this ground at least, for the existence of the Ideas. For man is begotten by man, each man by an individual father; and similarly in the arts; for the medical art is the formal cause of health.

37. Since there were three kinds of substance, two of them physical and one unmovable, regarding the latter we must assert that it is necessary that there should be an eternal unmovable substance. For substances are the first of existing things, and if they are all destructible, all things are destructible. But it is impossible that movement should either come into being or cease to be; for it must always have existed. Nor can time come into being or cease to be; for there could not be a

before and an after if time did not exist. Movement also is continuous, then, in the sense in which time is, for time is either the same thing as movement or an attribute of movement. And there is no continuous movement except movement in place, and of this only that which is circular is continuous.

But if there is something which is capable of moving things or acting on them, but is not actually doing so, there will not necessarily be movement: for that which has a potency need not exercise it. Nothing, then, is gained even if we suppose eternal substances, as the believers in the Forms do, unless there is to be in them some principle which can cause movement; and even this is not enough, nor is another substance besides the Forms enough; for if it does not *act,* there will be no movement. Further, even if it acts, this will not be enough, if its essence is potency; for there will not be *eternal* movement: for that which is potentially may possibly not be. There must, then, be such a principle, whose very essence is actuality. Further, then, these substances must be without matter; for they must be eternal, at least if anything else is eternal. Therefore they must be actuality.

Yet there is a difficulty; for it is thought that everything that acts is able to act, but that not everything that is able to act acts, so that the potency is prior. But if this is so, nothing at all might exist; for it is possible for all things to be capable of existing but not yet to exist. Yet if we follow the mythologists who generate the world from night, or the natural philosophers who say that all things were together, the same impossible result ensues. For how will there be movement, if there is no actual cause? Wood will surely not move itself—the carpenter's art must act on it; nor will the *menses* nor the earth set themselves in motion, but the seeds must act on the earth and the *semen* on the *menses*.

This is why some suppose eternal actuality—e.g. Leucippus and Plato; for they say there is always movement. But why and what this movement is they do not say, nor, if the world moves in this way or that, do they tell us the cause of its doing so. Now nothing is moved at random, but there must be some cause, e.g. as a matter of fact a thing moves in one way by nature, and in another by force or through the influence of reason or something else. Further, what sort of movement is primary? This makes a vast difference. But again Plato, at least, cannot even say what it is that he sometimes supposes to be the source of movement —that which moves itself; for the *soul* is later, and simultaneous with the heavens, according to his account. To suppose potency prior to actuality, then, is in a sense right, and in a sense not; and we have specified these senses.

That actuality is prior is testified by Anaxagoras (for his 'reason' is actuality) and by Empedocles in his doctrine of love and strife, and by those who say that there is always movement, e.g. Leucippus.

Therefore chaos or night did not exist for an infinite time, but the same things have always existed (either passing through a cycle of changes or obeying some other law), since actuality is prior to potency. If, then, there is a constant cycle, something must always remain, acting in the same way. And if there is to be generation and destruction, there must be something else which is always acting in different ways. This must, then, act in one way in virtue of itself, and in another in virtue of something else—either of a third agent, therefore, or of the first. But it must be in virtue of the first. For otherwise this again causes the motion both of the third agent and of the second. Therefore it is better to say 'the first'. For it was the cause of eternal movement; and something else is the cause of variety, and evidently both together are the cause of eternal variety. This, accordingly, is the character which the motions actually exhibit. What need then is there to seek for other principles?

Since (1) this is a possible account of the matter, and (2) if it were not true, the world would have proceeded out of night and 'all things together' and out of non-being, these difficulties may be taken as solved. There is, then, something which is always moved with an unceasing motion, which is motion in a circle; and this is plain not in theory only but in fact. Therefore the first heavens must be eternal. There is therefore also something which moves them. And since that which is moved and moves is intermediate, there is a mover which moves without being moved, being eternal, substance, and actuality. And the object of desire and the object of thought move in this way; they move without being moved. The primary objects of desire and of thought are the same. For the apparent good is the object of appetite, and the real good is the primary object of rational desire. But desire is consequent on opinion rather than opinion on desire; for the thinking is the starting-point. And thought is moved by the object of thought, and one side of the list of opposites is in itself the object of thought; and in this, substance is first, and in substance, that which is simple and exists actually. (The one and the simple are not the same; for 'one' means a measure, but 'simple' means that the thing itself has a certain nature.) But the good, also, and that which is in itself desirable are on this same side of the list; and the first in any class is always best, or analogous to the best.

That the final cause may be something unmovable, is shown by the distinction of its meanings. For the final cause is (*a*) something for whose good the action is done, and (*b*) something at which the action aims; and of these the latter is unmovable though the former is not. The final cause, then, produces motion by being loved, and by that which it moves, it moves all other things. Now if something is moved it is capable of being otherwise than as it is. Therefore if the actuality of the heavens is primary motion, then in so far as they are in motion, in *this* respect they are capable of being otherwise,—in place, even if not in substance. But since there is something which moves while itself unmoved, existing actually, this can in no way be otherwise than as it is. For motion in space is the first of the kinds of change, and motion in a circle the first kind of spatial motion; and this the first mover *produces*. The first mover, then, of necessity exists; and in so far as it is necessary, it is good, and in this sense a first principle. For the necessary has all these senses—that which is necessary perforce because it is contrary to the natural impulse, that without which the good is impossible, and that which cannot be otherwise but is *absolutely* necessary.

On such a principle, then, depend the heavens and the world of nature. And its life is such as the best which we enjoy, and enjoy for but a short time. For it is ever in this state (which we cannot be), since its actuality is also pleasure. (And therefore are waking, perception, and thinking most pleasant, and hopes and memories are so because of their reference to these.) And thought in itself deals with that which is best in itself, and that which is thought in the fullest sense with that which is best in the fullest sense. And thought thinks itself because it shares the nature of the object of thought; for it becomes an object of thought in coming into contact with and thinking its objects, so that thought and object of thought are the same. For that which is *capable* of receiving the object of thought, i.e. the •essence, is thought. And it is *active* when it *possesses* this object. Therefore the latter [possession] rather than the former [receptivity] is the divine element which thought seems to contain, and the act of contemplation is what is most pleasant and best. If, then, God is always in that good state in which we sometimes are, this compels our wonder; and if in a better this compels it yet more. And God *is* in a better state. And life also belongs to God; for the actuality of thought is life, and God is that actuality; and God's essential actuality is life most good and eternal. We say therefore that God is a living being, eternal, most good, so that life and duration continuous and eternal belong to God; for this *is* God.

Those who suppose, as the Pythagoreans and Speusippus do, that supreme beauty and goodness are not present in the beginning, because the beginnings both of plants and of animals are *causes,* but beauty and completeness are in the *effects* of these, are wrong in their opinion. For the seed comes from other individuals which are prior and complete, and the first thing is not seed but the complete being, e.g. we must say that before the seed there is a man,—not the man produced from the seed, but another from whom the seed comes.

It is clear then from what has been said that there is a substance which is eternal and unmovable and separate from sensible things. It has been shown also that this substance cannot have any magnitude, but is without parts and indivisible. For it produces movement through infinite time, but nothing finite has infinite power. And, while every magnitude is either infinite or finite, it cannot, for the above reason, have finite magnitude, and it cannot have infinite magnitude because there is no infinite magnitude at all. But it is also clear that it is impassive and unalterable; for all the other changes are posterior to change of place. It is clear, then, why the first mover has these attributes.

We must not ignore the question whether we have to suppose one such substance or more than one, and if the latter, how many; we must also mention, regarding the opinions expressed by others, that they have said nothing, that can even be clearly stated, about the number of the substances. For the theory of Ideas has no special discussion of the subject; for those who believe in Ideas say the Ideas are numbers, and they speak of numbers now as unlimited, now as limited by the number 10; but as for the reason why there should be just so many numbers, nothing is said with any demonstrative exactness.

We however must discuss the subject, starting from the presuppositions and distinctions we have mentioned. The first principle or primary being is not movable either in itself or accidentally, but produces the primary eternal and single movement. And since that which is moved must be moved by something, and the first mover must be in itself unmovable, and eternal movement must be produced by something eternal and a single movement by a single thing, and since we see that besides the simple spatial movement of the universe, which we say the first and unmovable substance produces, there are other spatial movements—those of the planets—which are eternal (for the body which moves in a circle is eternal and unresting; we have proved these points in the physical treatises), each of *these* movements also must be caused by a substance unmovable in itself and eternal. For the nature of the stars is eternal, being a kind of substance, and the mover is eternal and prior to the moved, and that which is prior to a substance must be a substance. Evidently, then, there must be substances which are of the same number as the movements of the stars, and in their nature eternal, and in themselves unmovable, and without magnitude, for the reason before mentioned.

That the movers are substances, then, and that one of these is first and another second according to the same order as the movements of the stars, is evident. But in the number of movements we reach a problem which must be treated from the standpoint of that one of the mathematical sciences which is most akin to philosophy—viz. of astronomy; for this science speculates about substance which is perceptible but eternal, but the other mathematical sciences, i.e. arithmetic and geometry, treat of no substance. That the movements are more numerous than the bodies that are moved, is evident to those who have given even moderate attention to the matter; for each of the planets has more than one movement. But as to the actual number of these movements, we now—to give some notion of the subject—quote what some of the mathematicians say; that our thought may have some definite number to grasp; but, for the rest, we must partly investigate for ourselves, partly learn from other investigators, and if those who study this subject form an opinion contrary to what we have now stated, we must esteem both parties indeed, but follow the more accurate.

Eudoxus supposed that the motion of the sun or of the moon involves, in either case, three spheres, of which the first is the sphere of the fixed stars, and the second moves in the circle which runs along the middle of the zodiac, and the third in the circle which is inclined across the breadth of the zodiac; but the circle in which the moon moves is inclined at a greater angle than that in which the sun moves. And the motion of the planets involves, in each case, four spheres, and of these also the first and second are the same as the first two mentioned above (for the sphere of the fixed stars is that which moves all the other spheres, and that which is placed beneath this and has its movement in the circle which bisects the zodiac is common to all), but the *poles* of the third sphere of each planet are in the circle which bisects the zodiac, and the motion of the fourth sphere is in the circle which is inclined at an angle to the equator of the third sphere; and the poles of the third spheres are different for the other planets, but those of Venus and Mercury are the same.

Callippus made the position of the spheres, i.e. the order of their intervals, the same as Eudoxus did, but while he assigned the same number as Eudoxus did to Jupiter and to Saturn, he thought two more spheres should be added to the sun and two to the moon, if we were to explain the observed facts, and one more to each of the other planets.

But it is necessary, if all the spheres combined are to explain the phenomena, that for each of the planets there should be other spheres (one fewer than those hitherto assigned) which counteract those already mentioned and bring back to the same position the first or outermost sphere of the star which in each case is situated below the star in question; for only thus can all the forces at work produce the observed motion of the planets. Since, then, the spheres by which the planets themselves are moved are—eight for Saturn and Jupiter and twenty-five for the others, and of these only those by which the lowest-situated planet is moved need not be counteracted, the spheres which counter-

act those of the first or outermost two planets will be
six in number, and the spheres which counteract those
of the next four planets will be sixteen, and the number of all the spheres—those which move the planets
and those which counteract these—will be fifty-five.
And if one were not to add to the moon and to the
sun the movements we mentioned, all the spheres will
be forty-nine in number.

Let this then be taken as the number of the spheres,
so that both the unmovable and the perceptible substances and principles may *probably* be taken as just
so many; the assertion of *necessity* must be left to
more powerful thinkers.

If there can be no spatial movement which does not
conduce to the moving of a star, and if further every
being and every substance which is immune from change
and in virtue of itself has attained to the best must
be considered an end, there can be no other being apart
from these we have named, but this must be the number
of the substances. For if there are others, they will
cause change as being a final cause of movement; but
there *cannot* be other movements besides those mentioned. And it is reasonable to infer this from a consideration of the bodies that are moved; for if everything that moves is for the sake of that which is moved,
and every movement belongs to something that is moved,
no movement can be for the sake of itself or of another
movement, but all movements must be for the sake of
the stars. For if a movement is to be for the sake
of a movement, this latter also will have to be for the
sake of something else; so that since there cannot be
an infinite regress, the end of every movement will be
one of the divine bodies which move through the
heaven.

Evidently there is but one heaven. For if there are

many heavens as there are many men, the moving principles, of which each heaven will have one, will be one in form but in number many. But all things that are many in number have matter. (For one and the same formula applies to *many* things, e.g. the formula of man; but Socrates is *one*.) But the primary essence has not matter; for it is complete reality. So the unmovable first mover is one both in formula and in number; therefore also that which is moved always and continuously is one alone; therefore there is one heaven alone.

Our forefathers in the most remote ages have handed down to us their posterity a tradition, in the form of a myth, that these substances are gods and that the divine encloses the whole of nature. The rest of the tradition has been added later in mythical form with a view to the persuasion of the multitude and to its legal and utilitarian expediency; they say these gods are in the form of men or like some of the other animals, and they say other things consequent on and similar to these which we have mentioned. But if we were to separate the first point from these additions and take it alone—that they thought the first substances to be gods, we must regard this as an inspired utterance, and reflect that, while probably each art and science has often been developed as far as possible and has again perished, these opinions have been preserved until the present, like relics of the ancient treasure. Only thus far, then, is the opinion of our ancestors and our earliest predecessors clear to us.

The nature of the divine thought involves certain problems; for while thought is held to be the most divine of things observed by us, the question what it must be in order to have that character involves difficulties. For if it thinks nothing, what is there here of dignity?

It is just like one who sleeps. And if it thinks, but
this depends on something else, then (as that which is
its substance is not the act of thinking, but a potency)
it cannot be the best substance; for it is through thinking that its value belongs to it. Further, whether its
substance is the faculty of thought or the act of thinking, what does it think? Either itself or something
else; and if something else, either the same always or
something different. Does it matter, then, or not,
whether it thinks the good or any chance thing? Are
there not some things about which it is incredible that
it should think? Evidently, then, it thinks that which
is most divine and precious, and it does not change;
for change would be change for the worse, and this
would be already a movement. First, then, if 'thought'
is not the act of thinking but a potency, it would be reasonable to suppose that the continuity of its thinking
is wearisome to it. Secondly, there would evidently
be something else more precious than thought, viz. that
which is thought. For both thinking and the act of
thought will belong even to one who has the worst of
thoughts. Therefore if this ought to be avoided (and
it ought, for there are even some things which it is
better not to see than to see), the act of thinking cannot be the best of things. Therefore it must be itself
that thought thinks (since it is the most excellent of
things), and its thinking is a thinking on thinking.

But evidently knowledge and perception and opinion
and understanding have always something else as their
object, and themselves only by the way. Further, if
thinking and being thought are different, in respect of
which does goodness belong to thought? For the act
of thinking and the object of thought have not the same
essence. We answer that in some cases the knowledge
is the object. In the productive sciences (if we ab-

stract from the matter) the substance in the sense of
essence, and in the theoretical sciences the formula or
the act of thinking, *is* the object. As, then, thought
and the object of thought are not different in the case
of things that have not matter, they will be the same,
i.e. the divine thinking will be one with the object of
its thought.

A further question is left—whether the object of the
divine thought is composite; for if it were, thought
would change in passing from part to part of the whole.
We answer that everything which has not matter is
indivisible. As human thought, or rather the thought
of composite objects, is in a certain period of time
(for it does not possess the good at this moment or
at that, but its best, being something *different* from it,
is attained only in a whole period of time), so throughout eternity is the thought which has *itself* for its
object.

We must consider also in which of two ways the
nature of the universe contains the good or the highest
good, whether as something separate and by itself, or
as the order of the parts. Probably in both ways, as
an army does. For the good is found both in the order
and in the leader, and more in the latter; for he does
not depend on the order but it depends on him. And
all things are ordered together somehow, but not all
alike,—both fishes and fowls and plants; and the world
is not such that one thing has nothing to do with another, but they are connected. For all are ordered
together to one end. . . .

Those who say mathematical number is first and go
on to generate one kind of substance after another and
give different principles for each, make the substance
of the universe a mere series of episodes (for one substance has no influence on another by its existence or

non-existence), and they give us many governing principles; but the world must not be governed badly.

'The rule of many is not good; one is the ruler.'

38. Of things that are, some are by nature, some
through other causes. 'By nature' the animals and their
parts are, and the plants and the simple bodies (earth,
fire, air, water)—these are the like we say are by nature.

All the things mentioned present a feature in which
they differ from things which are *not* constituted by
nature. Each of them has *within itself* a principle
of its change and of its coming to rest (in respect of
place or of growth and decrease or by way of alteration). On the other hand a bed and a coat and other
similar sorts of things *qua* receiving these designations
—i.e. in so far as they are products of art—have no
innate impulse to pass from one state to another. But
in so far as they happen to be composed of stone or
of earth or of a mixture of the two, they do have
such an impulse, and just to that extent—which seems
to indicate that nature is a source or cause of being
changed and of being at rest in that to which it belongs
primarily in virtue of itself and not in virtue of a coin-
cident attribute.

39. In general, art partly completes what nature is unable to elaborate, and partly imitates her. If therefore
artificial products are for the sake of an end, so clearly
also are natural products. The relation of the later to
the earlier terms of the series is the same in both.

This is most obvious in the animals other than man;
they make things neither by art nor after inquiry or
deliberation—wherefore people discuss whether it is by
intelligence or by what it is that these creatures work,
spiders, ants, and the like. By gradual advance in this

direction we come to see that in plants too that is produced which is conducive to the end—leaves e.g. grow to provide shade for the fruit. If then it is both by nature and for an end that the swallow makes its nest and the spider its web, and plants grow leaves for the sake of the fruit and send their roots down (not up) for the sake of nourishment, it is plain that this kind of cause is applicable to things which come to be and are by nature. And since 'nature' means two things, the matter and the form, of which the latter is the end, and since all the rest is for the sake of the end, the form must be cause—that for which.

Now mistakes come to pass even in the operations of art; the writer makes a mistake in writing and the doctor pours out the wrong dose. Hence clearly mistakes are possible in the operation of nature also. If then we find in art that successful production has an aim and that where mistakes occur there was an aim in what was attempted, only it was not attained, so must it be also in natural products, and monstrosities will be mistakes in adjusting the means towards the end. . . .

Those things are natural which, by a continuous movement originated from an internal principle, arrive at some completion; the same completion is not reached from every principle, nor any chance completion, but always the tendency in each is towards the same end, if there is no impediment. The end and the means towards it may come about by chance. We say, for instance, that a guest has come by chance, taken a ball, and gone away, when he does so as if he had come for a purpose, though it was not for that that he came. This is incidental, for chance is an incidental cause. But when this takes place always or for the most part, it is not incidental or by chance. In natural products the sequence is invariable, if there is no impediment. It is absurd to suppose that purpose is not present because we do not observe the agent deliberating.

40. That place is something seems to be clear from the fact of displacement; for where there is now water, later—when the water has gone out as though from a vessel—there is air; and when some other body occupies this same place, the place certainly seems to be different from all its changing occupants; for in that in which there is now air there was water before, so that plainly the place or space was something different from both, into which and out of which they moved. . . .

As a vessel is a movable place, so a place is an unmovable vessel. And so when in something that is moved that which is in it is moved and changes its place, e.g. a boat in a river, its container serves as a vessel rather than as a place. It is the nature of place to be unmovable; and so the *whole* river is more truly a place because the *whole* river is unmoved. Therefore the innermost *un*moved boundary of a container —that is what a thing's place is. And for this reason the centre of the material universe and the innermost part of the rotating system are thought to be, more than anything else, strictly speaking 'down' and 'up' respectively for all men, because the former is always at rest, while the innermost part of the circle remains always identically situated. Therefore, since the light is that which by nature moves up and the heavy that which by nature moves down, that which contains a body in the direction of the centre of the universe, and the centre itself, and its lower limit and that which contains it in the direction of the innermost part of the rotating system and the innermost part itself, are its upper limit; and for this reason place is thought to be a kind of surface and as it were a vessel or container. Further, a thing's place is 'together with' the thing; for limits are 'together with' the limited.

A body, then, which has another body surrounding it is in place, and that which has not is not. . . . And some things are in place potentially, others actually. And so when a homogeneous body is continuous, its parts are in place potentially, but when they have been separated and touch one another like a heap, they are in place actually. And some things are in place *per se* (e.g. every body that is capable either of locomotion or of increase is somewhere *per se,* while the universe is not as a whole anywhere or in any place, since no body contains it; but on the line on which the parts are moved there is a place for them; for they are contiguous one with another); other things are in place *per accidens,* e.g. the soul, and the material universe; for all its parts are in a sense in place; for on the circle one contains another. And so the body that is above us moves in a circle, yet the All is not anywhere. For that which is somewhere not only is itself something but there must be something else besides in which it is contained; but there is nothing apart from the All or whole and outside the All, and therefore all things are in the material universe; for the material universe is presumably the All. But their place is not the material universe, but a part of it, the innermost limit that touches the moving body, being itself at rest; and for this reason, while earth is in water, water in air, air in ether, ether in the material universe, the material universe is not in anything else. It is evident from this that all the problems can be solved if this is what 'place' means. For it is not necessary either that a thing's place should increase with it, or that a point should have a place, or that there should be two bodies

in the same place or a bodily 'interval' (for that which
is between places is some particular body or other,
not an interval of body); and place is also somewhere
—not as in a place, however, but as the limit is in the
limited. For not everything is in a place, but only movable bodies.

41. Since time is thought to be, more than anything, a
movement or change, we shall have to consider this
point. Now the change or movement of each thing is
in the changing thing only, or wherever the moving or
changing thing itself chances to be; but time is alike
everywhere and with all things. Again, change may be
faster or slower, but time cannot; for the slow or
fast is determined by time, that which moves much in
a little time being fast, that which moves little in
much time slow; but time is not determined by time,
neither by being a certain amount nor by being a certain kind of it. Evidently then it is not movement;
let us treat movement and change as equivalent.

But neither can it exist apart from change; for when
the state of our own mind does not change at all or
we do not notice it changing, we do not realize that
time has elapsed, any more than the Seven Sleepers do
when they are awakened; for they connect the earlier
'now' with the later and make them one, cutting out
the interval because of their failure to perceive it.
If then the non-realization of the existence of time happens when we do not distinguish any change but the
soul seems to stay in one indivisible state, and when
we perceive and distinguish a change we say time has
elapsed, evidently time is not independent of movement
or change. It is evident, then, that time is neither
movement nor independent of movement. And since
we are inquiring what time is we must start by grasp-

ing what it is in movement. For we perceive movement
and time together; for even if it be dark and we experience nothing through the body, if there be some
movement in the soul we at once think some time has
elapsed. But further, when we think some time has
elapsed, we think that simultaneously there has been
some movement. Therefore time is either movement
or some element in movement. Since, then, it is not
movement, it must be some element in movement. Now
since that which is moved is moved from something
into something, and every spatial magnitude is continuous, movement corresponds to magnitude; for because magnitude is continuous movement is continuous,
and because of movement time is so; for the length of
the time is always thought to correspond to that of the
movement. Now what is before and after in place is
the primary thing. And here before and after are
determined by position; but since there is a before and
after in magnitude, there must be an analogous before
and after in movement. But further, in time also there
is a before and after, because time always corresponds
to movement. Now their beforeness and afterness are
in movement, i.e. in the subject that underlies movement,
but their being is different and is not movement.

But further, we recognize time only when we have
distinguished movement, distinguishing it by a before
and after; and we say time has elapsed only when
we have perceived a before and after in movement. Now
we effect this distinction by judging that the before and
the after are different and that there is something else
between them; for when we perceive the extremes to
be different from the mean and the soul pronounces the
'nows' to be two, one before and one after, it is then
that we say there is time and this that we pronounce
to be time; for that which is bounded by a 'now' is

thought to be time; and let this be assumed. When, then we perceive the 'now' as one and not either as before and after in movement, or as the same thing but as an element in something before and in something after, we do not think there has been any lapse of time, because we do not think there has been any movement. But when we perceive a before and after, then we say that there is time; for this is what time is, the number of movement in respect of before and after. Time is not movement, then, but the respect in which movement is numerable. This is evidenced by the fact that we judge by number what is more and what is less, and by time what is more movement and what is less; time then is a sort of number. But since 'number' is used in two senses (both of that which is numbered or numerable and of that by which we number it), time is that which is numbered, not that by which we number.

42. The question as to the nature of the whole, whether it is infinite in size or limited in its total mass, is a matter for subsequent inquiry. We will now speak of those parts of the whole which are specifically distinct. Let us take this as our starting-point. All natural bodies and magnitudes we hold to be, as such, capable of locomotion; for nature, we say, is their principle of movement. But all movement that is in place, all locomotion, as we term it, is either straight or circular or a combination of these two, which are the only simple movements. And the reason of this is that these two, the straight and the circular line, are the only simple magnitudes. Now revolution about the centre is circular motion, while the upward and downward movements are in a straight line, 'upward' meaning motion away from the centre, and 'downward' motion towards

it. All simple motion, then, must be motion either away from or towards or about the centre. This seems to be in exact accord with what we said above: as body found its completion in three dimensions, so its movement completes itself in three forms.

Bodies are either simple or compounded of such; and by simple bodies I mean those which possess a principle of movement in their own nature, such as fire and earth with their kinds, and whatever is akin to them. Necessarily, then, movements also will be either simple or in some sort compound—simple in the case of the simple bodies, compound in that of the composite —and in the latter case the motion will be that of the simple body which prevails in the composition. Supposing, then, that there is such a thing as simple movement, and that circular movement is an instance of it, and that both movement of a simple body is simple and simple movement is of a simple body (for if it is movement of a compound it will be in virtue of a prevailing simple element), then there must necessarily be some simple body which revolves naturally and in virtue of its own nature with a circular movement. By constraint, of course, it may be brought to move with the motion of something else different from itself, but it cannot so move naturally, since there is one sort of movement natural to each of the simple bodies.

Again, if the unnatural movement is the contrary of the natural and a thing can have no more than one contrary, it will follow that circular movement, being a simple motion, must be unnatural, if it is not natural, to the body moved. If then (1) the body, whose movement is circular, is fire or some other element, its natural motion must be the contrary of the circular motion. But a single thing has a single contrary; and upward and downward motion are the contraries of one another.

If, on the other hand, (2) the body moving with this circular motion which is unnatural to it is something different from the elements, there will be some other motion which is natural to it. But this cannot be. For if the natural motion is upward, it will be fire or air, and if downward, water or earth. Further, this circular motion is necessarily primary. For the perfect is naturally prior to the imperfect, and the circle is a perfect thing. This cannot be said of any straight line: —not of an infinite line; for, if it were perfect, it would have a limit and an end: nor of any finite line; for in every case there is something beyond it, since any finite line can be extended. And so, since the prior movement belongs to the body which is naturally prior, and circular movement is prior to straight, and movement in a straight line belongs to simple bodies —fire moving straight upward and earthy bodies straight downward towards the centre—since this is so, it follows that circular movement also must be the movement of some simple body. For the movement of composite bodies is, as we said, determined by that simple body which preponderates in the composition. These premisses clearly give the conclusion that there is in nature some bodily substance other than the formations we know, prior to them all and more divine than they.

43. It is equally reasonable to assume that this body will be ungenerated and indestructible and exempt from increase and alteration, since everything that comes to be comes into being from its contrary and in some substrate, and passes away likewise in a substrate by the action of the contrary into the contrary, as we explained in our opening discussions. Now the motions of contraries are contrary. If then this body can have

no contrary, because there can be no contrary motion
to the circular, nature seems justly to have exempted
from contraries the body which was to be ungenerated
and indestructible. For it is in contraries that generation and decay subsist. Again, that which is subject
to increase increases upon contact with a kindred body,
which is resolved into its matter. But there is nothing
out of which this body can have been generated. And
if it is exempt from increase and diminution, the same
reasoning leads us to suppose that it is also unalterable.
For alteration is movement in respect of quality; and
qualitative states and dispositions, such as health and
disease, do not come into being without changes of properties. But all natural bodies which change their properties we see to be subject without exception to increase
and diminution. This is the case, for instance, with the
bodies of animals and their parts and with vegetable
bodies, and similarly also with those of the elements.
And so, if the body which moves with a circular motion
cannot admit of increase or diminution, it is reasonable
to suppose that it is also unalterable.

The reasons why the primary body is eternal and
not subject to increase or diminution, but unaging and
unalterable and unmodified, will be clear from what
has been said to any one who believes in our assumptions. Our theory seems to confirm experience and
to be confirmed by it. For all men have some conception of the nature of the gods, and all who believe in
the existence of gods at all, whether barbarian or Greek,
agree in allotting the highest place to the deity, surely
because they suppose that immortal is linked with immortal and regard any other supposition as inconceivable. If then there is, as there certainly is, anything
divine, what we have just said about the primary bodily
substance was well said. The mere evidence of the

senses is enough to convince us of this, at least with human certainty. For in the whole range of time past, so far as our inherited records reach, no change appears to have taken place either in the whole scheme of the outermost heaven or in any of its proper parts. The common name, too, which has been handed down from our distant ancestors even to our own day, seems to show that they conceived of it in the fashion which we have been expressing. The same ideas, one must believe, recur in men's minds not once or twice but again and again. And so, implying that the primary body is something else beyond earth, fire, air, and water, they gave the highest place a name of its own, *æther*, derived from the fact that it 'runs always' for an eternity of time.

44. The activity of God is immortality, i.e. eternal life. Therefore the movement of that which is divine must be eternal. But such is the heaven, viz. a divine body, and for that reason to it is given the circular body whose nature it is to move always in a circle. Why, then, is not the whole body of the heaven of the same character as that part? Because there must be something at rest at the centre of the revolving body; and of that body no part can be at rest, either elsewhere or at the centre. It could do so only if the body's natural movement were towards the centre. But the circular movement is natural, since otherwise it could not be eternal: for nothing unnatural is eternal. The unnatural is subsequent to the natural, being a derangement of the natural which occurs in the course of its generation. Earth then has to exist; for it is earth which is at rest at the centre. (At present we may take this for granted: it shall be explained later.) But if earth must exist, so must fire. For, if one of a pair

of contraries naturally exists, the other, if it is really contrary, exists also naturally. In some form it must be present, since the matter of contraries is the same. Also, the positive is prior to its privation (warm, for instance, to cold), and rest and heaviness stand for the privation of lightness and movement. But further, if fire and earth exist, the intermediate bodies must exist also: for each element stands in a contrary relation to every other. (This, again, we will here take for granted and try later to explain.) With these four elements generation clearly is involved, since none of them can be eternal: for contraries interact with one another and destroy one another. Further, it is inconceivable that a movable body should be eternal, if its movement cannot be regarded as naturally eternal: and these bodies we know to possess movement. Thus we see that generation is necessarily involved. But if so, there must be at least one other circular motion: for a single movement of the whole heaven would necessitate an identical relation of the elements of bodies to one another. This matter also shall be cleared up in what follows: but for the present so much is clear, that the reason why there is more than one circular body is the necessity of generation, which follows on the presence of fire, which, with that of the other bodies, follows on that of earth; and earth is required because eternal movement in one body necessitates eternal rest in another.

45. Those of our predecessors who have entered upon this inquiry have for the most part spoken of light and heavy things only in the sense in which one of two things both endowed with weight is said to be the lighter. And this treatment they consider a sufficient analysis also of the notions of absolute heaviness and

absolute lightness, to which their account does not
apply. This, however, will become clearer as we advance. One use of the terms 'lighter' and 'heavier' is
that which is set forth in writing in the *Timaeus,* that
the body which is composed of the greater number of
identical parts is relatively heavy, while that which
is composed of a smaller number is relatively light.
As a larger quantity of lead or of bronze is heavier
than a smaller—and this holds good of all homogeneous masses, the superior weight always depending upon
a numerical superiority of equal parts—in precisely
the same way, they assert, lead is heavier than wood.
For all bodies, in spite of the general opinion to the
contrary, are composed of identical parts and of a
single material. But this analysis says nothing of
the absolutely heavy and light. The facts are that
fire is always light and moves upward, while earth
and all earthy things move downwards or towards the
centre. It cannot then be the fewness of the triangles
(of which, in their view, all these bodies are composed)
which disposes fire to move upward. If it were, the
greater the quantity of fire the slower it would move,
owing to the increase of weight due to the increased
number of triangles. But the palpable fact, on the
contrary, is that the greater the quantity, the lighter
the mass is and the quicker its upward movement: and,
similarly, in the reverse movement from above downward, the small mass will move quicker and the large
slower. Further, since to be lighter is to have fewer
of these homogeneous parts and to be heavier is to have
more, and air, water, and fire are composed of the same
triangles, the only difference being in the number of
such parts, which must therefore explain any distinction of relatively light and heavy between these bodies,
it follows that there must be a certain quantum of air

which is heavier than water. But the facts are directly opposed to this. The larger the quantity of air the more readily it moves upward, and any portion of air without exception will rise up out of the water.

So much for one view of the distinction between light and heavy. To others the analysis seems insufficient; and their views on the subject, though they belong to an older generation than ours, have an air of novelty. It is apparent that there are bodies which, when smaller in bulk than others, yet exceed them in weight. It is therefore obviously insufficient to say that bodies of equal weight are composed of an equal number of primary parts: for that would give equality of bulk. Those who maintain that the primary or atomic parts, of which bodies endowed with weight are composed, are planes, cannot so speak without absurdity; but those who regard them as solids are in a better position to assert that of such bodies the larger is the heavier. But since in composite bodies the weight obviously does not correspond in this way to the bulk, the lesser bulk being often superior in weight (as, for instance, if one be wool and the other bronze), there are some who think and say that the cause is to be found elsewhere. The void, they say, which is imprisoned in bodies, lightens them and sometimes makes the larger body the lighter. The reason is that there is more void. And this would also account for the fact that a body composed of a number of solid parts equal to, or even smaller than, that of another is sometimes larger in bulk than it. In short, generally and in every case a body is relatively light when it contains a relatively large amount of void. This is the way they put it themselves, but their account requires an addition. Relative lightness must depend not only on an excess of void, but also on a defect of solid: for if the ratio of solid to void exceeds a certain proportion, the relative lightness will disappear. Thus fire, they say, is the lightest of things just for this reason, that it has the most void. But it would follow that a large mass of gold, as containing more void than a small mass of fire, is lighter than it, unless it also contains many times as much solid. The addition is therefore necessary.

Of those who deny the existence of a void some, like Anaxagoras and Empedocles, have not tried to analyse the notions of light and heavy at all; and those who, while still denying the existence of a void, have attempted this, have failed to explain why there are bodies which are absolutely heavy and light, or in other words why some move upward and others downward. The fact, again, that the body of greater bulk is sometimes lighter than smaller bodies is one which they have passed over in silence, and what they have said gives no obvious suggestion for reconciling their views with the observed facts.

But those who attribute the lightness of fire to its containing so much void are necessarily involved in practically the same difficulties. For though fire be supposed to contain less solid than any other body, as well as more void, yet there will be a certain quantum of fire in which the amount of solid or plenum is in excess of the solids contained in some small quantity of earth. They may reply that there is an excess of void also. But the question is, how will they discriminate the absolutely heavy? Presumably, either by its excess of solid or by its defect of void. On the former view there could be an amount of earth so small as to contain less solid than a large mass of fire. And similarly, if the distinction rests on the amount of void, there will be a body, lighter than the absolutely light, which nevertheless moves downward as constantly as the other moves upward. But that cannot be so, since the absolutely light is always lighter than bodies which have weight and move downward, while, on the other hand, that which is lighter need not be light, because in common speech we distinguish a lighter and a heavier (viz. water and earth) among bodies endowed with weight. Again, the suggestion of a certain ratio between the void and the solid in a body is no more equal to solving the problem before us. This manner of speaking will issue in a similar impossibility. For any two portions of fire, small or great, will exhibit the same ratio of solid to void; but the upward movement of the greater is quicker than that of the less, just as the downward movement of a mass of gold or lead, or of any other body endowed with weight, is quicker in proportion to its size. This, however, should not be the case if the ratio is the ground of distinction between heavy things and light. There is also an absurdity in attributing the upward movement of bodies to a void which does not itself move. If, however, it is the nature of a void to move upward and of a plenum to move downward, and therefore each causes a like movement in other things, there was no need to raise the question why composite bodies are some light and some heavy; they had only to explain why these two things are themselves light and heavy respectively, and to give, further, the reason why the plenum and the void are not eternally separated. It is also unreasonable to imagine a place for the void, as if the void were not itself a kind of place. But if the void is to move, it must have a place out of which and into which the change carries it. Also what is the cause of its movement? Not, surely, its voidness: for it is not the void only which is moved, but also the solid.

Similar difficulties are involved in all other methods

of distinction, whether they account for the relative
lightness and heaviness of bodies by distinctions of size,
or proceed on any other principle, so long as they
attribute to each the same matter, or even if they
recognize more than one matter, so long as that means
only a pair of contraries. If there is a single matter,
as with those who compose things of triangles, nothing can be absolutely heavy or light: and if there is
one matter and its contrary—the void, for instance, and
the plenum—no reason can be given for the relative
lightness and heaviness of the bodies intermediate between the absolutely light and heavy when compared
either with one another or with these themselves. The
view which bases the distinction upon differences of
size is more like a mere fiction than those previously
mentioned, but, in that it is able to make distinctions
between the four elements, it is in a stronger position
for meeting the foregoing difficulties. Since, however,
it imagines that these bodies which differ in size are
all made of one substance, it implies, equally with the
view that there is but one matter, that there is nothing absolutely light and nothing which moves upward
(except as being passed by other things or forced up
by them); and since a multitude of small atoms are
heavier than a few large ones, it will follow that much
air or fire is heavier than a little water or earth, which
is impossible.

These, then, are the views which have been advanced
by others and the terms in which they state them. We
may begin our own statement by settling a question
which to some has been the main difficulty—the question
why some bodies move always and naturally upward
and others downward, while others again move both
upward and downward. After that we will inquire
into light and heavy and the explanation of the various

phenomena connected with them. The local movement of each body into its own place must be regarded as similar to what happens in connexion with other forms of generation and change. There are, in fact, three kinds of movement, affecting respectively the size, the form, and the place of a thing, and in each it is observable that change proceeds from a contrary to a contrary or to something intermediate: it is never the change of any chance subject in any chance direction, nor, similarly, is the relation of the mover to its object fortuitous: the thing altered is different from the thing increased, and precisely the same difference holds between that which produces alteration and that which produces increase. In the same manner it must be thought that that which produces local motion and that which is so moved are not fortuitously related. Now, that which produces upward and downward movement is that which produces weight and lightness, and that which is moved is that which is potentially heavy or light, and the movement of each body to its own place is motion towards its own form. (It is best to interpret in this sense the common statement of the older writers that 'like moves to like'. For the words are not in every sense true to fact. If one were to remove the earth to where the moon now is, the various fragments of earth would each move not towards it but to the place in which it now is. In general, when a number of similar and undifferentiated bodies are moved with the same motion this result is necessarily produced, viz. that the place which is the natural goal of the movement of each single part is also that of the whole. But since the place of a thing is the boundary of that which contains it, and the continent of all things that move upward or downward is the extremity and the centre, and this boundary comes to be, in a sense, the form of that which is contained, it is to its like that a body moves when it moves to its own place. For the successive members of the series are like one another: water, I mean, is like air and air like fire, and between intermediates the relation may be converted, though not between them and the extremes; thus air is like water, but water is like earth: for the relation of each outer body to that which is next within it is that of form to matter.)

Thus to ask why fire moves upward and earth downward is the same as to ask why the healable, when moved and changed *quâ* healable, attains health and not whiteness; and similar questions might be asked concerning any other subject of alteration. Of course the subject of increase, when changed *quâ* increasable, attains not health but a superior size. The same applies in the other cases. One thing changes in quality, another in quantity: and so in place, a light thing goes upward, a heavy thing downward. The only difference is that in the last case, viz. that of the heavy and the light, the bodies are thought to have a spring of change within themselves, while the subjects of healing and increase are thought to be moved purely from without. Sometimes, however, even they change of themselves, i.e. in response to a slight external movement reach health or increase, as the case may be. And since the same thing which is healable is also receptive of disease, it depends on whether it is moved *quâ* healable or *quâ* liable to disease whether the motion is towards health or towards disease. But the reason why the heavy and the light appear more than these things to contain within themselves the source of their movements is that their matter is nearest to being. This is indicated by the fact that locomotion belongs to bodies only when isolated from

other bodies, and is generated last of the several kinds
of movement; in order of being then it will be first.
Now whenever air comes into being out of water, light
out of heavy, it goes to the upper place. It is forthwith light: becoming is at an end, and in that place it
has being. Obviously, then, it is a potentiality, which,
in its passage to actuality, comes into that place and
quantity and quality which belong to its actuality.
And the same fact explains why what is already actually fire or earth moves, when nothing obstructs it,
towards its own place. For motion is equally immediate in the case of nutriment, when nothing hinders,
and in the case of the thing healed, when nothing stays
the healing. But the movement is also due to the
original creative force and to that which removes the
hindrance or off which the moving thing rebounded, as
was explained in our opening discussions, where we
tried to show how none of these things moves itself.

46. Our own doctrine is that although there is a matter
of the perceptible bodies (a matter out of which the
so-called 'elements' come-to-be), it has no separate existence, but is always bound up with a contrariety. A
more precise account of these presuppositions has been
given in another work: we must, however, give a detailed explanation of the primary bodies as well, since
they too are similarly derived from the matter. We
must reckon as an 'originative source' and as 'primary'
the matter which underlies, though it is inseparable
from, the contrary qualities: for 'the hot' is not matter
for 'the cold' nor 'the cold' for 'the hot', but the *substratum* is matter for them both. We therefore have
to recognize three 'originative sources': *firstly* that
which is potentially perceptible body, *secondly* the contrarieties (I mean, e.g., heat and cold), and *thirdly*

Fire, Water, and the like. *Only* 'thirdly', however: for these bodies change into one another (they are not immutable as Empedocles and other thinkers assert, since 'alteration' would then have been impossible), whereas the contrarieties do not change.

Nevertheless, even so the question remains: What sorts of contrarieties, and how many of them, are to be accounted 'originative sources' of body? For all the other thinkers assume and use them without explaining why they are *these* or why they are just *so many*.

Since, then, we are looking for 'originative sources' of perceptible body; and since 'perceptible' is equivalent to 'tangible', and 'tangible' is that of which the perception is touch; it is clear that not all the contrarieties constitute 'forms' and 'originative sources' of body, but only those which correspond to touch. For it is in accordance with a contrariety—a contrariety, moreover, of *tangible* qualities—that the primary bodies are differentiated. That is why neither whiteness (and blackness), nor sweetness (and bitterness), nor (similarly) any quality belonging to the other perceptible contrarieties either, constitutes an 'element'. And yet vision is prior to touch, so that its object also is prior to the object of touch. The object of vision, however, is a quality of tangible body not *qua* tangible, but *qua* something else—*qua* something which may well be naturally prior to the object of touch.

Accordingly, we must segregate the tangible differences and contrarieties, and distinguish which amongst them are primary. Contrarieties correlative to touch are the following: hot-cold, dry-moist, heavy-light, hard-soft, viscous-brittle, rough-smooth, coarse-fine. Of these (i) heavy and light are neither active nor susceptible. Things are not called 'heavy' and 'light' because they act upon, or suffer action from, other things. But the 'elements' must be reciprocally active and susceptible, since they 'combine' and are transformed into one another. On the other hand (ii) hot and cold, and dry and moist, are terms, of which the first pair implies *power to act* and the second pair *susceptibility*. 'Hot' is that which 'associates' things of the same kind (for 'dissociating', which people attribute to Fire as its function, *is* 'associating' things of the same class, since its effect is to eliminate what is foreign), while 'cold' is that which brings together, i.e. 'associates', homogeneous and heterogeneous things alike. And 'moist' is that which, being readily adaptable in shape, is not determinable by any limit of its own: while 'dry' is that which is readily determinable by its own limit, but not readily adaptable in shape.

From moist and dry are derived (iii) the fine and coarse, viscous and brittle, hard and soft, and the remaining tangible differences. For (*a*) since the moist has no determinate shape, but is readily adaptable and follows the outline of that which is in contact with it, it is characteristic of it to be 'such as to fill up'. Now 'the fine' is 'such as to fill up'. For 'the fine' consists of subtle particles; but that which consists of small particles is 'such as to fill up', inasmuch as it is in contact whole with whole—and 'the fine' exhibits this character in a superlative degree. Hence it is evident that the fine derives from the moist, while the coarse derives from the dry. Again (*b*) 'the viscous' derives from the moist: for 'the viscous' (e.g. oil) is a 'moist' modified in a certain way. 'The brittle', on the other hand, derives from the dry: for 'brittle' is that which is *completely* dry—so completely, that its solidification has actually been due to failure of moisture. Further (*c*) 'the soft' derives from the moist. For 'soft' is that which yields to pressure by retiring into itself, though it does not yield by total displacement as the moist does—which explains why the moist is not 'soft', although 'the soft' derives from the moist. 'The hard', on the other hand, derives from the dry: for 'hard' is that which is solidified, and the solidified is dry.

The terms 'dry' and 'moist' have more senses than one. For 'the damp', as well as the moist, is opposed to the dry: and again 'the solidified', as well as the dry, is opposed to the moist. But all these qualities derive from the dry and moist we mentioned first. For (i) the dry is opposed to the damp: i.e. 'damp' is that which has foreign moisture on its surface ('sodden' being that which is penetrated to its core), while 'dry' is that which has lost foreign moisture. Hence it is evident that the damp will derive from the moist, and 'the dry' which is opposed to it will derive from the primary dry. Again (ii) the 'moist' and the solidified derive in the same way from the primary pair. For 'moist' is that which contains moisture *of its own* deep within it ('sodden' being that which is deeply penetrated by *foreign* moisture), whereas 'solidified' is that which has lost this inner moisture. Hence these too derive from the primary pair, the 'solidified' from the dry and the 'liquefiable' from the moist.

It is clear, then, that all the other differences reduce to the first four, but that these admit of no further reduction. For the hot is not *essentially* moist or dry, nor the moist *essentially* hot or cold: nor are the cold and the dry derivative forms, either of one another or of the hot and the moist. Hence these must be four.

The elementary qualities are four, and any four terms can be combined in six couples. Contraries, however, refuse to be coupled: for it is impossible for the same thing to be hot and cold, or moist and dry. Hence it

is evident that the 'couplings' of the elementary qualities will be four: hot with dry and moist with hot, and
again cold with dry and cold with moist. And these
four couples have attached themselves to the *apparently*
'simple' bodies (Fire, Air, Water, and Earth) in a manner consonant with theory. For Fire is hot and dry,
whereas Air is hot and moist (Air being a sort of
aqueous vapour); and Water is cold and moist, while
Earth is cold and dry. Thus the differences are reasonably distributed among the primary bodies, and the number of the latter is consonant with theory. For all
who make the simple bodies 'elements' postulate either
one, or two, or three, or four. Now (i) those who assert
there is *one* only, and then generate everything else
by condensation and rarefaction, are in effect making
their 'originative sources' two, viz. the rare and the
dense, or rather the hot and the cold: for it is these
which are the moulding forces, while the 'one' underlies
them as a 'matter'. But (ii) those who postulate *two*
from the start—as Parmenides postulated Fire and
Earth—make the intermediates (e.g. Air and Water)
blends of these. The same course is followed (iii) by
those who advocate *three*. (We may compare what
Plato does in 'The Divisions': for he makes 'the middle'
a blend.) Indeed, there is practically no difference
between those who postulate *two* and those who postulate *three,* except that the former split the middle 'element' into two, while the latter treat it as only one. But
(iv) some advocate *four* from the start, e.g. Empedocles:
yet he too draws them together so as to reduce them to
the two, for he opposes all the others to Fire.

In fact, however, fire and air, and each of the bodies
we have mentioned, are not simple, but blended. The
'simple' bodies are indeed similar in nature to them,
but not identical with them. Thus the 'simple' body

corresponding to fire is 'such-as-fire', not fire: that which corresponds to air is 'such-as-air': and so on with the rest of them. But fire is an excess of heat, just as ice is an excess of cold. For freezing and boiling are excesses of heat and cold respectively. Assuming, therefore, that ice is a freezing of moist and cold, fire analogously will be a boiling of dry and hot: a fact, by the way, which explains why nothing comes-to-be either out of ice or out of fire.

The 'simple' bodies, since they are four, fall into two pairs which belong to the two regions, each to each: for Fire and Air are forms of the body moving towards the 'limit', while Earth and Water are forms of the body which moves towards the 'centre'. Fire and Earth, moreover, are extremes and purest: Water and Air, on the contrary, are intermediates and more like blends. And, further, the members of either pair are contrary to those of the other, Water being contrary to Fire and Earth to Air; for the qualities constituting Water and Earth are contrary to those that constitute Fire and Air. Nevertheless, since they are four, each of them is characterized *par excellence* by a single quality: Earth by dry rather than by cold, Water by cold rather than by moist, Air by moist rather than by hot, and Fire by hot rather than by dry.

47. We have assumed, and have proved, that coming-to-be and passing-away happen to things continuously; and we assert that motion causes coming-to-be. That being so, it is evident that, if the motion be single, *both* processes cannot occur since they are contrary to one another: for it is a law of nature that the same cause, provided it remain in the same condition, always produces the same effect, so that, from a single motion, either coming-to-be or passing-away will always result.

The movements must, on the contrary, be more than one, and they must be contrasted with one another either by the sense of their motion or by its irregularity: for contrary effects demand contraries as their causes.

This explains why it is not the primary motion that causes coming-to-be and passing-away, but the motion along the inclined circle: for this motion not only possesses the necessary continuity, but includes a duality of movements as well. For if coming-to-be and passing-away are always to be continuous, there must be some body always being moved (in order that these changes may not fail) and moved with a duality of movements (in order that both changes, not one only, may result). Now the continuity of this movement is caused by the motion of the whole: but the approaching and retreating of the moving body are caused by the inclination. For the consequence of the inclination is that the body becomes alternately remote and near; and since its distance is thus unequal, its movement will be irregular. Therefore, if it generates by approaching and by its proximity, it—this very same body—destroys by retreating and becoming remote: and if it generates by many successive approaches, it also destroys by many successive retirements.

48. Let us proceed to the theory of winds. Its basis is a distinction we have already made. We recognize two kinds of evaporation, one moist, the other dry. The former is called vapour: for the other there is no general name but we must call it a sort of smoke, applying to the whole of it a word that is proper to one of its forms. The moist cannot exist without the dry nor the dry without the moist: whenever we speak of either we mean that it predominates. Now when the sun in its circular course approaches, it draws up by its heat

the moist evaporation: when it recedes the cold makes
the vapour that had been raised condense back into
water which falls and is distributed through the earth.
(This explains why there is more rain in winter and
more by night than by day: though the fact is not recognized because rain by night is more apt to escape observation than by day.)   But there is a great quantity
of fire and heat in the earth, and the sun not only draws
up the moisture that lies on the surface of it, but warms
and dries the earth itself.   Consequently, since there
are two kinds of evaporation, as we have said, one like
vapour, the other like smoke, both of them are necessarily generated.   That in which moisture predominates
is the source of rain, as we explained before, while
the dry evaporation is the source and substance of all
winds.   That things must necessarily take this course is
clear from the resulting phenomena themselves, for the
evaporation that is to produce them must necessarily
differ; and the sun and the warmth in the earth not
only can but must produce these evaporations.

Since the two evaporations are specifically distinct,
wind and rain obviously differ and their substance is
not the same, as those say who maintain that one and
the same air when in motion is wind, but when it con-
denses again is water.   Air, as we have explained in an
earlier book, is made up of these as constituents.   Vapour is moist and cold (for its fluidity is due to its
moistness, and because it derives from water it is naturally cold, like water that has not been warmed):
whereas the smoky evaporation is hot and dry.   Hence
each contributes a part, and air is moist and hot.

49. We have already stated that the rainbow is a reflection: we have now to explain what sort of reflection

it is, to describe its various concomitants, and to assign their causes.

Sight is reflected from all smooth surfaces, such as are air and water among others. Air must be condensed if it is to act as a mirror, though it often gives a reflection even uncondensed when the sight is weak. Such was the case of a man whose sight was faint and indistinct. He always saw an image in front of him and facing him as he walked. This was because his sight was reflected back to him. Its morbid condition made it so weak and delicate that the air close by acted as a mirror, just as distant and condensed air normally does, and his sight could not push it back. So promontories in the sea 'loom' when there is a south-east wind, and everything seems bigger, and in a mist, too, things seem bigger: so, too, the sun and the stars seem bigger when rising and setting than on the meridian. But things are best reflected from water, and even in process of formation it is a better mirror than air, for each of the particles, the union of which constitutes a raindrop, is necessarily a better mirror than mist. Now it is obvious and has already been stated that a mirror of this kind renders the colour of an object only, but not its shape. Hence it follows that when it is on the point of raining and the air in the clouds is in process of forming into raindrops but the rain is not yet actually there, if the sun is opposite, or any other object bright enough to make the cloud a mirror and cause the sight to be reflected to the object then the reflection must render the colour of the object without its shape. Since each of the mirrors is so small as to be invisible and what we see is the continuous magnitude made up of them all, the reflection necessarily gives us a continuous magnitude made up of one colour; each of the mirrors contributing the same colour to the whole. We may deduce that since these conditions are realizable there will be an appearance due to reflection whenever the sun and the cloud are related in the way described and we are between them. But these are just the conditions under which the rainbow appears. So it is clear that the rainbow is a reflection of sight to the sun.

So the rainbow always appears opposite the sun whereas the halo is round it. They are both reflections, but the rainbow is distinguished by the variety of its colours. The reflection in the one case is from water which is dark and from a distance; in the other from air which is nearer and lighter in colour. White light through a dark medium or on a dark surface (it makes no difference) looks red. We know how red the flame of green wood is: this is because so much smoke is mixed with the bright white firelight: so, too, the sun appears red through smoke and mist. That is why in the rainbow reflection the outer circumference is red (the reflection being from small particles of water), but not in the case of the halo. The other colours shall be explained later. Again, a condensation of this kind cannot persist in the neighbourhood of the sun: it must either turn to rain or be dissolved, but opposite to the sun there is an interval during which the water is formed. If there were not this distinction haloes would be coloured like the rainbow. Actually no complete or circular halo presents this colour, only small and fragmentary appearances called 'rods'. But if a haze due to water or any other dark substance formed there we should have had, as we maintain, a complete rainbow like that which we do find round lamps. A rainbow appears round these in winter, generally with southerly winds. Persons whose eyes are moist see it most clearly because their sight is weak and easily reflected. It is due to the moistness of the air and the soot which the flame gives off and which mixes with the air and makes it a mirror, and to the blackness which that mirror derives from the smoky nature of the soot. The light of the lamp appears as a circle which is not white but purple. It shows the colours of the rainbow; but because the sight that is reflected is too weak and the mirror too dark, red is absent. The rainbow that is seen when oars are raised out of the sea involves the same relative positions as that in the sky, but its colour is more like that round the lamps, being purple rather than red. The reflection is from very small particles continuous with one another, and in this case the particles are fully formed water. We get a rainbow, too, if a man sprinkles fine drops in a room turned to the sun so that the sun is shining in part of the room and throwing a shadow in the rest. Then if one man sprinkles in the room, another, standing outside, sees a rainbow where the sun's rays cease and make the shadow. Its nature and colour is like that from the oars and its cause is the same, for the sprinkling hand corresponds to the oar.

That the colours of the rainbow are those we described and how the other colours come to appear in it will be clear from the following considerations. We must recognize, as we have said, and lay down: first, that white colour on a black surface or seen through a black medium gives red; second, that sight when strained to a distance becomes weaker and less; third, that black is in a sort the negation of sight: an object is black because sight fails; so everything at a distance looks blacker, because sight does not reach it. The theory of these matters belongs to the account of the senses, which are the proper subjects of such an inquiry; we need only state about them what is necessary for us. At all events, that is the reason why distant objects and objects seen in a mirror look darker and smaller and smoother, and why the reflection of clouds in water is darker than the clouds themselves. This latter is clearly the case: the reflection diminishes the sight that reaches them. It makes no difference whether the change is in the object seen or in the sight, the result being in either case the same.

The following fact further is worth noticing. When there is a cloud near the sun and we look at it it does not look coloured at all but white, but when we look at the same cloud in water it shows a trace of rainbow colouring. Clearly, then, when sight is reflected it is weakened and, as it makes dark look darker, so it makes white look less white, changing it and bringing it nearer to black. When the sight is relatively strong the change is to red; the next stage is green, and a further degree of weakness gives violet. No further change is visible, but three completes the series of colours (as we find three does in most other things), and the change into the rest is imperceptible to sense. Hence also the rainbow appears with three colours; this is true of each of the two, but in a contrary way. The outer band of the primary rainbow is red: for the largest band reflects most sight to the sun, and the outer band is largest. The middle band and the third go on the same principle. So if the principles we laid down about the appearance of colours are true the rainbow necessarily has three colours, and these three and no others. The appearance of yellow is due to contrast, for the red is whitened by its juxtaposition with green. We can see this from the fact that the rainbow is purest when the cloud is blackest; and then the red shows most yellow. (Yellow in the rainbow comes between red and green.) So the whole of the red shows white by contrast with the blackness of the cloud around: for it

is white compared to the cloud and the green. Again,
when the rainbow is fading away and the red is dis-
solving, the white cloud is brought into contact with
the green and becomes yellow. But the moon rainbow
affords the best instance of this colour contrast. It
looks quite white: this is because it appears on the
dark cloud and at night. So, just as fire is intensified
by added fire, black beside black makes that which
is in some degree white look quite white. Bright dyes
too show the effect of contrast. In woven and em-
broidered stuffs the appearance of colours is profoundly
affected by their juxtaposition with one another (purple,
for instance, appears different on white and on black
wool), and also by differences of illumination. Thus
embroiderers say that they often make mistakes in their
colours when they work by lamplight, and use the
wrong ones.

50. Generation from the egg proceeds in an identical
manner with all birds, but the full periods from conception to birth differ, as has been said. With the common
hen after three days and three nights there is the first
indication of the embryo; with larger birds the interval
being longer, with smaller birds shorter. Meanwhile
the yolk comes into being, rising towards the sharp
end, where the primal element of the egg is situated,
and where the egg gets hatched; and the heart appears, like a speck of blood, in the white of the egg.
This point beats and moves as though endowed with
life, and from it two vein-ducts with blood in them
trend in a convoluted course as the egg-substance goes
on growing, towards each of the two circumjacent in-
teguments; and a membrane carrying bloody fibres
now envelops the yolk, leading off from the vein-ducts.
A little afterwards the body is differentiated, at first

very small and white. The head is clearly distinguished,
and in it the eyes, swollen out to a great extent. This
condition of the eyes lasts on for a good while, as it
is only by degrees that they diminish in size and col-
lapse. At the outset the under portion of the body
appears insignificant in comparison with the upper portion. Of the two ducts that lead from the heart, the
one proceeds towards the circumjacent integument, and
the other, like a navel-string, towards the yolk. The
life-element of the chick is in the white of the egg, and
the nutriment comes through the navel-string out of
the yolk.

When the egg is now ten days old the chick and all
its parts are distinctly visible. The head is still larger
than the rest of its body, and the eyes larger than the
head, but still devoid of vision. The eyes, if removed
about this time, are found to be larger than beans, and
black; if the cuticle be peeled off them there is a white
and cold liquid inside, quite glittering in the sunlight,
but there is no hard substance whatsoever. Such is the
condition of the head and eyes. At this time also the
larger internal organs are visible, as also the stomach
and the arrangement of the viscera; and the veins that
seem to proceed from the heart are now close to the
navel. From the navel there stretch a pair of veins;
one towards the membrane that envelops the yoke (and,
by the way, the yolk is now liquid, or more so than is
normal), and the other towards that membrane which
envelops collectively the membrane wherein the chick
lies, the membrane of the yolk, and the intervening
liquid. For, as the chick grows, little by little one
part of the yolk goes upward, and another part downward, and the white liquid is between them; and the
white of the egg is underneath the lower part of the
yolk, as it was at the outset. On the tenth day the

white is at the extreme outer surface, reduced in amount, glutinous, firm in substance, and sallow in colour.

The disposition of the several constituent parts is as follows. First and outermost comes the membrane of the egg, not that of the shell, but underneath it. Inside this membrane is a white liquid; then comes the chick, and a membrane round about it, separating it off so as to keep the chick free from the liquid; next after the chick comes the yolk, into which one of the two veins was described as leading, the other one leading into the enveloping white substance. A membrane with a liquid resembling serum envelops the entire structure. Then comes another membrane right round the embryo, as has been described, separating it off against the liquid. Underneath this comes the yolk, enveloped in another membrane (into which yolk proceeds the navel-string that leads from the heart and the big vein), so as to keep the embryo free of both liquids.

About the twentieth day, if you open the egg and touch the chick, it moves inside and chirps; and it is already coming to be covered with down, when, after the twentieth day is past, the chick begins to break the shell.

51. As regards the shape of the womb, the reader is referred to my treatise on Anatomy. The womb is diverse in diverse fishes, as for instance in the sharks as compared one with another or as compared with the skate. That is to say, in some sharks the eggs adhere in the middle of the womb round about the backbone, as has been stated, and this is the case with the dog-fish; as the eggs grow they shift their place; and since the womb is bifurcate and adheres to the midriff, as in the rest of similar creatures, the eggs pass into one or other of the two compartments. This womb and the womb

of the other sharks exhibit, as you go a little way off
from the midriff, something resembling white breasts,
which never make their appearance unless there be
conception.

Dog-fish and skate have a kind of egg-shell, in
which is found an egg-like liquid. The shape of the
egg-shell resembles the tongue of a bagpipe, and hair-
like ducts are attached to the shell. With the dog-fish,
which is called by some the 'dappled shark', the young
are born when the shell-formation breaks in pieces and
falls out; with the ray, after it has laid the egg the
shell-formation breaks up and the young move out. The
spiny dog-fish has its eggs close to the midriff above
the breast-like formations; when the egg descends,
as soon as it gets detached the young is born. The
mode of generation is the same in the case of the fox-
shark.

The so-called smooth shark has its eggs in betwixt
the wombs like the dog-fish; these eggs shift into each
of the two horns of the womb and descend, and the
young develop with the navel-string attached to the
womb, so that, as the egg-substance gets used up, the
embryo is sustained to all appearance just as in the
case of quadrupeds. The navel-string is long and
adheres to the under part of the womb (each navel-
string being attached as it were by a sucker), and also
to the centre of the embryo in the place where the liver
is situated. If the embryo be cut open, even though
it has the egg-substance no longer, the food inside is
egg-like in appearance. Each embryo, as in the case
of quadrupeds, is provided with a chorion and separate
membranes. When young the embryo has its head upwards, but downwards when it gets strong and is completed in form. Males are generated on the left-hand
side of the womb, and females on the right-hand side.

and males and females on the same side together. If the embryo be cut open, then, as with quadrupeds, such internal organs as it is furnished with, as for instance the liver, are found to be large and supplied with blood.

All cartilaginous fishes have at one and the same time eggs above close to the midriff (some larger, some smaller), in considerable numbers, and also embryos lower down. And this circumstance leads many to suppose that fishes of this species pair and bear young every month, inasmuch as they do not produce all their young at once, but now and again and over a lengthened period. But such eggs as have come down below within the womb are simultaneously ripened and completed in growth.

Dog-fish in general can extrude and take in again their young, as can also the angel-fish and the electric ray—and, by the way, a large electric ray has been seen with about eighty embryos inside it—but the spiny dog-fish is an exception to the rule, being prevented by the spine of the young fish from so doing. Of the flat cartilaginous fish, the trygon and the ray cannot extrude and take in again in consequence of the roughness of the tails of the young. The batrachus or fishing-frog also is unable to take in its young owing to the size of the head and the prickles; and, by the way, as was previously remarked, it is the only one of these fishes that is not viviparous.

52. The drones, as a rule, keep inside the hive; when they go out of doors, they soar up in the air in a stream, whirling round and round in a kind of gymnastic exercise; when this is over, they come inside the hive and feed to repletion ravenously. The kings never quit the hive, except in conjunction with the entire swarm, either for food or for any other reason. They say that,

if a young swarm go astray, it will turn back upon its route and by the aid of scent seek out its leader. It is said that if he is unable to fly he is carried by the swarm, and that if he dies the swarm perishes; and that, if this swarm outlives the king for a while and constructs combs, no honey is produced and the bees soon die out. Bees scramble up the stalks of flowers and rapidly gather the bees-wax with their front legs; the front legs wipe it off on to the middle legs, and these pass it on to the hollow curves of the hind-legs; when thus laden, they fly away home, and one may see plainly that their load is a heavy one. On each expedition the bee does not fly from a flower of one kind to a flower of another, but flies from one violet, say, to another violet, and never meddles with another flower until it has got back to the hive; on reaching the hive they throw off their load, and each bee on his return is accompanied by three or four companions. One cannot well tell what is the substance they gather, nor the exact process of their work. Their mode of gathering wax has been observed on olive-trees, as owing to the thickness of the leaves the bees remain stationary for a considerable while. After this work is over, they attend to the grubs. There is nothing to prevent grubs, honey, and drones being all found in one and the same comb. As long as the leader is alive, the drones are said to be produced apart by themselves; if he be no longer living, they are said to be reared by the bees in their own cells, and under these circumstances to become more spirited: for this reason they are called 'sting-drones', not that they really have stings, but that they have the wish, without the power, to use such weapons. The cells for the drones are larger than the others; sometimes the bees construct cells for the drones apart, but usually they put them in amongst their own; and when this is the case the bee-keepers cut the drone-cells out of the combs.

There are several species of bees, as has been said, two of 'kings', the better kind red, the other black and variegated, and twice as big as the working-bee. The best working-bee is small, round, and speckled: another kind is long and like an anthrene wasp; another kind is what is called the robber-bee, black and flat-bellied; then there is the drone, the largest of all, but devoid of sting, and lazy. There is a difference between the progeny of bees that inhabit cultivated land and of those from the mountains: the forest-bees are more shaggy, smaller, more industrious and more fierce. Working-bees make their combs all even, with the superficial covering quite smooth. Each comb is of one kind only: that is, it contains either bees only, or grubs only, or drones only; if it happen, however, that they make in one and the same comb all these kinds of cells, each separate kind will be built in a continuous row right through. The long bees build uneven combs, with the lids of the cells protuberant, like those of the anthrene; grubs and everything else have no fixed places, but are put anywhere; from these bees come inferior kings, a large quantity of drones, and the so-called robber-bee; they produce either no honey at all, or honey in very small quantities. Bees brood over the combs and so mature them; if they fail to do so, the combs are said to go bad and to get covered with a sort of spider's web. If they can keep brooding over the part undamaged, the damaged part simply eats itself away; if they cannot so brood, the entire comb perishes; in the damaged combs small worms are engendered, which take on wings and fly away. When the combs keep settling down, the bees restore the level surface, and put props underneath the combs to give themselves free passage-room; for if such free passage be lacking they cannot brood, and the cobwebs come on. When the robber-bee and the drone appear, not only do they do no work themselves, but they actually damage the work of the other bees; if they are caught in the act, they are killed by the working-bees. These bees also kill without mercy most of their kings, and especially kings of the inferior sort; and this they do for fear a multiplicity of kings should lead to a dismemberment of the hive. They kill them especially when the hive is deficient in grubs, and a swarm is not intended to take place; under these circumstances they destroy the cells of the kings if they have been prepared, on the ground that these kings are always ready to lead out swarms. They destroy also the combs of the drones if a failure in the honey supply be threatening and the hive runs short of provisions; under such circumstances they fight desperately with all who try to take their honey, and eject from the hive all the resident drones; and oftentimes the drones are to be seen sitting apart in the hive.

The little bees fight vigorously with the long kind, and try to banish them from the hives; if they succeed, the hive will be unusually productive, but if the bigger bees get left mistresses of the field they pass the time in idleness, and do no good at all but die out before the autumn. Whenever the working-bees kill an enemy they try to do so out of doors; and whenever one of their own body dies, they carry the dead bee out of doors also. The so-called robber-bees spoil their own combs, and, if they can do so unnoticed, enter and spoil the combs of other bees; if they are caught in the act they are put to death. It is no easy task for them to escape detection, for there are sentinels on guard at every entry; and, even if they do escape detection on entering, afterwards from a surfeit of food they cannot fly, but go rolling about in front of the hive, so that their chances of escape are small indeed. The kings are never themselves seen outside the hive except with a swarm in flight: during which time all the other bees cluster around them. . . .

Bees have fear only of one another. They fight with one another and with wasps. Away from the hive they attack neither their own species nor any other creature, but in the close proximity of the hive they kill whatever they get hold of. Bees that sting die from their inability to extract the sting without at the same time extracting their intestines. True, they often recover, if the person stung takes the trouble to press the sting out; but once it loses its sting the bee must die. They can kill with their stings even large animals; in fact, a horse has been known to have been stung to death by them. The kings are the least disposed to show anger or to inflict a sting. Bees that die are removed from the hive, and in every way the creature is remarkable for its cleanly habits; in point of fact, they often fly away to a distance to void their excrement because it is malodorous; and, as has been said, they are annoyed by all bad smells and by the scent of perfumes, so much so that they sting people that use perfumes. They perish from a number of accidental causes, and when their kings become too numerous and try each to carry away a portion of the swarm. The toad also feeds on bees; he comes to the doorway of the hive, puffs himself out as he sits on the watch, and devours the creatures as they come flying out; the bees can in no way retaliate, but the bee-keeper makes a point of killing him. As for the class of bee that has been spoken of as inferior or good-for-nothing, and as constructing its combs so roughly, some bee-keepers say that it is the young bees that act so from inexperience; and the bees of the current year are termed young. The young bees do not sting as the others do; and it is for this reason that swarms may be safely carried, as it is of young bees that they are composed. When honey runs short they expel the drones, and the bee-keepers supply the bees with figs and sweet-tasting articles of food. The elder bees do the indoor work, and are rough and hairy from staying indoors; the young bees do the outer carrying, and are comparatively smooth. They kill the drones also when in their work they are confined for room; the drones, by the way, live in the innermost recess of the hive. On one occasion, when a hive was in a poor condition, some of the occupants assailed a foreign hive; proving victorious in a combat they took to carrying off the honey; when the bee-keeper tried to kill them, the other bees came out and tried to beat off the enemy but made no attempt to sting the man.

The diseases that chiefly attack prosperous hives are first of all the clerus—this consists in a growth of little worms on the floor, from which, as they develop, a kind of cobweb grows over the entire hive, and the combs decay; another diseased condition is indicated in a lassitude on the part of the bees and in malodorousness of the hive. Bees feed on thyme; and the white thyme is better than the red. In summer the place for the hive should be cool, and in winter warm. They are very apt to fall sick if the plant they are at work on be mildewed. In a high wind they carry a stone by way of ballast to steady them. If a stream be near at hand, they drink from it and from it only, but before they drink they first deposit their load; if there be no water near at hand, they disgorge their honey as they drink elsewhere, and at once make off to work. There are two seasons for making honey, spring and autumn;

the spring honey is sweeter, whiter, and in every way better than the autumn honey. Superior honey comes from fresh comb, and from young shoots; the red honey is inferior, and owes its inferiority to the comb in which it is deposited, just as wine is apt to be spoiled by its cask; consequently, one should have it looked to and dried. When the thyme is in flower and the comb is full, the honey does not harden. The honey that is golden in hue is excellent. White honey does not come from thyme pure and simple; it is good as a salve for sore eyes and wounds. Poor honey always floats on the surface and should be skimmed off; the fine clear honey rests below. When the floral world is in full bloom, then they make wax; consequently you must then take the wax out of the hive, for they go to work on new wax at once. The flowers from which they gather honey are as follows: the spindle-tree, the melilot-clover, king's-spear, myrtle, flowering-reed, withy, and broom. When they work at thyme, they mix in water before sealing up the comb. As has been already stated, they all either fly to a distance to discharge their excrement or make the discharge into one single comb. The little bees, as has been said, are more industrious than the big ones; their wings are battered; their colour is black, and they have a burnt-up aspect. Gaudy and showy bees, like gaudy and showy women, are good-for-nothings.

53. Consider how the physician or how the builder sets about his work. He starts by forming for himself a definite picture, in the one case perceptible to mind, in the other to sense, of his end—the physician of health, the builder of a house—and this he holds forward as the reason and explanation of each subsequent step that he takes, and of his acting in this or that way

as the case may be. Now in the works of nature the
good end and the final cause is still more dominant
than in works of art such as these, nor is necessity a
factor with the same significance in them all; though
almost all writers, while they try to refer their origin to
this cause, do so without distinguishing the various
senses in which the term necessity is used. For there
is absolute necessity, manifested in eternal phenomena;
and there is hypothetical necessity, manifested in everything that is generated by nature as in everything that
is produced by art, be it a house or what it may. For
if a house or other such final object is to be realized, it
is necessary that such and such material shall exist;
and it is necessary that first this and then that shall
be produced, and first this and then that set in motion,
and so on in continuous succession, until the end and
final result is reached, for the sake of which each prior
thing is produced and exists. As with these productions
of art, so also is it with the productions of nature.
The mode of necessity, however, and the mode of ratio-
cination are different in natural science from what
they are in the theoretical sciences; of which we have
spoken elsewhere. For in the latter the starting-point
is that which is; in the former that which is to be. For
it is that which is yet to be—health, let us say, or a
man—that, owing to its being of such and such characters, necessitates the pre-existence or previous production of this and that antecedent; and not this or that
antecedent which, because it exists or has been generated,
makes it necessary that health or a man is in, or shall
come into, existence. Nor is it possible to trace back
the series of necessary antecedents to a starting-point,
of which you can say that, existing itself from eternity,
it has determined their existence as its consequent.
These however, again, are matters that have been dealt

with in another treatise. There too it was stated in what cases absolute and hypothetical necessity exist; in what cases also the proposition expressing hypothetical necessity is simply convertible, and what cause it is that determines this convertibility.

Another matter which must not be passed over without consideration is, whether the proper subject of our exposition is that with which the ancient writers concerned themselves, namely, what is the process of formation of each animal; or whether it is not rather, what are the characters of a given creature when formed. For there is no small difference between these two views. The best course appears to be that we should follow the method already mentioned, and begin with the phenomena presented by each group of animals, and, when this is done, proceed afterwards to state the causes of those phenomena, and to deal with their evolution. For elsewhere, as for instance in house-building, this is the true sequence. The plan of the house, or the house, has this and that form; and because it has this and that form, therefore is its construction carried out in this or that manner. For the process of evolution is for the sake of the thing finally evolved, and not this for the sake of the process. Empedocles, then, was in error when he said that many of the characters presented by animals were merely the results of incidental occurrences during their development; for instance, that the backbone was divided as it is into vertebrae, because it happened to be broken owing to the contorted position of the foetus in the womb. In so saying he overlooked the fact that propagation implies a creative seed endowed with certain formative properties. Secondly, he neglected another fact, namely, that the parent animal pre-exists, not only in idea, but actually in time. For man is generated from man;

and thus it is the possession of certain characters by the parent that determines the development of like characters in the child. The same statement holds good also for the operations of art, and even for those which are apparently spontaneous. For the same result as is produced by art may occur spontaneously. Spontaneity, for instance, may bring about the restoration of health. The products of art, however, require the pre-existence of an efficient cause homogeneous with themselves, such as the statuary's art, which must necessarily precede the statue; for this cannot possibly be produced spontaneously. Art indeed consists in the conception of the result to be produced before its realization in the material. As with spontaneity, so with chance; for this also produces the same result as art, and by the same process.

The fittest mode, then, of treatment is to say, a man has such and such parts, because the conception of a man includes their presence, and because they are necessary conditions of his existence, or, if we cannot quite say this, which would be best of all, then the next thing to it, namely, that it is either quite impossible for him to exist without them, or, at any rate, that it is better for him that they should be there; and their existence involves the existence of other antecedents. Thus we should say, because man is an animal with such and such characters, therefore is the process of his development necessarily such as it is; and therefore is it accomplished in such and such an order, this part being formed first, that next, and so on in succession; and after a like fashion should we explain the evolution of all other works of nature.

Now that with which the ancient writers, who first philosophized about Nature, busied themselves, was the material principle and the material cause. They inquired what this is, and what its character; how the universe is generated out of it, and by what motor influence, whether, for instance, by antagonism or friendship, whether by intelligence or spontaneous action, the substratum of matter being assumed to have certain inseparable properties; fire, for instance, to have a hot nature, earth a cold one; the former to be light, the latter heavy. For even the genesis of the universe is thus explained by them. After a like fashion do they deal also with the development of plants and of animals. They say, for instance, that the water contained in the body causes by its currents the formation of the stomach and the other receptacles of food or of excretion; and that the breath by its passage breaks open the outlets of the nostrils; air and water being the materials of which bodies are made; for all represent nature as composed of such or similar substances.

But if men and animals and their several parts are natural phenomena, then the natural philosopher must take into consideration not merely the ultimate substances of which they are made, but also flesh, bone, blood, and all the other homogeneous parts; not only these, but also the heterogeneous parts, such as face, hand, foot; and must examine how each of these comes to be what it is, and in virtue of what force. For to say what are the ultimate substances out of which an animal is formed, to state, for instance, that it is made of fire or earth, is no more sufficient than would be a similar account in the case of a couch or the like. For we should not be content with saying that the couch was made of bronze or wood or whatever it might be, but should try to describe its design or mode of composition in preference to the material; or, if we did deal with the material, it would at any rate be with the concretion of material and form. For a couch is such and such a form embodied in this or that matter, or such and such a matter with this or that form; so that its shape and structure must be included in our description. For the formal nature is of greater importance than the material nature.

Does, then, configuration and colour constitute the essence of the various animals and of their several parts? For if so, what Democritus says will be strictly correct. For such appears to have been his notion. At any rate he says that it is evident to every one what form it is that makes the man, seeing that he is recognizable by his shape and colour. And yet a dead body has exactly the same configuration as a living one; but for all that is not a man. So also no hand of bronze or wood or constituted in any but the appropriate way can possibly be a hand in more than name. For like a physician in a painting, or like a flute in a sculpture, in spite of its name it will be unable to do the office which that name implies. Precisely in the same way no part of a dead body, such I mean as its eye or its hand, is really an eye or a hand. To say, then, that shape and colour constitute the animal is an inadequate statement, and is much the same as if a woodcarver were to insist that the hand he had cut out was really a hand. Yet the physiologists, when they give an account of the development and causes of the animal form, speak very much like such a craftsman. What, however, I would ask, are the forces by which the hand or the body was fashioned into its shape? The woodcarver will perhaps say, by the axe or the auger; the physiologist, by air and by earth. Of these two answers the artificer's is the better, but it is nevertheless insufficient. For it is not enough for him to say that by the stroke of his tool this part was formed into a concavity, that into a flat surface; but he must state the reasons why he struck his blow in such a way as to effect this, and what his final object was; namely, that the piece of wood should develop eventually into this or that shape. It is plain, then, that the teaching of the old physiologists is inadequate, and that the true method is to state what the definitive characters are that distinguish the animal as a whole; to explain what it is both in substance and in form, and to deal after the same fashion with its several organs; in fact, to proceed in exactly the same way as we should do, were we giving a complete description of a couch.

If now this something that constitutes the form of the living being be the soul, or part of the soul, or something that without the soul cannot exist; as would seem to be the case, seeing at any rate that when the soul departs, what is left is no longer a living animal, and that none of the parts remain what they were before, excepting in mere configuration, like the animals that in the fable are turned into stone; if, I say, this be so, then it will come within the province of the natural philosopher to inform himself concerning the soul, and to treat of it, either in its entirety, or, at any rate, of that part of it which constitutes the essential character of an animal; and it will be his duty to say what this soul or this part of a soul is; and to discuss the attributes that attach to this essential character, especially as nature is spoken of in two senses, and the nature of a thing is either its matter or its essence; nature as essence including both the motor cause and the final cause. Now it is in the latter of these two senses that either the whole soul or some part of it constitutes the nature of an animal; and inasmuch as it is the presence of the soul that enables matter to constitute the animal nature, much more than it is the presence of matter which so enables the soul, the inquirer into nature is bound on every ground to treat of the soul rather than of the matter. For though the wood of which they are made constitutes the couch and the tripod, it only does so because it is capable of receiving such and such a form.

What has been said suggests the question, whether it is the whole soul or only some part of it, the consideration of which comes within the province of natural science. Now if it be of the whole soul that this should treat, then there is no place for any other philosophy beside it. For as it belongs in all cases to one and the same science to deal with correlated subjects—one and the same science, for instance, deals with sensation and with the objects of sense—and as therefore the intelligent soul and the objects of intellect, being correlated, must belong to one and the same science, it follows that natural science will have to include the whole universe in its province. But perhaps it is not the whole soul, nor all its parts collectively, that constitutes the source of motion; but there may be one part, identical with that in plants, which is the source of growth, another, namely the sensory part, which is the source of change of quality, while still another, and this not the intellectual part, is the source of locomotion. I say not the intellectual part; for other animals than man have the power of locomotion, but in none but him is there intellect. Thus then it is plain that it is not of the whole soul that we have to treat. For it is not the whole soul that constitutes the animal nature, but only some part or parts of it.

Moreover, it is impossible that any abstraction can form a subject of natural science, seeing that everything that Nature makes is means to an end. For just as human creations are the products of art, so living objects are manifestly the products of an analogous cause or

principle, not external but internal, derived like the hot
and the cold from the environing universe. And that the
heaven, if it had an origin, was evolved and is maintained
by such a cause, there is therefore even more reason to
believe, than that mortal animals so originated. For
order and definiteness are much more plainly manifest in
the celestial bodies than in our own frame; while change
and chance are characteristic of the perishable things of
earth. Yet there are some who, while they allow that
every animal exists and was generated by nature, nevertheless hold that the heaven was constructed to be
what it is by chance and spontaneity; the heaven, in
which not the faintest sign of hap-hazard or of dis-
order is discernible! Again, whenever there is plainly
some final end, to which a motion tends should nothing
stand in the way, we always say that such final end
is the aim or purpose of the motion; and from this it
is evident that there must be a something or other really
existing, corresponding to what we call by the name
of Nature. For a given germ does not give rise to
any chance living being, nor spring from any chance
one; but each germ springs from a definite parent and
gives rise to a definite progeny. And thus it is the
germ that is the ruling influence and fabricator of the
offspring.

54. Some writers propose to reach the definitions of
the ultimate forms of animal life by bipartite division.
But this method is often difficult, and often impracticable.

Sometimes the final differentia of the subdivision is
sufficient by itself, and the antecedent differentiae are
mere surplusage. Thus in the series Footed, Two-
footed, Cleft-footed, the last term is all-expressive by

itself, and to append the higher terms is only an idle iteration.

Again it is not permissible to break up a natural group, Birds for instance, by putting its members under different bifurcations, as is done in the published dichotomies, where some birds are ranked with animals of the water, and others placed in a different class. The group Birds and the group Fishes happen to be named, while other natural groups have no popular names; for instance, the groups that we may call Sanguineous and Bloodless are not known popularly by any designations. If such natural groups are not to be broken up, the method of Dichotomy cannot be employed, for it necessarily involves such breaking up and dislocation. The group of the Many-footed, for instance, would, under this method, have to be dismembered, and some of its kinds distributed among land animals, others among water animals.

Again, privative terms inevitably form one branch of dichotomous division, as we see in the proposed dichotomies. But privative terms in their character of privatives admit of no subdivision. For there can be no specific forms of a negation, of Featherless for instance or of Footless, as there are of Feathered and of Footed. Yet a generic differentia must be subdivisible; for otherwise what is there that makes it generic rather than specific? There are to be found generic, that is specifically subdivisible, differentiae; Feathered for instance and Footed. For feathers are divisible into Barbed and Unbarbed, and feet into Manycleft, and Twocleft, like those of animals with bifid hoofs, and Uncleft or Undivided, like those of animals with solid hoofs. Now even with differentiae capable of this specific subdivision it is difficult enough so to make the classification, as that each animal shall be comprehended in some one subdivision and in not more than one; but far more difficult, nay impossible, is it to do this, if we start with a dichotomy into two contradictories. (Suppose for instance we start with the two contradictories, Feathered and Unfeathered; we shall find that the ant, the glow-worm, and some other animals fall under both divisions.) For each differentia must be presented by some species. There must be some species, therefore, under the privative heading. Now specifically distinct animals cannot present in their essence a common undifferentiated element, but any apparently common element must really be differentiated. (Bird and Man for instance are both Two-footed, but their two-footedness is diverse and differentiated. So any two sanguineous groups must have some difference in their blood, if their blood is part of their essence.) From this it follows that a privative term, being insusceptible of differentiation, cannot be a generic differentia; for, if it were, there would be a common undifferentiated element in two different groups.

Again, if the species are ultimate indivisible groups, that is, are groups with indivisible differentiae, and if no differentia be common to several groups, the number of differentiae must be equal to the number of species. If a differentia though not divisible could yet be common to several groups, then it is plain that in virtue of that common differentia specifically distinct animals would fall into the same division. It is necessary then, if the differentiae, under which are ranged all the ultimate and indivisible groups, are specific characters, that none of them shall be common; for otherwise, as already said, specifically distinct animals will come into one and the same division. But this would violate one of the requisite conditions, which are as follows.

No ultimate group must be included in more than a single division; different groups must not be included in the same division; and every group must be found in some division. It is plain then that we cannot get at the ultimate specific forms of the animal, or any other, kingdom by bifurcate division. If we could, the number of ultimate differentiae would equal the number of ultimate animal forms. For assume an order of beings whose prime differentiae are White and Black. Each of these branches will bifurcate, and their branches again, and so on till we reach the ultimate differentiae, whose number will be four or some other power of two, and will also be the number of the ultimate species comprehended in the order.

(A species is constituted by the combination of differentia and matter. For no part of an animal is purely material or purely immaterial; nor can a body, independently of its condition, constitute an animal or any of its parts, as has repeatedly been observed.)

Further, the differentiae must be elements of the essence, and not merely essential attributes. Thus if Figure is the term to be divided, it must not be divided into figures whose angles are equal to two right angles, and figures whose angles are together greater than two right angles. For it is only an attribute of a triangle and not part of its essence that its angles are equal to two right angles.

Again, the bifurcations must be opposites, like White and Black, Straight and Bent; and if we characterize one branch by either term, we must characterize the other by its opposite, and not, for example, characterize one branch by a colour, the other by a mode of progression, swimming for instance.

Furthermore, living beings cannot be divided by the functions common to body and soul, by Flying, for instance, and Walking, as we see them divided in the dichotomies already referred to. For some groups, Ants for instance, fall under both divisions, some ants flying while others do not. Similarly as regards the division into Wild and Tame; for it also would involve the disruption of a species into different groups. For in almost all species in which some members are tame, there are other members that are wild. Such, for example, is the case with Men, Horses, Oxen, Dogs in India, Pigs, Goats, Sheep; groups which, if double, ought to have what they have not, namely, different appellations; and which, if single, prove that Wildness and Tameness do not amount to specific differences. And whatever single element we take as a basis of division the same difficulty will occur.

The method then that we must adopt is to attempt to recognize the natural groups, following the indications afforded by the instincts of mankind, which led them for instance to form the class of Birds and the class of Fishes, each of which group combines a multitude of differentiae, and is not defined by a single one as in dichotomy. The method of dichotomy is either impossible (for it would put a single group under different divisions or contrary groups under the same division), or it only furnishes a single ultimate differentia for each species, which either alone or with its series of antecedents has to constitute the ultimate species.

If, again, a new differential character be introduced at any stage into the division, the necessary result is that the continuity of the division becomes merely a unity and continuity of agglomeration, like the unity and continuity of a series of sentences coupled together by conjunctive particles. For instance, suppose we have the bifurcation Feathered and Featherless, and

then divide Feathered into Wild and Tame, or into
White and Black. Tame and White are not a differentiation of Feathered, but are the commencement of an
independent bifurcation, and are foreign to the series
at the end of which they are introduced.

As we said then, we must define at the outset by a
multiplicity of differentiae. If we do so, privative
terms will be available, which are unavailable to the
dichotomist.

The impossibility of reaching the definition of any
of the ultimate forms by dichotomy of the larger group,
as some propose, is manifest also from the following
considerations. It is impossible that a single differentia, either by itself or with its antecedents, shall
express the whole essence of a species. (In saying a
single differentia by itself I mean such an isolated
differentia as Cleft-footed; in saying a single differentia
with antecedent I mean, to give an instance, Many-cleft-
footed preceded by Cleft-footed. The very continuity
of a series of successive differentiae in a division is
intended to show that it is their combination that expresses the character of the resulting unit, or ultimate
group. But one is misled by the usages of language
into imagining that it is merely the final term of the
series, Many-cleft-footed for instance, that constitutes
the whole differentia, and that the antecedent terms,
Footed, Cleft-footed, are superfluous. Now it is evident that such a series cannot consist of many terms.
For if one divides and subdivides, one soon reaches the
final differential term, but for all that will not have
got to the ultimate division, that is, to the species.)
No single differentia, I repeat, either by itself or with
its antecedents, can possibly express the essence of a
species. Suppose, for example, Man to be the animal
to be defined; the single differentia will be Cleft-footed,

either by itself or with its antecedents, Footed and Two-footed. Now if man was nothing more than a Cleft-footed animal, this single differentia would duly represent his essence. But seeing that this is not the case, more differentiae than this one will necessarily be required to define him; and these cannot come under one division; for each single branch of a dichotomy ends in a single differentia, and cannot possibly include several differentiae belonging to one and the same animal.

It is impossible then to reach any of the ultimate animal forms by dichotomous division.

It deserves inquiry why a single name denoting a higher group was not invented by mankind, as an appellation to comprehend the two groups of Water animals and Winged animals. For even these have certain attributes in common. However, the present nomenclature is just. Groups that only differ in degree, and in the more or less of an identical element that they possess, are aggregated under a single class; groups whose attributes are not identical but analogous are separated. For instance, bird differs from bird by gradation, or by excess and defect; some birds have long feathers, others short ones, but all are feathered. Bird and Fish are more remote and only agree in having analogous organs; for what in the bird is feather, in the fish is scale. Such analogies can scarcely, however, serve universally as indications for the formation of groups, for almost all animals present analogies in their corresponding parts.

The individuals comprised within a species, such as Socrates and Coriscus, are the real existences; but inasmuch as these individuals possess one common specific form, it will suffice to state the universal attributes of the species, that is, the attributes common to all its individuals, once for all, as otherwise there will be endless reiteration, as has already been pointed out.

But as regards the larger groups—such as Birds—which comprehend many species, there may be a question. For on the one hand it may be urged that as the ultimate species represent the real existences, it will be well, if practicable, to examine these ultimate species separately, just as we examine the species Man separately; to examine, that is, not the whole class Birds collectively, but the Ostrich, the Crane, and the other indivisible groups or species belonging to the class.

On the other hand, however, this course would involve repeated mention of the same attribute, as the same attribute is common to many species, and so far would be somewhat irrational and tedious. Perhaps, then, it will be best to treat generically the universal attributes of the groups that have a common nature and contain closely allied subordinate forms, whether they are groups recognized by a true instinct of mankind, such as Birds and Fishes, or groups not popularly known by a common appellation, but withal composed of closely allied subordinate groups; and only to deal individually with the attributes of a single species, when such species—man, for instance, and any other such, if such there be—stands apart from others, and does not constitute with them a larger natural group.

It is generally similarity in the shape of particular organs, or of the whole body, that has determined the formation of the larger groups. It is in virtue of such a similarity that Birds, Fishes, Cephalopoda, and Testacea have been made to form each a separate class. For within the limits of each such class, the parts do not differ in that they have no nearer resemblance than that of analogy—such as exists between the bone of

man and the spine of fish—but differ merely in respect
of such corporeal conditions as largeness smallness,
softness hardness, smoothness roughness, and other similar oppositions, or, in one word, in respect of degree.

55. Of things constituted by nature some are ungenerated, imperishable, and eternal, while others are subject
to generation and decay. The former are excellent beyond compare and divine, but less accessible to knowledge. The evidence that might throw light on them,
and on the problems which we long to solve respecting
them, is furnished but scantily by sensation; whereas
respecting perishable plants and animals we have abun-
dant information, living as we do in their midst, and
ample data may be collected concerning all their various
kinds, if only we are willing to take sufficient pains.
Both departments, however, have their special charm.
The scanty conceptions to which we can attain of celestial things give us, from their excellence, more pleasure
than all our knowledge of the world in which we live;
just as a half glimpse of persons that we love is more
delightful than a leisurely view of other things, whatever their number and dimensions. On the other hand,
in certitude and in completeness our knowledge of
terrestrial things has the advantage. Moreover, their
greater nearness and affinity to us balances somewhat
the loftier interest of the heavenly things that are the
objects of the higher philosophy. Having already
treated of the celestial world, as far as our conjectures
could reach, we proceed to treat of animals, without
omitting, to the best of our ability, any member of the
kingdom, however ignoble. For if some have no graces
to charm the sense, yet even these, by disclosing to
intellectual perception the artistic spirit that designed
them, give immense pleasure to all who can trace links

of causation, and are inclined to philosophy. Indeed, it would be strange if mimic representations of them were attractive, because they disclose the mimetic skill of the painter or sculptor, and the original realities themselves were not more interesting, to all at any rate who have eyes to discern the reasons that determined their formation. We therefore must not recoil with childish aversion from the examination of the humbler animals. Every realm of nature is marvellous: and as Heraclitus, when the strangers who came to visit him found him warming himself at the furnace in the kitchen and hesitated to go in, is reported to have bidden them not to be afraid to enter, as even in that kitchen divinities were present, so we should venture on the study of every kind of animal without distaste; for each and all will reveal to us something natural and something beautiful. Absence of haphazard and conduciveness of everything to an end are to be found in Nature's works in the highest degree, and the resultant end of her generations and combinations is a form of the beautiful.

If any person thinks the examination of the rest of the animal kingdom an unworthy task, he must hold in like disesteem the study of man. For no one can look at the primordia of the human frame—blood, flesh, bones, vessels, and the like—without much repugnance. Moreover, when any one of the parts or structures, be it which it may, is under discussion, it must not be supposed that it is its material composition to which attention is being directed or which is the object of the discussion, but the relation of such part to the total form. Similarly, the true object of architecture is not bricks, mortar, or timber, but the house; and so the principal object of natural philosophy is not the material elements, but their composition, and the totality of the form, independently of which they have no existence.

The course of exposition must be first to state the attributes common to whole groups of animals, and then to attempt to give their explanation. Many groups, as already noticed, present common attributes, that is to say, in some cases absolutely identical affections, and absolutely identical organs,—feet, feathers, scales, and the like; while in other groups the affections and organs are only so far identical as that they are analogous. For instance, some groups have lungs, others have no lung, but an organ analogous to a lung in its place; some have blood, others have no blood, but a fluid analogous to blood, and with the same office. To treat of the common attributes in connexion with each individual group would involve, as already suggested, useless iteration. For many groups have common attributes. So much for this topic.

As every instrument and every bodily member subserves some partial end, that is to say, some special action, so the whole body must be destined to minister to some plenary sphere of action. Thus the saw is made for sawing, for sawing is a function, and not sawing for the saw. Similarly, the body too must somehow or other be made for the soul, and each part of it for some subordinate function, to which it is adapted.

We have, then, first to describe the common functions, common, that is, to the whole animal kingdom, or to certain large groups, or to the members of a species. In other words, we have to describe the attributes common to all animals, or to assemblages, like the class of Birds, of closely allied groups differentiated by gradation, or to groups like Man not differentiated into subordinate groups. In the first case the common attributes may be called analogous, in the second generic, in the third specific.

When a function is ancillary to another, a like relation manifestly obtains between the organs which discharge these functions; and similarly, if one function is prior to and the end of another, their respective organs will stand to each other in the same relation. Thirdly, the existence of these parts involves that of other things as their necessary consequents.

Instances of what I mean by functions and affections are Reproduction, Growth, Copulation, Waking, Sleep, Locomotion, and other similar vital actions. Instances of what I mean by parts are Nose, Eye, Face, and other so-called members or limbs, and also the more elementary parts of which these are made. So much for the method to be pursued. Let us now try to set forth the causes of all vital phenomena, whether universal or particular, and in so doing let us follow that order of exposition which conforms, as we have indicated, to the order of nature.

56. The nature and the number of the parts of which animals are severally composed are matters which have already been set forth in detail in the book of Researches about Animals. We have now to inquire what are the causes that in each case have determined this composition, a subject quite distinct from that dealt with in the Researches.

Now there are three degrees of composition; and of these the first in order, as all will allow, is composition out of what some call the elements, such as earth, air, water, fire. Perhaps, however, it would be more accurate to say composition out of the elementary forces; nor indeed out of all of these, but out of a limited number of them, as defined in previous treatises. For fluid and solid, hot and cold, form the material of all composite bodies; and all other differences are secondary to these, such differences, that is, as heaviness or lightness, density or rarity, roughness or smoothness, and any other such properties of matter as there may be. The second degree of composition is that by which the homogeneous parts of animals, such as bone, flesh, and the like, are constituted out of the primary substances. The third and last stage is the composition which forms the heterogeneous parts, such as face, hand, and the rest.

Now the order of actual development and the order of logical existence are always the inverse of each other. For that which is posterior in the order of development is antecedent in the order of nature, and that is genetically last which in nature is first.

(That this is so is manifest by induction; for a house does not exist for the sake of bricks and stones, but these materials for the sake of the house; and the same is the case with the materials of other bodies. Nor is induction required to show this. It is included in our conception of generation. For generation is a process from a something to a something; that which is generated having a cause in which it originates and a cause in which it ends. The originating cause is the primary efficient cause, which is something already endowed with tangible existence, while the final cause is some definite form or similar end; for man generates man, and plant generates plant, in each case out of the underlying material.)

In order of time, then, the material and the generative process must necessarily be anterior to the being that is generated; but in logical order the definitive character and form of each being precedes the material. This is evident if one only tries to define the process of

formation. For the definition of house-building includes and presupposes that of the house; but the definition of the house does not include nor presuppose that
of house-building; and the same is true of all other
productions. So that it must necessarily be that the
elementary material exists for the sake of the homogeneous parts, seeing that these are genetically posterior
to it, just as the heterogeneous parts are posterior
genetically to them. For these heterogeneous parts
have reached the end and goal, having the third degree of composition, in which degree generation or
development often attains its final term.

Animals, then, are composed of homogeneous parts,
and are also composed of heterogeneous parts. The
former, however, exist for the sake of the latter. For
the active functions and operations of the body are
carried on by these; that is, by the heterogeneous parts,
such as the eye, the nostril, the whole face, the fingers,
the hand, and the whole arm. But inasmuch as there
is a great variety in the functions and motions not only
of aggregate animals but also of the individual organs,
it is necessary that the substances out of which these
are composed shall present a diversity of properties.
For some purposes softness is advantageous, for others
hardness; some parts must be capable of extension,
others of flexion.

57. In all animals, at least in all the perfect kinds,
there are two parts more essential than the rest, namely
the part which serves for the ingestion of food, and the
part which serves for the discharge of its residue. For
without food growth and even existence is impossible.
Intervening again between these two parts there is
invariably a third, in which is lodged the vital principle.
. . . There is a heart, then, in all sanguineous animals,

and the reason for this has already been given. For that sanguineous animals must necessarily have blood is self-evident. And, as the blood is fluid, it is also a matter of necessity that there shall be a receptacle for it; and it is apparently to meet this requirement that nature has devised the blood-vessels. These, again, must necessarily have one primary source. For it is preferable that there shall be one such, when possible, rather than several. This primary source of the vessels is the heart. For the vessels manifestly issue from it and do not go through it. Moreover, being as it is homogeneous, it has the character of a blood-vessel. Again its position is that of a primary or dominating part. For nature, when no other more important purpose stands in her way, places the more honourable part in the more honourable position; and the heart lies about the centre of the body, but rather in its upper than its lower half, and also more in front than behind. This is most evident in the case of man, but even in other animals there is a tendency in the heart to assume a similar position, in the centre of the necessary part of the body, that is to say of the part which terminates in the vent for excrement. For the limbs vary in position in different animals, and are not to be counted with the parts which are necessary for life. For life can be maintained even when they are removed; while it is self-evident that the addition of them to an animal is not destructive of it.

58. Continuous with the head and neck is the trunk with the anterior limbs. In man the forelegs and forefeet are replaced by arms and by what we call hands. For of all animals man alone stands erect, in accordance with his god-like nature and essence. For it is the function of the god-like to think and to be wise; and

no easy task were this under the burden of a heavy body, pressing down from above and obstructing by its weight the motions of the intellect and of the general sense. When, moreover, the weight and corporeal substance become excessive, the body must of necessity incline towards the ground. In such cases therefore nature, in order to give support to the body, has replaced the arms and hands by forefeet, and has thus converted the animal into a quadruped. . . .

Now it is the opinion of Anaxagoras that the possession of these hands is the cause of man being of all animals the most intelligent. But it is more rational to suppose that his endowment with hands is the consequence rather than the cause of his superior intelligence. For the hands are instruments or organs, and the invariable plan of nature in distributing the organs is to give each to such animal as can make use of it; nature acting in this matter as any prudent man would do. For it is a better plan to take a person who is already a flute-player and give him a flute, than to take one who possesses a flute and teach him the art of flute-playing. For nature adds that which is less to that which is greater and more important, and not that which is more valuable and greater to that which is less. Seeing then that such is the better course, and seeing also that of what is possible nature invariably brings about the best, we must conclude that man does not owe his superior intelligence to his hands, but his hands to his superior intelligence. For the most intelligent of animals is the one who would put the most organs to use; and the hand is not to be looked on as one organ but as many; for it is, as it were, an instrument for further instruments. This instrument, therefore,—the hand— of all instruments the most variously serviceable, has been given by nature to man, the animal of all animals the most capable of acquiring the most varied handicrafts.

Much in error, then, are they who say that the construction of man is not only faulty, but inferior to that of all other animals; seeing that he is, as they point out, barefooted, naked, and without weapon of which to avail himself. For other animals have each but one mode of defence, and this they can never change; so that they must perform all the offices of life and even, so to speak, sleep with sandals on, never laying aside whatever serves as a protection to their bodies, nor changing such single weapon as they may chance to possess. But to man numerous modes of defence are open, and these, moreover, he may change at will; as also he may adopt such weapon as he pleases, and at such times as suit him. For the hand is talon, hoof, and horn, at will. So too it is spear, and sword, and whatsoever other weapon or instrument you please; for all these can it be from its power of grasping and holding them all.

59. Some animals bring to perfection and produce into the world a creature like themselves, as all those which bring their young into the world alive; others produce something undeveloped which has not yet acquired its own form; in this latter division the sanguinea lay eggs, the bloodless animals either lay an egg or give birth to a scolex. The difference between egg and scolex is this: an egg is that from a part of which the young comes into being, the rest being nutriment for it; but the whole of a scolex is developed into the whole of the young animal. Of the vivipara, which bring into the world an animal like themselves, some are internally viviparous (as men, horses, cattle, and of marine animals dolphins and the other cetacea); others

first lay eggs within themselves, and only after this are externally viviparous (as the cartilaginous fishes). Among the ovipara some produce the egg in a perfect condition (as birds and all oviparous quadrupeds and footless animals, e.g. lizards and tortoises and most snakes; for the eggs of all these do not increase when once laid). The eggs of others are imperfect; such are those of fishes, crustaceans, and cephalopods, for their eggs increase after being produced.

All the vivipara are sanguineous, and the sanguinea are either viviparous or oviparous, except those which are altogether infertile. Among bloodless animals the insects produce a scolex, alike those that are generated by copulation and those that copulate themselves though not so generated. For there are some insects of this sort, which though they come into being by spontaneous generation are yet male and female; from their union something is produced, only it is imperfect; the reason of this has been previously stated.

These classes admit of much cross-division. Not all bipeds are viviparous (for birds are oviparous), nor are they all oviparous (for man is viviparous), nor are all quadrupeds oviparous (for horses, cattle, and countless others are viviparous), nor are they all viviparous (for lizards, crocodiles, and many others lay eggs). Nor does the presence or absence of feet make the difference between them, for not only are some footless animals viviparous, as vipers and the cartilaginous fishes, while others are oviparous, as the other fishes and serpents, but also among those which have feet many are oviparous and many viviparous, as the quadrupeds above mentioned. And some which have feet, as man, and some which have not, as the whale and dolphin, are internally viviparous. By this character then it is not possible to divide them, nor is any of the locomotive organs the cause of this difference, but it is those animals which are more perfect in their nature and participate in a purer element which are viviparous, for nothing is internally viviparous unless it receive and breathe out air. But the more perfect are those which are hotter in their nature and have more moisture and are not earthy in their composition. And the measure of natural heat is the lung when it has blood in it, for generally those animals which have a lung are hotter than those which have not, and in the former class again those whose lung is not spongy nor solid nor containing only a little blood, but soft and full of blood. And as the animal is perfect but the egg and the scolex are imperfect, so the perfect is naturally produced from the more perfect. If animals are hotter as shown by their possessing a lung but drier in their nature, or are colder but have more moisture, then they either lay a perfect egg or are viviparous after laying an egg within themselves. For birds and scaly reptiles because of their heat produce a perfect egg, but because of their dryness it is only an egg; the cartilaginous fishes have less heat than these but more moisture, so that they are intermediate, for they are both oviparous and viviparous within themselves, the former because they are cold, the latter because of their moisture; for moisture is vivifying, whereas dryness is furthest removed from what has life. Since they have neither feathers nor scales such as either reptiles or other fishes have, all which are signs rather of a dry and earthy nature, the egg they produce is soft; for the earthy matter does not come to the surface in their eggs any more than in themselves. This is why they lay eggs in themselves, for if the egg were laid externally it would be destroyed, having no protection.

Animals that are cold and rather dry than moist also

lay eggs, but the egg is imperfect; at the same time, because they are of an earthy nature and the egg they produce is imperfect, therefore it has a hard integument that it may be preserved by the protection of the shell-like covering. Hence fishes, because they are scaly, and crustacea, because they are of an earthy nature, lay eggs with a hard integument.

The cephalopods, having themselves bodies of a sticky nature, preserve in the same way the imperfect eggs they lay, for they deposit a quantity of sticky material about the embryo.

All insects produce a scolex. Now all the insects are bloodless, wherefore all creatures that produce a scolex from themselves are so. But we cannot say simply that all bloodless animals produce a scolex, for the classes overlap one another: (1) the insects, (2) the animals that produce a scolex, (3) those that lay their egg imperfect, as the scaly fishes, the crustacea, and the cephalopoda. I say that these form a gradation, for the eggs of these latter resemble a scolex, in that they increase after oviposition, and the scolex of insects again as it develops resembles an egg; how so we shall explain later.

We must observe how rightly Nature orders generation in regular gradation. The more perfect and hotter animals produce their young perfect in respect of quality (in respect of quantity this is so with no animal, for the young always increase in size after birth), and these generate living animals within themselves from the first. The second class do not generate perfect animals within themselves from the first (for they are only viviparous after first laying eggs), but still they are externally viviparous. The third class do not produce a perfect animal, but an egg, and this egg is perfect. Those whose nature is still colder than these produce an egg, but an imperfect one, which is perfected outside the body; as the class of scaly fishes, the crustacea, and the cephalopods. The fifth and coldest class does not even lay an egg from itself; but so far as the young ever attain to this condition at all, it is outside the body of the parent, as has been said already. For insects produce a scolex first; the scolex after developing becomes egg-like (for the so-called chrysalis or pupa is equivalent to an egg); then from this it is that a perfect animal comes into being, reaching the end of its development in the second change.

Some animals then, as said before, do not come into being from semen, but all the sanguinea do so which are generated by copulation, the male emitting semen into the female; when this has entered into her the young are formed and assume their peculiar character, some within the animals themselves when they are viviparous, others in eggs.

There is a considerable difficulty in understanding how the plant is formed out of the seed or any animal out of the semen. Everything that comes into being or is made must (1) be made out of something, (2) be made by the agency of something, and (3) must become something. Now that out of which it is made is the material; this some animals have in its first form within themselves, taking it from the female parent, as all those which are not born alive but produced as a scolex or an egg; others receive it from the mother for a long time by sucking, as the young of all those which are not only externally but also internally viviparous. Such, then, is the material out of which things come into being, but we now are inquiring not out of what the parts of an animal are made, but by what agency. Either it is something external which makes them, or else something existing in the seminal fluid and the semen; and this must either be soul or a part of soul, or something containing soul.

Now it would appear irrational to suppose that any of either the internal organs or the other parts is made by something external, since one thing cannot set up a motion in another without touching it, nor can a thing be affected in any way by another if it does not set up a motion in it. Something then of the sort we require exists in the embryo itself, being either a part of it or separate from it. To suppose that it should be something else separate from it is irrational. For after the animal has been produced does this something perish or does it remain in it? But nothing of the kind appears to be in it, nothing which is not a part of the whole plant or animal. Yet, on the other hand, it is absurd to say that it perishes after making either all the parts or only some of them. If it makes some of the parts and then perishes, what is to make the rest of them? Suppose this something makes the heart and then perishes, and the heart makes another organ, by the same argument either all the parts must perish or all must remain. Therefore it is preserved and does not perish. Therefore it is a part of the embryo itself which exists in the semen from the beginning; and if indeed there is no part of the soul which does not exist in some part of the body, it would also be a part containing soul in it from the beginning.

How, then, does it make the other parts? Either all the parts, as heart, lung, liver, eye, and all the rest, come into being together or in succession, as is said in the verse ascribed to Orpheus, for there he says that an animal comes into being in the same way as the knitting of a net. That the former is not the fact is plain even to the senses, for some of the parts

are clearly visible as already existing in the embryo
while others are not; that it is not because of their
being too small that they are not visible is clear, for
the lung is of greater size than the heart, and yet appears later than the heart in the original development.
Since, then, one is earlier and another later, does the
one make the other, and does the later part exist on
account of the part which is next to it, or rather does
the one come into being only *after* the other? I mean,
for instance, that it is not the fact that the heart, having come into being first, then makes the liver, and the
liver again another organ, but that the liver only comes
into being *after* the heart, and not by the agency of
the heart, as a man becomes a man *after* being a boy,
not by his agency. An explanation of this is that, in
all the productions of Nature or of art, what already
exists potentially is brought into being only by what
exists actually; therefore if one organ formed another
the form and the character of the later organ would
have to exist in the earlier, e.g. the form of the liver
in the heart. And otherwise also the theory is strange
and fictitious.

Yet again, if the whole animal or plant is formed
from semen or seed, it is impossible that any part of
it should exist ready made in the semen or seed, whether
that part be able to make the other parts or no. For
it is plain that, if it exists in it from the first, it was
made by that which made the semen. But semen must
be made first, and that is the function of the generating
parent. So, then, it is not possible that any part should
exist in it, and therefore it has not within itself that
which makes the parts.

But neither can this agent be external, and yet it
must needs be one or other of the two. We must try,
then, to solve this difficulty, for perhaps some one of

the statements made cannot be made without qualification, e.g. the statement that the parts cannot be made by what is external to the semen. For if in a certain sense they cannot, yet in another sense they can. (Now it makes no difference whether we say 'the semen' or 'that from which the semen comes,' in so far as the semen has in itself the movement initiated by the other.) It is possible, then, that A should move B, and B move C; that, in fact, the case should be the same as with the automatic machines shown as curiosities. For the parts of such machines while at rest have a sort of potentiality of motion in them, and when any external force puts the first of them in motion, immediately the next is moved in actuality. As, then, in these automatic machines the external force moves the parts in a certain sense (not by touching any part at the moment, but by having touched one previously), in like manner also that from which the semen comes, or in other words that which made the semen, sets up the movement in the embryo and makes the parts of it by having first touched something though not continuing to touch it. In a way it is the innate motion that does this, as the act of building builds the house. Plainly, then, while there is something which makes the parts, this does not exist as a definite object, nor does it exist in the semen at the first as a complete part.

But how is each part formed? We must answer this by starting in the first instance from the principle that, in all products of Nature or art, a thing is made by something actually existing out of that which is potentially such as the finished product. Now the semen is of such a nature, and has in it such a principle of motion, that when the motion is ceasing each of the parts comes into being, and that as a part having life or soul. For there is no such thing as face or flesh

without life or soul in it; it is only equivocally that
they will be called face or flesh if the life has gone
out of them, just as if they had been made of stone
or wood. And the homogeneous parts and the organic
come into being together. And just as we should not
say that an axe or other instrument or organ was made
by the fire alone, so neither shall we say that foot or
hand were made by heat alone. The same applies also
to flesh, for this too has a function. While, then, we
may allow that hardness and softness, stickiness and
brittleness, and whatever other qualities are found in
the parts that have life and soul, may be caused by
mere heat and cold, yet, when we come to the principle
in virtue of which flesh is flesh and bone is bone, that
is no longer so; what makes them is the movement set
up by the male parent, who is in actuality what that
out of which the offspring is made is in potentiality.
This is what we find in the products of art; heat and
cold may make the iron soft and hard, but what makes
a sword is the movement of the tools employed, this
movement containing the principle of the art. For the
art is the starting-point and form of the product; only
it exists in something else, whereas the movement of
Nature exists in the product itself, issuing from another
nature which has the form in actuality.

60. The next question to raise and to answer is this.
If, in the case of those animals which emit semen into the
female, that which enters makes no part of the resulting embryo, where is the material part of it diverted if
(as we have seen) it acts by means of the power residing
in it? It is not only necessary to decide whether what
is forming in the female receives anything material, or
not, from that which has entered her, but also concerning the soul in virtue of which an animal is so called

(and this is in virtue of the sensitive part of the soul) —does this exist originally in the semen and in the unfertilized embryo or not, and if it does whence does it come? For nobody would put down the unfertilized embryo as soulless or in every sense bereft of life (since both the semen and the embryo of an animal have every bit as much life as a plant), and it is productive up to a certain point. That then they possess the nutritive soul is plain (and plain is it from the discussions elsewhere about soul why this soul must be acquired first). As they develop they also acquire the sensitive soul in virtue of which an animal is an animal. For e.g. an animal does not become at the same time an animal and a man or a horse or any other particular animal. For the end is developed last, and the peculiar character of the species is the end of the generation in each individual. Hence arises a question of the greatest difficulty, which we must strive to solve to the best of our ability and as far as possible. When and how and whence is a share in reason acquired by those animals that participate in this principle? It is plain that the semen and the unfertilized embryo, while still separate from each other, must be assumed to have the nutritive soul potentially, but not actually, except that (like those unfertilized embryos that are separated from the mother) it absorbs nourishment and performs the function of the nutritive soul. For at first all such embryos seem to live the life of a plant. And it is clear that we must be guided by this in speaking of the sensitive and the rational soul. For all three kinds of soul, not only the nutritive, must be possessed potentially before they are possessed in actuality. And it is necessary either (1) that they should all come into being in the embryo without existing previously outside it, or (2) that they should all exist previously, or

(3) that some should so exist and others not. Again, it is necessary that they should either (1) come into being in the material supplied by the female without entering with the semen of the male, or (2) come from the male and be imparted to the material in the female. If the latter, then either all of them, or none, or some must come into being in the male from outside.

Now that it is impossible for them all to pre-exist is clear from this consideration. Plainly those principles whose activity is bodily cannot exist without a body, e.g. walking cannot exist without feet. For the same reason also they cannot enter from outside. For neither is it possible for them to enter by themselves, being inseparable from a body, nor yet in a body, for the semen is only a secretion of the nutriment in process of change. It remains, then, for the reason alone so to enter and alone to be divine, for no bodily activity has any connexion with the activity of reason.

Now it is true that the faculty of all kinds of soul seems to have a connexion with a matter different from and more divine than the so-called elements; but as one soul differs from another in honour and dishonour, so differs also the nature of the corresponding matter. All have in their semen that which causes it to be productive; I mean what is called vital heat. This is not fire nor any such force, but it is the spiritus included in the semen and the foam-like, and the natural principle in the spiritus, being analogous to the element of the stars. Hence, whereas fire generates no animal and we do not find any living thing forming in either solids or liquids under the influence of fire, the heat of the sun and that of animals does generate them. Not only is this true of the heat that works through the semen, but whatever other residuum of the animal nature there may be, this also has still a vital principle in it. From such considerations it is clear that the heat in animals neither is fire nor derives its origin from fire.

Let us return to the material of the semen, in and with which comes away from the male the spiritus conveying the principle of soul. Of this principle there are two kinds; the one is not connected with matter, and belongs to those animals in which is included something divine (to wit, what is called the reason), while the other is inseparable from matter. This material of the semen dissolves and evaporates because it has a liquid and watery nature. Therefore we ought not to expect it always to come out again from the female or to form any part of the embryo that has taken shape from it; the case resembles that of the fig-juice which curdles milk, for this too changes without becoming any part of the curdling masses.

It has been settled, then, in what sense the embryo and the semen have soul, and in what sense they have not; they have it potentially but not actually.

Now semen is a secretion and is moved with the same movement as that in virtue of which the body increases (this increase being due to subdivision of the nutriment in its last stage). When it has entered the uterus it puts into form the corresponding secretion of the female and moves it with the same movement wherewith it is moved itself. For the female's contribution also is a secretion, and has all the parts in it potentially though none of them actually; it has in it potentially even those parts which differentiate the female from the male, for just as the young of mutilated parents are sometimes born mutilated and sometimes not, so also the young born of a female are sometimes female and sometimes male instead. For the female is, as it were, a mutilated male, and the catamenia are semen, only not pure; for there is only one thing they have not in them, the principle of soul. For this reason, whenever a wind-egg is produced by any animal, the egg so forming has in it the parts of both sexes potentially, but has not the principle in question, so that it does not develop into a living creature, for this is introduced by the semen of the male. When such a principle has been imparted to the secretion of the female it becomes an embryo.

Liquid but corporeal substances become surrounded by some kind of covering on heating, like the solid scum which forms on boiled foods when cooling. All bodies are held together by the glutinous; this quality, as the embryo develops and increases in size, is acquired by the sinewy substance, which holds together the parts of animals, being actual sinew in some and its analogue in others. To the same class belong also skin, blood-vessels, membranes, and the like, for these differ in being more or less glutinous and generally in excess and deficiency.

61. We must now investigate the qualities by which the parts of animals differ. I mean such qualities of the parts as blueness and blackness in the eyes, height and depth of pitch in the voice, and differences in colour whether of the skin or of hair and feathers. Some such qualities are found to characterize the whole of a kind of animals sometimes, while in other kinds they occur at random, as is especially the case in man. Further, in connexion with the changes in the time of life, all animals are alike in some points, but are opposed in others as in the case of the voice and the colour of the hair, for some do not grow grey visibly in old age, while man is subject to this more than any other animal. And some of these affections appear immediately after

birth, while others become plain as age advances or in old age.

Now we must no longer suppose that the cause of these and all such phenomena is the same. For whenever things are not the product of Nature working upon the animal kingdom as a whole, nor yet characteristic of each separate kind, then none of these things is such as it is or is so developed for any final cause. The eye for instance exists for a final cause, but it is not blue for a final cause unless this condition be characteristic of the kind of animal. In fact in some cases this condition has no connexion with the essence of the animal's being, but we must refer the causes to the material and the motive principle or efficient cause, on the view that these things come into being by Necessity. For, as was said originally in the outset of our discussion, when we are dealing with definite and ordered products of Nature, we must not say that each *is* of a certain quality because it *becomes* so, but rather that they *become* so and so because they *are* so and so, for the process of Becoming or development attends upon Being and is for the sake of Being, not *vice versa*.

The ancient Nature-philosophers however took the opposite view. The reason of this is that they did not see that the causes were numerous, but only saw the material and efficient and did not distinguish even these, while they made no inquiry at all into the formal and final causes.

Everything then exists for a final cause, and all those things which are included in the definition of each animal, or which either are means to an end or are ends in themselves, come into being both through this cause and the rest. But when we come to those things which come into being without falling under the heads just mentioned, their course must be sought in the movement or process of coming into being, on the view that the differences which mark them arise in the actual formation of the animal. An eye, for instance, the animal must have of necessity (for the fundamental idea of the animal is of such a kind), but it will have an eye of a particular kind of necessity in another sense, not the sense mentioned just above, because it is its nature to act or be acted on in this or that way.

START

62. A tentative description of the soul as subject to movement would be more plausible in view of the following considerations. We say that the soul is pained or rejoices, is confident or afraid, and again is angry and perceives and thinks; and all of these are thought to be movements. From this one might suppose that it is moved; but that is not necessary. For however much pain and enjoyment and thinking are movements and each of them is a being moved, the being moved is produced by the soul, e.g. to be angry or afraid is the heart's being moved in a particular way, and thinking is a movement either (as is probable) of the heart or of something else, and some of these phenomena take place owing to certain parts being in locomotion and others owing to their being altered in quality (which parts these are, and how they are moved, is another question); to say, then, that the soul is angry is like saying that the soul weaves or builds; it were better, perhaps, not to say that the soul pities or learns or thinks, but that the man does so with his soul; but this not in the sense that the movement is in the soul, but that it sometimes reaches the soul and sometimes proceeds from it; e.g. perception proceeds from particular outward things, while reminiscence proceeds from the soul to the movements, or permanent traces of movement, in the sense-organs. But reason seems to come to be present

in us as an independent substance, and not to be destroyed. For it would have been destroyed, if at all, by the dulling that characterizes old age, but in fact the same presumably happens as happens in the case of the sense-organs; if an old man were to get a particular kind of eye, he would see like a young man. Therefore old age consists not in something having happened to the soul, but in something having happened to that in which the soul resides, just as happens in intoxication and disease. Similarly, then, thought and scientific contemplation dies away through the destruction of something else within, but is itself impassive. Thinking, and love and hate, however, are not affections of reason but of that which possesses this, *qua* possessing it. And so too when this possessor perishes we neither remember nor love; for these did not belong to reason but to the composite being which has perished; while reason is presumably something more divine and impassive.

63. Since knowing and perceiving and the forming of opinions belong to the soul, and so do appetite and rational wish and in general the desires, and locomotion also is originated in animals by the soul, and so too is increase, maturity, and decay, we ask whether each of these belongs to the whole soul; do we both think and perceive and move, and do and suffer each of the things we do and suffer, with the whole soul, or different things with different parts? And does life itself reside in one of these parts or in more than one or in all, or is something else the cause of it? Some say the soul is divisible and one part thinks and another feels appetition. What then can it be that holds together the soul, if it is by nature divisible? Surely not the body; for the soul is thought rather, on the contrary, to hold the body together; at all events when it has passed out the

body is dissipated and rots. If then something else makes the soul one, that rather than anything else must be soul. But of that again we shall have to ask whether it is single or has many parts. For if it is one, why should we not say straight off that the soul is one? And if it is divisible, again the argument will enquire what it is that holds it together, and so will proceed to infinity. One might also ask with regard to each of its parts what power each has in the body. For if the whole soul holds together the entire body, each of its parts should hold together some part of the body. But this seems impossible; what sort of part the reason is to hold together or how it will do so, it is difficult even to imagine. And the plants and some of the animals, viz. of the insects, seem to live when divided, which implies that they have a soul that is the same in species, even if not in number; for each of the two parts has perception and locomotion for a certain time. And if they do not endure, there is nothing strange in this; for they have not the instruments for the preservation of their nature. But none the less in each of the two parts all the parts of the soul are present, and the souls are one in species with each other and with the whole, which implies that they are not separate from each other but that it is the *whole* soul that is divisible. And the originative principle even in plants seems to be in a sense soul; for this is the only thing in which both animals and plants share; and while this can be separated from the perceptive principle, no creature has perception without having this other principle.

64. So much for the theories about soul handed down by our predecessors; let us as it were make a fresh start, by trying to determine what soul is and what would be the most general definition of it. We say, then, that

one class of things is substance, and that one element
in this is the material, which is not in itself an individual,
and another is shape or form, in respect of which—and
of no less—we speak of a thing as individual, and
thirdly the compound of these two. Now matter is a
potentiality, but form is an actuality, and actuality is
of two kinds, that of which knowledge is an instance
and that of which actual knowing is an instance. Now
it is bodies, above all other things, that are thought to
be substances, and of bodies natural bodies; for these
are the source of the others. And of natural bodies
some have life while others have not; by life we mean
self-originated nutrition, increase, and decay. Therefore every natural body sharing in life will be a substance, and a substance in the sense of a concrete
substance. But since it is in fact a body possessed of
a certain character (i.e. having life), the body cannot be the soul; for body is not an attribute of a subject but rather a subject or matter. It is necessary then
that the soul should be the substance, in the sense of
form, of a natural body potentially having life. Now
substance is actuality. It is then the actuality of such
a body. But 'actuality' is used in two senses, one illus-
trated by knowledge, the other by the exercise of knowledge. It is evident then that soul is actuality in the
sense in which knowledge is so, for the presence of
the soul is compatible both with sleep and with waking,
and waking is analogous to the exercise of knowledge
sleep, to the possession and non-actualization of it; and
knowledge is prior in a single individual to its actualization. So the soul is the *first* actualization of a natural
body potentially having life. And such a body is one
that is organic. The parts even of plants are organs,
but quite simple; e.g. the leaf is the sheath of the pod,
and the pod of the fruit; the roots are analogous to

the mouth; for both of them draw in the nutriment. If, then, we *must* say something applicable to every soul, it will be 'the first actualization of a natural organic body'. For this reason, too, we should not ask whether soul and body are one, any more than whether the wax and its shape are one, or in general the matter of each thing and that whose matter it is; for while 'one' and 'being' have several senses, it is to actuality that they are strictly applicable.

We have stated generally what soul is; it is the substance, so far as this is expressible in a definition, i.e. the essence, of a body of a certain kind, just as, if some tool—e.g. an axe—were a natural body, its axeness would be its substance, and this would be its soul, and if this were taken away it would no longer be an axe except in an equivocal sense. But it is in fact only an axe; for it is not of such a body that the soul is the essence and definition, but of a natural body of a particular kind, having an origin of movement and of rest in itself.

We must also, however, view our statement in the light of the parts of the body. For if the eye were an animal, the sight would have been its soul; for this is the essence of the eye so far as this is expressible in a definition. The eye is the matter of sight, and when sight fails it is no longer an eye except in an equivocal sense, like a stone eye or a painted eye. What is true of a part must be applied to the whole living body; for as a part of the sensitive faculty is to a part of the body, so is the whole sensitive faculty to the whole sentient body as such. Now it is not the body which has lost its soul that is potentially such as to be alive, but that which has its soul; the seed in animals, the fruit in plants, is potentially such a body. As, then, cutting and seeing are actualities, so is waking, and as

sight and the faculty of the organ of sight, so is the
soul; and the body is that which is potentially existent;
but as the pupil + sight are the eye, so in the other case
the soul + the body are the animal. *what is left over is wut thatbu*

Now, that the soul is not separable from the body—
or certain parts of the soul, if it is divisible—is clear
enough; for in certain cases the actuality belongs to
the parts of the body themselves. Still there is nothing
to prevent *some* parts of the soul being separable, because they are not actualities of any body. Further,
it is not clear whether the soul is the actuality of the
body in the way in which the sailor is the actuality
of the ship. Let this suffice as an outline or provisional
sketch of the soul.

But since it is from the things that are not clear but
are more obvious that we get to what is clear and in
order of explanation more intelligible, let us try to
proceed in this way with regard to soul; for the definitory statement must not make plain merely the fact,
as most definitions do, but the reason also must be
present in it and appear in it. In fact, however, most
definitions of terms are like mere conclusions; e.g. what
is quadrature? The construction of a square rectilinear
figure equal to an oblong one. Such a definition is a
statement of the conclusion. But that which says that
quadrature is the finding of a mean proportional states
the reason of the thing.

We say, then, as starting-point of our consideration,
that the animate is distinguished from the inanimate by
living. Now 'live' has various senses, and if life in
even one of them is present we say the thing is alive,—
e.g. reason, sense-perception, local movement and rest,
and again the movement connected with nutrition, viz.
decay and growth. So all plants too are thought to be
alive; for they evidently have in themselves such a

power or principle by which they acquire growth and decay in each of two opposite directions; they do not grow up and not down, but in both, indeed in all, directions and feed and live continuously so long as they can absorb nutriment. This faculty can be separated from the others, but the others cannot be separated from this, in mortal beings. This is evident in the case of plants, for they have no other faculty of soul.

Life, then, belongs to living things in virtue of this principle, but it is perception that first makes an animal; for even the animals that do not move or change their place, but have perception, we describe as animals and not merely as alive. And of perception that which belongs first to all animals is touch. And as the nutritive power can be separated from touch and from all sensation, so touch can be separated from the other senses. By the nutritive we mean that part of the soul in which even plants share; all animals evidently possess actual perception; why each of these facts is so we shall state later.

For the present let it suffice to say that soul is the principle of the capacities we have named and is delimited by them—the nutritive, the sensitive, the ratiocinative, and movement. Whether each of these is soul or a part of soul, and if a part, whether in such a way as to be separable in definition only or also in place, is not hard to see with regard to some of them, though some raise a problem. For as in the case of the plants some evidently live when divided and separated from one another, which implies that the soul in them is, though actually single in each plant, potentially more than one, so too we see it happening in the case of other differences of the soul in insects that are cut in two; for each of the parts has both sentience and locomotion, and if sentience, then also imagination and desire; for where there is sensation, there is also pain and pleasure, and where there are these, there is necessarily also appetite. But with regard to reason and the contemplative power this is not yet clear, but this *seems* to be another class of soul, and this alone is capable of existing separately, as the eternal from the perishable. It is evident from what has been said that the other parts of the soul are not separable, as some say; but that they are different in definition is evident; for to be capable of perception and to be capable of holding opinions are different, if perceiving is different from opining. So too with each of the other faculties that have been named. Again, to some of the animals belong all these faculties, to some some of them, to others one only (and this will produce a differentiation of the animals); why this is so must be examined later. And something similar happens with regard to the senses; some animals have them all, some have some, and some have only the one most necessary one, touch.

Since 'that by which we live and perceive' has two meanings, as has the phrase 'that by which we know' (which may mean either knowledge or the soul, for we describe ourselves as knowing by virtue of each of these), and similarly 'that by which we are healthy' may mean either health, or some part of the body or even the whole body; and of these knowledge and health are a shape or form or definition and as it were an actuality of that which is capable of receiving them— i.e. of receiving knowledge and health respectively (for the activity of agents seems to reside in the patient which they put into a certain condition); and the soul is that by which, primarily, we live and perceive and think; it follows that it must be a sort of definition or form, not matter or substratum. For, substance being used in three senses, as we pointed out, of which one is

form, one matter, and one the resultant of these, and
of these matter is potentiality, form actuality,—this
being so, since the resultant of the two is a living being,
it is not body that is the actuality of soul, but soul is
the actuality of a certain kind of body. And therefore
those are right who hold that soul is neither independent
of body nor itself a body; for it is not a body, but
something belonging to body, and therefore is present in
a body, and in a body of a certain kind; our predecessors were mistaken when they fitted it into a body without going on to define in what, or what kind of, body it
exists, although it does not even appear to be the case
that any chance thing will admit any chance thing. And
this result is what might be expected; for the actuality
of each thing naturally comes into being in that which
exists potentially, and in its proper matter. That soul
is an actuality, then, or definition of that which has
the capacity of possessing soul, is evident from these
considerations.

Of the faculties of soul, all the above-named belong
to some creatures, as we have mentioned, while to some
belong only some of them and to some one only. We
have given the name of faculties to the nutritive, the
desiring, the perceptive, the locomotive, and the thinking power. Plants possess the nutritive faculty only;
other creatures this and the perceptive faculty. And
if they possess the perceptive faculty, they possess
also the desiring faculty; for desire includes appetite,
anger, and rational wish, and all the animals have *one*
of the senses, touch, and that which has sense-perception has pleasure and pain and the pleasant and
painful, and that which has these has also appetite;
for this is desire of the pleasant. Again they have
perception of food; for touch is the perception of food;
it is by things dry or wet, and hot or cold, that all living

things are nourished, and the perception of these is touch, which perceives the other sensible qualities only incidentally. For sound and colour and scent contribute nothing to nutrition, and flavour (which does) is one of the tangible qualities apprehended by touch. And hunger and thirst are appetites, and hunger is for the dry and warm, and thirst for the cold and wet; and flavour is a sort of seasoning of these qualities. We must clear up the nature of these later; for the present it is enough to say that the animals that have touch have also desire. The subject of imagination is obscure, and must be examined later. Some animals have in addition to these the power of locomotion, and some have also the power of thinking, and reason; men have this, and so has any other creature (if there be such) that is higher in worth than man.

Clearly, then, there can be one definition of soul only in the same way as there can be one of figure; there is no figure apart from the triangle and its successors, and here there is no soul apart from those we have named. There can be framed, however, in the case of the figures a common definition which shall apply to all figures and be peculiar to none. And so too in the case of the souls we have named. So it would be absurd, here as elsewhere, to seek the common definition which will not be the proper definition of any existing thing nor correspond to the particular indivisible species, neglecting the definition that *has* these characteristics.

The facts about soul are akin to the state of affairs about figures; the prior is always present potentially in its successor, both in the case of figures and in that of living things; e.g., the triangle in the quadrilateral, the nutritive power in the perceptive. Therefore we must ask, species by species, what is the soul of each, e.g.

what is the soul of the plant and what that of man or of
the beast. We must, however, examine into the reason
why the faculties are thus related by succession. The
perceptive faculty is not found without the nutritive; but
the nutritive is separated from the perceptive in plants.
Again apart from the faculty of touch none of the other
senses is found, but touch is found without the others;
for many of the animals have neither sight nor hearing
nor smell. Of creatures that have perception, too, some
have the power of locomotion and others have not. What
comes last and is possessed by fewest is reasoning and
thought; for among mortals those that possess reasoning possess also all the others, but those that possess
each of these do not all possess reasoning; some do
not possess even imagination, and others live by this
alone. The theoretical reason is matter for another
inquiry. It is clear, however, that an account of each
of the faculties is also the most appropriate account of
soul.

65. In speaking of each sense we must speak first
about its objects. By the object of sense we may mean
any one of three things, two of which we say that we
perceive *per se*, and one incidentally. Of the two one is
peculiar to a particular sense, the other common to all.
By the peculiar object I mean that which we cannot perceive by any other sense, and about which we cannot be
mistaken; sight perceives colour in this way, hearing
sound, and taste flavour; touch, no doubt, takes account
of several differences; but at all events each sense judges
about these objects and is not mistaken in thinking
that it perceives colour, or sound, but only in its judgment as to what or where the coloured or sounding
body is. Such objects then, are said to be peculiar
to each sense; the common objects are movement, rest,

number, figure, size; such things are peculiar to no
sense but common to all. For there are particular
movements that are perceptible both by touch and by
sight. What is said to be incidentally perceptible is
such facts as that the white object is the son of Diares;
we perceive this incidentally, because what we perceive
thus is incidental to the whiteness. And so we suffer
no modification from the incidental sensible as such.
Of the objects perceptible *per se,* the peculiar sensibles
are sensible in the strict sense and are the things to
which the essence of each sense is naturally relative.

The object of sight is the visible. The visible is
colour and something else that can be described but
has in fact no name; what we mean will be best explained
when we have got some distance on. The visible, then,
is colour. Now this is what is on the surface of that
which is *per se* visible; *per se* not in the sense of 'by
virtue of its definition', but because it has in itself the
cause of its visibility. Every colour is capable of causing change in that which is actually transparent, and
this is its nature. Hence colour is not visible without
light, but every colour, whatever it be the colour of,
is seen in light. So we must first discuss the nature of
light.

We assume that there are some things that are transparent. By 'transparent' I mean that which is visible,
but not visible in itself or without qualification, but on
account of the colour of something else. Such are air,
water, and many solids; for it is not *qua* water or *qua*
air that water and air are transparent but because there
is a nature that is identically present in both of these,
as well as in the eternal substance of the heavens. Light
is the actuality of this, of the transparent *qua* transparent. In that in which this is present, darkness also
is potentially present. Light is as it were the colour

of the transparent, when this is made actually transparent by fire or by something such as the substance of
the heavens; for this too has some quality one and the
same with that of fire. We have stated, then, what the
transparent is and what light is, viz. that light is neither
fire nor body at all nor an emanation from any body
(for even so it would be a kind of body), but the presence of fire or of something like it in the transparent;
that it is not a body follows also from the fact that
two bodies cannot be at once in the same place. Light
is thought to be contrary to darkness; now darkness is
the absence from the transparent of the quality we have
indicated; so that clearly the presence of this quality is
light. Empedocles, and anyone else that may have said
the same, are wrong in saying that light moves and
comes to be, at a particular time, between the earth
and that which surrounds it, without our perceiving it;
for this contradicts both the evidence of argument and
the observed facts; over a short distance it might escape
us, but that it should escape our notice over the whole
distance from east to west is too big an assumption.

What is receptive of colour is the colourless, and of
sound the soundless. What is colourless is the transparent and the invisible or the scarcely visible, of which
nature the dark is thought to be. The transparent is
of this nature, but not when it is actually transparent
but when it is potentially so; for the same nature is
sometimes darkness and sometimes light. Not all things
are visible in light, but only the proper colour of each
thing; for some things are not seen in the light but
produce a sensation in the dark, e.g. the things that present a fire-like and shining appearance (they have no
one name), such as fungus, horn, the heads, scales, and
eyes of fish (but the proper colour of none of these is
seen in the dark). Why these are seen is another ques-

tion; for the present this much is plain, that that which is seen in *light* is colour. This is why it is not seen without light; for this was what its being colour was— its being capable of causing change in the actually transparent, and the actuality of the transparent is light. This is indicated clearly by the fact that if we place the coloured object on the eye itself, we shall not see; the colour causes change in what is transparent, e.g. in the air, and this, being continuous, causes change in the sense-organ. . . .

We must conclude, therefore, that there is, as has been stated before, some one faculty in the soul with which the latter perceives all its percepts, though it perceives each different genus of sensibles through a different organ.

May we not, then, conceive this faculty which perceives White and Sweet to be one *qua* indivisible in its actualization, but different, when it has become divisible in its actualization?

Or is what occurs in the case of the perceiving Soul conceivably analogous to what holds true in that of the things themselves? For the same numerically one thing is white and sweet, and has many other qualities, if the fact is not that the qualities are really separable in the object from one another, but that the *being* of each quality is different. In the same way therefore we must assume also, in the case of the Soul, that the faculty of perception in general is in itself numerically one and the same, but different in its *being;* different, that is to say, in genus as regards some of its objects, in species as regards others. Hence too, we may conclude that one can perceive coinstantaneously with a faculty which is numerically one and the same, but not the same in its relationship.

SENSE ⟹ RECIEVES THE FORMS WITHOUT THE MATTER

66. With regard to all sense in general we must lay it down that sense is that which is capable of receiving the sensible forms without the matter. Just as wax receives the imprint of the signet-ring without the iron or gold, and takes the imprint of gold or bronze but not *qua* gold or bronze; so too the sense as relative to each object is affected by that which has colour or flavour or sound, but not *qua* the particular thing it is said to be but *qua* possessing a certain quality and in virtue of a ratio. The primary sense-organ is that in which such a power is resident. The organ is the same as the faculty, but its being is different; for that which perceives must be a spatial magnitude of some kind, but a thing's being perceptive, i.e. sense itself, is not a magnitude, but a certain ratio or power in the organ. These considerations make it plain also why excessive amounts of sensible qualities sometimes destroy the sense-organs; if the movement is too strong for the organ, the ratio is destroyed(and this was the sense), as the harmony and the pitch of the lyre are destroyed when the strings are plucked too violently. It is evident also why it is that plants do not perceive, though they have a certain psychical part and are affected by the very qualities that are tangible; for they are both cooled and heated. The reason is that they have no mean, no principle such as to receive the forms of sensible things, but can only be affected by them + their matter.

67. With regard to the part of the soul by which it knows and thinks, whether this be separable, or not separable in spatial magnitude but only in definition, we must examine its specific character and how it is that knowing takes place. Now if knowing is like perceiving, it must be either a being affected by the knowable object

or something else like this. This part of the soul, then, must be impassive, but capable of receiving the form and potentially like this form but not identical with it, and reason must be related to knowable objects as the faculty of perception is to perceptible objects. It must therefore, since it knows all things, be unmixed, as Anaxagoras says, in order that it may master its objects, i.e., that it may come to know them; for that which is alien hinders and obstructs by intruding its own form; so that it has not even eny other nature than this, that it has a capacity. The part of the soul called reason, therefore (by reason I mean that by which the soul thinks and judges), is not actually any existing thing before it knows. And so it is not plausible to suppose it to be mixed with the body; for it would come to have a certain character, cold or hot, or would even have an organ, as the power of sense-perception has; but in fact it has nothing of the kind. And well did they speak who said the soul is the place of forms, except that it is not the whole soul but that which has the power of knowing, nor is it actually, but potentially, the forms. That the impassivity of the perceptive faculty and of that of knowing is not alike is plain if we look at the sense-organs and at sense-perception. For sense-perception cannot receive a sensation from an excessive sense-object, e.g. that of sound from great sounds, nor can we get a sensation of sight or smell from excessively strong colours and scents; but reason when it has come to know something that is in a high degree knowable, does not know inferior objects less, but even more; for the power of sense-perception is not independent of body, but reason *is* separable. When it has become its several objects and is in a state answering to the 'knowledge' of the man who is actually a man of science (and this exists when he can exercise his knowledge if he wishes), even when it exists, in a sense, potentially, but not in the same way as before it was taught or discovered the truth; and at this stage it can know itself as well.

Since magnitude is not the same as the essence of magnitude nor water the same as the essence of water (and so too in many other cases, though not in all; for in some the two things are the same), we discern flesh and the essence of flesh either with different faculties or with the same faculty in a different condition; for flesh is never found without matter, but, like the 'snub', is a 'this in that'. By the perceptive faculty, then, we discern the hot and the cold and all the qualities of which flesh is a ratio; and with a faculty which is either separable, or related to the former as a bent line is to itself when it has been straightened out, we discern the essence of flesh. Again, in the case of abstractions, the 'straight' is like the 'snub'; for it involves a continuum; but its essence, if the being straight is not the same as that which is straight, is something different; let it be twoness. We discern this, then, by a different faculty or by the same faculty in a different state. And in general, therefore, the operations of reason correspond to the degrees of separability of things from their matter.

But one might ask, if reason is simple and impassive and has nothing in common with anything else, as Anaxagoras maintains, how will it know, if knowing is a way of being affected. For it is in so far as two things have something in common (so we think) that the one acts and the other is acted on. Further, a difficulty arises from the fact that reason itself is knowable. For either reason will belong to other things as well, if it is not in virtue of anything else that it is itself knowable and the knowable is one in species, or it will have something intermixed with it, which makes it knowable as it makes other things. Perhaps we should use our old distinction between two meanings of the phrase 'being acted on in virtue of a common element', and point out that reason is in a sense potentially its own objects, but is nothing actually until it knows. They must be present as in a tablet in which there is as yet nothing actually written; that is what happens in the case of reason. And it itself is knowable too, just as its objects are. For in the case of immaterial things the knower and the known are the same; speculative knowledge and that which is known in this way are the same. We must, however, inquire into the reason why we do not always know. On the other hand in things possessing matter each of the objects of knowledge is potentially present. Therefore the objects of knowledge will not possess reason (for reason is the power of becoming such objects *without* their matter), but *it* will possess knowability.

Just as in nature as a whole there is an element that serves as matter for each class of things (this is that which is potentially all these things), and another which is their cause and is active in the sense that it makes them all (an art is so related to its matter), these distinctions must exist in the soul as well. The one reason is analogous to matter because it becomes all things; the other is analogous to the agent because it makes all things, in the manner of a positive state like light; for in a sense light, too, makes the potentially existing colours actually existing colours. And this reason is capable of separate existence and impassive and unmixed, being in its essence an actuality. For the active is always of higher worth than the passive, and the originative source than the matter. Actual knowledge is identical with its object; potential knowledge is prior

in time in the individual, but in general it is not prior
in time; reason does not at one time function and at
another not. When it has been separated it is only
that which it is essentially, and this alone is immortal
and eternal (we do not remember, however, because this
reason is impassive and the passive reason is perishable); and without this nothing thinks.

STOP

68. Next comes the subject of Recollection, in dealing
with which we must assume as fundamental the truths
elicited above in our introductory discussions. For recollection is not the 'recovery' or 'acquisition' of memory;
since at the instant when one at first learns or experiences, he does not thereby 'recover' a memory, inasmuch
as none has preceded, nor does he acquire one *ab initio*.
It is only at the instant when the aforesaid state or
affection is implanted in the soul that memory exists,
and therefore memory is not itself implanted concur-
rently with the continuous implantation of the sensory
experience.

Further: at the very individual and concluding instant
when first the sensory experience or scientific knowledge has been completely implanted, there is then already established in the person affected the sensory
affection, or the scientific knowledge (if one ought to
apply the term 'scientific knowledge' to the mnemonic
state or affection; and indeed one may well remember,
in the 'incidental' sense, some of the things which are
properly objects of scientific knowledge); but to remember, strictly and properly speaking, is an activity which
will not be immanent until the original experience has
undergone lapse of time. For one remembers now what
one saw or otherwise experienced formerly; the moment of the original experience and the moment of
the memory of it are never identical.

Again, it is obviously possible, without any present act of recollection, to remember as a continued consequence of the original perception or other experience; whereas when one recovers some scientific knowledge which he had before, or some perception, or some other experience, the state of which we above declared to be memory, it is then, and then only, that this recovery may amount to a recollection of any of the things aforesaid. But recollecting always implies remembering, and actualized memory follows.

But secondly, even the assertion that recollection is the reinstatement in consciousness of something which was there before but had disappeared requires qualification. This assertion may be true, but it may also be false; for the same person may twice learn or twice discover the same fact. Accordingly, the act of recollecting ought to be distinguished from these acts; i.e. recollecting must imply in those who recollect the presence of some spring over and above that from which they originally learn.

Acts of recollection, as they occur in experience, are due to the fact that one movement has by nature another that succeeds it in regular order.

If this order be necessary, whenever a subject experiences the former of two movements thus connected, it will experience the latter; if, however, the order be not necessary, but customary, only in the majority of cases will the subject experience the latter of the two movements. But it is a fact that there are some movements, by a single experience of which persons take the impress of custom more deeply than they do by experiencing others many times; hence upon seeing some things but once we remember them better than others which we may have seen frequently.

Whenever, therefore, we are recollecting, we are experiencing certain of the antecedent movements until finally we experience the one after which customarily comes that which we seek. This explains why we hunt up the series, having started in thought either from a present intuition or some other, and from something either similar, or contrary, to what we seek, or else from that which is contiguous with it. Such is the empirical ground of the process of recollection; for the mnemonic movements involved in these starting-points are in some cases identical, in others, again, simultaneous, with those of the idea we seek, while in others they comprise a portion of them, so that the remnant which one experienced after that portion is comparatively small.

Thus, then, it is that persons seek to recollect, and thus, too, it is that they recollect even without the effort of seeking to do so, viz. when the movement implied in recollection has supervened on some other which is its condition. For, as a rule, it is when antecedent movements of the classes here described have first been excited, that the particular movement implied in recollection follows. We need not examine a series of which the beginning and end lie far apart, in order to see how we remember; one in which they lie near one another will serve equally well. For it is clear that the method is in each case the same, that is, one hunts up the objective series, without any previous search or previous recollection. For by the effect of custom the mnemonic movements tend to succeed one another in a certain order. Accordingly, therefore, when one wishes to recollect, this is what he will do: he will try to obtain a beginning of movement whose sequel shall be the movement which he desires to reawaken. This explains why attempts at recollection succeed soonest and best when they start from a beginning. For, in order of succession, the mnemonic movements are to one another as the objective facts. Accordingly, things arranged in a fixed order, like the successive demonstrations in geometry, are easy to remember, while badly arranged subjects are remembered with difficulty.

Recollecting differs also in this respect from relearning, that one who recollects will be able, somehow, to move, solely by his own effort, to the term next after the starting-point. When one cannot do this of himself, but only by external assistance, he no longer remembers. It often happens that, though a person cannot recollect at the moment, yet by seeking he can do so, and discovers what he seeks. This he succeeds in doing by setting up many movements, until finally he excites one of a kind which will have for its sequel the fact he wishes to recollect. For remembering is the existence, potentially, in the mind of a movement capable of stimulating it to the desired movement, and this, as has been said, in such a way that the person should be moved from within himself, i.e. in consequence of movements wholly contained within himself.

But one must get hold of a starting-point. This explains why it is that persons are supposed to recollect sometimes by starting from mnemonic *loci*. The cause is that they pass swiftly in thought from one point to another, e.g. from milk to white, from white to mist, and thence to moist, from which one remembers Autumn, if this be the season he is trying to recollect.

START

69. Every art and every inquiry, and similarly every action and pursuit, is thought to aim at some good; and for this reason the good has rightly been declared to be that at which all things aim. But a certain difference is found among ends; some are activities, others are products apart from the activities that produce

them.   Where there are ends apart from the actions, it is the nature of the products to be better than the activities.   Now, as there are many actions, arts, and sciences, their ends also are many; the end of the medical art is health, that of shipbuilding a vessel, that of strategy victory, that of economics wealth.   But where such arts fall under a single capacity—as bridle-making and the other arts concerned with the equipment of horses fall under the art of riding, and this and every military action under strategy, in the same way other arts fall under yet others—in all of these the ends of the master arts are to be preferred to all the subordinate ends; for it is for the sake of the former that the latter are pursued.   It makes no difference whether the activities themselves are the ends of the actions, or something else apart from the activities, as in the case of the sciences just mentioned.

If, then, there is some end of the things we do, which we desire for its own sake (everything else being desired for the sake of this), and if we do not choose everything for the sake of something else(for at that rate the process would go on to infinity, so that our desire would be empty and vain), clearly this must be the good and the chief good.   Will not the knowledge of it, then, have a great influence on life?   Shall we not, like archers who have a mark to aim at, be more likely to hit upon what is right?   If so, we must try, in outline at least, to determine what it is, and of which of the sciences or capacities it is the object.   It would seem to belong to the most authoritative art and that which is most truly the master art.   And politics appears to be of this nature; for it is this that ordains which of the sciences should be studied in a state, and which each class of citizens should learn and up to what point they should learn them; and we see even the most highly esteemed of capacities to fall under this, e.g. strategy, economics, rhetoric; now, since politics uses the rest of the sciences, and since, again, it legislates as to what we are to do and what we are to abstain from, the end of this science must include those of the others, so that this end must be the good for man. For even if the end is the same for a single man and for a state, that of the state seems at all events something greater and more complete whether to attain or to preserve; though it is worth while to attain the end merely for one man, it is finer and more godlike to attain it for a nation or for city-states. These, then, are the ends at which our inquiry aims, since it is political science, in one sense of that term.

70. Let us resume our inquiry and state, in view of the fact that all knowledge and every pursuit aims at some good, what it is that we say political science aims at and what is the highest of all goods achievable by action. Verbally there is very general agreement; for both the general run of men and people of superior refinement say that it is happiness, and identify living well and doing well with being happy; but with regard to what happiness is they differ, and the many do not give the same account as the wise. For the former think it is some plain and obvious thing, like pleasure, wealth, or honour; they differ, however, from one another—and often even the same man identifies it with different things, with health when he is ill, with wealth when he is poor; but, conscious of their ignorance, they admire those who proclaim some great ideal that is above their comprehension. Now some thought that apart from these many goods there is another which is self-subsistent and causes the goodness of all these as well. To examine all the opinions that have been

held were perhaps somewhat fruitless; enough to examine those that are most prevalent or that seem to be arguable.

Let us not fail to notice, however, that there is a difference between arguments from and those to the first principles   For Plato, too, was right in raising this question and asking, as he used to do, 'are we on the way from or to the first principles?'   There is a difference, as there is in a race-course between the course from the judges to the turning-point and the way back.   For, while we must begin with what is known, things are objects of knowledge in two senses —some to us, some without qualification.   Presumably, then, *we* must begin with things known to *us*.   Hence any one who is to listen intelligently to lectures about what is noble and just and, generally, about the subjects of political science must have been brought up in good habits.   For the fact is the starting-point, and if this is sufficiently plain to him, he will not at the start need the reason as well; and the man who has been well brought up has or can easily get starting-points.

71. We had perhaps better consider the universal good and discuss thoroughly what is meant by it, although such an inquiry is made an uphill one by the fact that the Forms have been introduced by friends of our own. Yet it would perhaps be thought to be better, indeed to be our duty, for the sake of maintaining the truth even to destroy what touches us closely, especially as we are philosophers or lovers of wisdom; for, while both are dear, piety requires us to honour truth above our friends.

The men who introduced this doctrine did not posit Ideas of classes within which they recognized priority and posteriority (which is the reason why they did not maintain the existence of an Idea embracing all numbers); but the term 'good' is used both in the category of substance and in that of quality and in that of relation, and that which is *per se,* i.e. substance, is prior in nature to the relative (for the latter is like an offshoot and accident of being); so that there could not be a common Idea set over all these goods. Further, since 'good' has as many senses as 'being' (for it is predicated both in the category of substance, as of God and of reason, and in quality, i.e. of the virtues, and in quantity, i.e. of that which is moderate, and in relation, i.e. of the useful, and in time, i.e. of the right opportunity, and in place, i.e. of the right locality and the like), clearly it cannot be something universally present in all cases and single; for then it could not have been predicated in all the categories but in one only. Further, since of the things answering to one Idea there is one science, there would have been one science of all the goods; but as it is there are many sciences even of the things that fall under one category, e.g. of opportunity, for opportunity in war is studied by strategics and in disease by medicine, and the moderate in food is studied by medicine and in exercise by the science of gymnastics. And one might ask the question, what in the world they *mean* by 'a thing itself', if (as is the case) in 'man himself' and in a particular man the account of man is one and the same. For in so far as they are man, they will in no respect differ; and if this is so, neither will 'good itself' and particular goods, in so far as they are good. But again it will not be good any the more for being eternal, since that which lasts long is no whiter than that which perishes in a day. The Pythagoreans seem to give a more plausible account of the good, when they place the one in the

column of goods; and it is they that Speusippus seems
to have followed.

But let us discuss these matters elsewhere; an objection to what we have said, however, may be discerned
in the fact that the Platonists have not been speaking
about *all* goods, and that the goods that are pursued
and loved for themselves are called good by reference
to a single Form, while those which tend to produce
or to preserve these somehow or to prevent their contraries are called so by reference to these, and in a
secondary sense. Clearly, then, goods must be spoken
of in two ways, and some must be good in themselves,
the others by reason of these. Let us separate, then,
things good in themselves from things useful, and
consider whether the former are called good by reference to a single Idea. What sort of goods would one
call good in themselves? Is it those that are pursued
even when isolated from others, such as intelligence,
sight, and certain pleasures and honours? Certainly,
if we pursue these also for the sake of something else,
yet one would place them among things good in themselves. Or is nothing other than the Idea of good good
in itself? In that case the Form will be empty. But
if the things we have named are also things good in
themselves, the account of the good will have to appear
as something identical in them all, as that of whiteness
is identical in snow and in white lead. But of honour,
wisdom, and pleasure, just in respect of their goodness, the accounts are distinct and diverse. The good,
therefore, is not some common element answering to
one Idea.

But what then do we mean by the good? It is
surely not like the things that only chance to have the
same name. Are goods one, then, by being derived from
one good or by all contributing to one good, or are

they rather one by analogy? Certainly as sight is in
the body, so is reason in the soul, and so on in other
cases. But perhaps these subjects had better be dismissed for the present; for perfect precision about
them would be more appropriate to another branch of
philosophy. And similarly with regard to the Idea;
even if there is some one good which is universally
predicable of goods or is capable of separate and independent existence, clearly it could not be achieved or
attained by man; but we are now seeking something
attainable. Perhaps, however, some one might think
it worth while to recognize this with a view to the goods
that *are* attainable and achievable; for having this
as a sort of pattern we shall know better the goods
that are good for us, and if we know them shall attain
them. This argument has some plausibility, but seems
to clash with the procedure of the sciences; for all of
these, though they aim at some good and seek to supply
the deficiency of it, leave on one side the knowledge of
the good. Yet that all the exponents of the arts should
be ignorant of, and should not even seek, so great an
aid is not probable. It is hard, too, to see how a weaver
or a carpenter will be benefited in regard to his own
craft by knowing this 'good itself', or how the man
who has viewed the Idea itself will be a better doctor
or general thereby. For a doctor seems not even to
study health in this way, but the health of man, or perhaps rather the health of a particular man; it is individuals that he is healing.

72. Presumably to say that happiness is the chief good
seems a platitude, and a clearer account of what it is
is still desired. This might perhaps be given, if we
could first ascertain the function of man. For just
as for a flute-player, a sculptor, or any artist, and, in

general, for all things that have a function or activity, the good and the 'well' is thought to reside in the function, so would it seem to be for man, if he has a function. Have the carpenter, then, and the tanner certain functions or activities, and has man none? Is he born without a function? Or as eye, hand, foot, and in general each of the parts evidently has a function, may one lay it down that man similarly has a function apart from all these? What then can this be? Life seems to be common even to plants, but we are seeking what is peculiar to man. Let us exclude, there-fore, the life of nutrition and growth. Next there would be a life of perception, but *it* also seems to be common even to the horse, the ox, and every animal. There remains, then, an active life of the element that has a rational principle; of this, one part has such a principle in the sense of being obedient to one, the other in the sense of possessing one and exercising thought. And, as 'life of the rational element' also has two meanings, we must state that life in the sense of activity is what we mean; for this seems to be the more proper sense of the term. Now if the function of man is an activity of soul which follows or implies a rational principle, and if we say 'a so-and-so' and 'a good so-and-so' have a function which is the same in kind, e.g. a lyre-player and a good lyre-player, and so without qualification in all cases, eminence in respect of goodness being added to the name of the function (for the function of a lyre-player is to play the lyre, and that of a good lyre-player is to do so well): if this is the case, human good turns out to be activity of soul in accordance with virtue, and if there are more than one virtue, in accordance with the best and most com-plete.

But we must add 'in a complete life'. For one swallow does not make a summer, nor does one day; and so too one day, or a short time, does not make a man blessed and happy.

73. Happiness then is the best, noblest, and most pleasant thing in the world, and these attributes are not severed as in the inscription at Delos—

Most noble is that which is justest, and best is health;
But pleasantest is it to win what we love.

For all these properties belong to the best activities; and these, or one—the best—of these, we identify with happiness.

Yet evidently, as we said, it needs the external goods as well; for it is impossible, or not easy, to do noble acts without the proper equipment. In many actions we use friends and riches and political power as instruments; and there are some things the lack of which takes the lustre from happiness, as good birth, goodly children, beauty; for the man who is very ugly in appearance or ill-born or solitary and childless is not very likely to be happy, and perhaps a man would be still less likely if he had thoroughly bad children or friends or had lost good children or friends by death. As we said, then, happiness seems to need this sort of prosperity in addition; for which reason some identify happiness with good fortune, though others identify it with virtue.

74. Since happiness is an activity of soul in accordance with perfect virtue, we must consider the nature of virtue; for perhaps we shall thus see better the nature of happiness. The true student of politics, too, is thought to have studied virtue above all things; for

he wishes to make his fellow-citizens good and obedient to the laws. As an example of this we have the law-givers of the Cretans and the Spartans, and any others of the kind that there may have been. And if this inquiry belongs to political science, clearly the pursuit of it will be in accordance with our original plan. But clearly the virtue we must study is human virtue; for the good we were seeking was human good and the happiness human happiness. By human virtue we mean not that of the body but that of the soul; and happiness also we call an activity of soul. But if this is so, clearly the student of politics must know somehow the facts about soul, as the man who is to heal the eyes or the body as a whole must know about the eyes or the body; and all the more since politics is more prized and better than medicine; but even among doctors the best educated spend much labour on acquiring knowledge of the body. The student of politics, then, must study the soul, and must study it with these objects in view, and do so just to the extent which is sufficient for the questions we are discussing; for further precision is perhaps something more laborious than our purposes require.

Some things are said about it, adequately enough, even in the discussions outside our school, and we must use these; e. g. that one element in the soul is irrational and one has a rational principle. Whether these are separated as the parts of the body or of anything divisible are, or are distinct by definition but by nature inseparable, like convex and concave in the circumference of a circle, does not affect the present question.

Of the irrational element one division seems to be widely distributed, and vegetative in its nature, I mean that which causes nutrition and growth; for it is this kind of power of the soul that one must assign to all nurslings and to embryos, and this same power to full-grown creatures; this is more reasonable than to assign some different power to them. Now the excellence of this seems to be common to all species and not specifically human; for this part or faculty seems to function most in sleep, while goodness and badness are least manifest in sleep (whence comes the saying that the happy are no better off than the wretched for half their lives; and this happens naturally enough, since sleep is an inactivity of the soul in that respect in which it is called good or bad), unless perhaps to a small extent some of the movements actually penetrate to the soul, and in this respect the dreams of good men are better than those of ordinary people. Enough of this subject, however; let us leave the nutritive faculty alone, since it has by its nature no share in human excellence.

There seems to be also another irrational element in the soul—one which in a sense, however, shares in a rational principle. For we praise the rational principle of the continent man and of the incontinent, and the part of their soul that has such a principle, since it urges them aright and towards the best objects; but there is found in them also another element naturally opposed to the rational principle, which fights against and resists that principle. For exactly as paralysed limbs when we intend to move them to the right turn on the contrary to the left, so is it with the soul; the impulses of incontinent people move in contrary directions. But while in the body we see that which moves astray, in the soul we do not. No doubt, however, we must none the less suppose that in the soul too there is something contrary to the rational principle, resisting and opposing it. In what sense it is distinct from the other elements does not concern us. Now even this seems to have a share in a rational principle, as we said; at any rate in the continent man it obeys the rational principle—and presumably in the temperate and brave man it is still more obedient; for in him it speaks, on all matters, with the same voice as the rational principle.

Therefore the irrational element also appears to be twofold. For the vegetative element in no way shares in a rational principle, but the appetitive and in general the desiring element in a sense shares in it, in so far as it listens to and obeys it; this is the sense in which we speak of 'taking account' of one's father or one's friends, not that in which we speak of 'accounting' for a mathematical property. That the irrational element is in some sense persuaded by a rational principle is indicated also by the giving of advice and by all reproof and exhortation. And if this element also must be said to have a rational principle, that which has a rational principle (as well as that which has not) will be twofold, one subdivision having it in the strict sense and in itself, and the other having a tendency to obey as one does one's father.

Virtue too is distinguished into kinds in accordance with this difference; for we say that some of the virtues are intellectual and others moral, philosophic wisdom and understanding and practical wisdom being intellectual, liberality and temperance moral. For in speaking about a man's character we do not say that he is wise or has understanding but that he is good-tempered or temperate; yet we praise the wise man also with respect to his state of mind; and of states of mind we call those which merit praise virtues.

Virtue, then, being of two kinds, intellectual and moral, intellectual virtue in the main owes both its birth and its growth to teaching (for which reason it requires experience and time), while moral virtue comes about as a result of habit, whence also its name (ἠθική) is one that is formed by a slight variation from the word ἔθος (habit). From this it is also plain that none of the moral virtues arises in us by nature; for nothing that exists by nature can form a habit contrary to its nature. For instance the stone which by nature moves downwards cannot be habituated to move upwards, not even if one tries to train it by throwing it up ten thousand times; nor can fire be habituated to move downwards, nor can anything else that by nature behaves in one way be trained to behave in another. Neither by nature, then, nor contrary to nature do the virtues arise in us; rather we are adapted by nature to receive them, and are made perfect by habit.

Again, of all the things that come to us by nature we first acquire the potentiality and later exhibit the activity (this is plain in the case of the senses; for it was not by often seeing or often hearing that we got these senses, but on the contrary we had them before we used them, and did not come to have them by using them); but the virtues we get by first exercising them, as also happens in the case of the arts as well. For the things we have to learn before we can do them, we learn by doing them, e.g. men become builders by building and lyre-players by playing the lyre; so too we become just by doing just acts, temperate by doing temperate acts, brave by doing brave acts.

75. Next we must consider what virtue is. Since things that are found in the soul are of three kinds—passions, faculties, states of character, virtue must be one of these. By passions I mean appetite, anger, fear, confidence, envy, joy, friendly feeling, hatred, longing, emulation, pity, and in general the feelings that are

accompanied by pleasure or pain; by faculties the things in virtue of which we are said to be capable of feeling these, e.g. of becoming angry or being pained or feeling pity; by states of character the things in virtue of which we stand well or badly with reference to the passions, e.g. with reference to anger we stand badly if we feel it violently or too weakly, and well if we feel it moderately; and similarly with reference to the other passions.

Now neither the virtues nor the vices are *passions,* because we are not called good or bad on the ground of our passions, but are so called on the ground of our virtues and our vices, and because we are neither praised nor blamed for our passions (for the man who feels fear or anger is not praised, nor is the man who simply feels anger blamed, but the man who feels it in a certain way), but for our virtues and our vices we *are* praised or blamed.

Again, we feel anger and fear without choice, but the virtues are modes of choice or involve choice. Further, in respect of the passions we are said to be moved, but in respect of the virtues and the vices we are said not to be moved but to be disposed in a particular way.

For these reasons also they are not *faculties;* for we are neither called good nor bad, nor praised nor blamed, for the simple capacity of feeling the passions; again, we have the faculties by nature, but we are not made good or bad by nature; we have spoken of this before.

If, then, the virtues are neither passions nor faculties, all that remains is that they should be *states of character.*

Thus we have stated what virtue is in respect of its genus.

We must, however, not only describe virtue as a state of character, but also say what sort of state it is. We may remark, then, that every virtue or excellence both brings into good condition the thing of which it is the excellence and makes the work of that thing be done well; e.g. the excellence of the eye makes both the eye and its work good; for it is by the excellence of the eye that we see well. Similarly the excellence of the horse makes a horse both good in itself and good at running and at carrying its rider and at awaiting the attack of the enemy. Therefore, if this is true in every case, the virtue of man also will be the state of character which makes a man good and which makes him do his own work well.

How this is to happen we have stated already, but it will be made plain also by the following consideration of the specific nature of virtue. In everything that is continuous and divisible it is possible to take more, less, or an equal amount, and that either in terms of the thing itself or relatively to us; and the equal is an intermediate between excess and defect. By the intermediate in the object I mean that which is equidistant from each of the extremes, which is one and the same for all men; by the intermediate relatively to us that which is neither too much nor too little—and this is not one, nor the same for all. For instance, if ten is many and two is few, six is the intermediate, taken in terms of the object; for it exceeds and is exceeded by an equal amount; this is intermediate according to arithmetical proportion. But the intermediate relatively to us is not to be taken so; if ten pounds are too much for a particular person to eat and two too little, it does not follow that the trainer will order six pounds; for this also is perhaps too much for the person who is to take it, or too little—too little for Milo, too much for the beginner in athletic exercises. The same is true of running and wrestling. Thus a master of any art avoids excess and defect, but seeks the intermediate and chooses this—the intermediate not in the object but relatively to us.

If it is thus, then, that every art does its work well —by looking to the intermediate and judging its works by this standard (so that we often say of good works of art that it is not possible either to take away or to add anything, implying that excess and defect destroy the goodness of works of art, while the mean preserves it; and good artists, as we say, look to this in their work), and if, further, virtue is more exact and better than any art, as nature also is, then virtue must have the quality of aiming at the intermediate. I mean moral virtue; for it is this that is concerned with passions and actions, and in these there is excess, defect, and the intermediate. For instance, both fear and confidence and appetite and anger and pity and in general pleasure and pain may be felt both too much and too little, and in both cases not well; but to feel them at the right times, with reference to the right objects, towards the right people, with the right motive, and in the right way, is what is both intermediate and best, and this is characteristic of virtue. Similarly with regard to actions also there is excess, defect, and the intermediate. Now virtue is concerned with passions and actions, in which excess is a form of failure, and so is defect, while the intermediate is praised and is a form of success; and being praised and being successful are both characteristics of virtue. Therefore virtue is a kind of mean, since, as we have seen, it aims at what is intermediate.

Again, it is possible to fail in many ways (for evil belongs to the class of the unlimited, as the Pythagoreans conjectured, and good to that of the limited), while to succeed is possible only in one way (for which reason also one is easy and the other difficult—to miss the mark easy, to hit it difficult); for these reasons also, then, excess and defect are characteristic of vice, and the mean of virtue;

For men are good in but one way, but bad in many.

Virtue, then, is a state of character concerned with choice, lying in a mean, i.e. the mean relative to us, this being determined by a rational principle, and by that principle by which the man of practical wisdom would determine it. Now it is a mean between two vices, that which depends on excess and that which depends on defect; and again it is a mean because the vices respectively fall short of or exceed what is right in both passions and actions, while virtue both finds and chooses that which is intermediate. Hence in respect of its substance and the definition which states its essence virtue is a mean, with regard to what is best and right an extreme.

76. We must, however, not only make this general statement, but also apply it to the individual facts. For among statements about conduct those which are general apply more widely, but those which are particular are more genuine, since conduct has to do with individual cases, and our statements must harmonize with the facts in these cases. We may take these cases from our table. With regard to feelings of fear and confidence courage is the mean; of the people who exceed, he who exceeds in fearlessness has no name (many of the states have no name), while the man who exceeds in confidence is rash, and he who exceeds in fear and falls short in confidence is a coward. With regard to pleasures and pains—not all of them, and not so much with regard

to the pains—the mean is temperance, the excess self-indulgence. Persons deficient with regard to the pleasures are not often found; hence such persons also have received no name. But let us call them 'insensible.'

With regard to giving and taking of money the mean is liberality, the excess and the defect prodigality and meanness. In these actions people exceed and fall short in contrary ways; the prodigal exceeds in spending and falls short in taking, while the mean man exceeds in taking and falls short in spending. (At present we are giving a mere outline or summary, and are satisfied with this; later these states will be more exactly determined.) With regard to money there are also other dispositions—a mean, magnificence (for the magnificent man differs from the liberal man; the former deals with large sums, the latter with small ones), an excess, tastelessness and vulgarity, and a deficiency, niggardliness; these differ from the states opposed to liberality, and the mode of their difference will be stated later.

With regard to honour and dishonour the mean is proper pride, the excess is known as a sort of 'empty vanity', and the deficiency is undue humility; and as we said liberality was related to magnificence, differing from it by dealing with small sums, so there is a state similarly related to proper pride, being concerned with small honours while that is concerned with great. For it is possible to desire honour as one ought, and more than one ought, and less, and the man who exceeds in his desires is called ambitious, the man who falls short unambitious, while the intermediate person has no name. The dispositions also are nameless, except that that of the ambitious man is called ambition. Hence the people who are at the extremes lay claim to the middle place; and we ourselves sometimes call the intermediate person ambitious and sometimes unambitious, and sometimes praise the ambitious man and sometimes the unambitious. The reason of our doing this will be stated in what follows; but now let us speak of the remaining states according to the method which has been indicated.

With regard to anger also there is an excess, a deficiency, and a mean. Although they can scarcely be said to have names, yet since we call the intermediate person good-tempered let us call the mean good temper; of the persons at the extremes let the one who exceeds be called irascible, and his vice irascibility, and the man who falls short an inirascible sort of person, and the deficiency inirascibility.

There are also three other means, which have a certain likeness to one another, but differ from one another: for they are all concerned with intercourse in words and actions, but differ in that one is concerned with truth in this sphere, the other two with pleasantness; and of this one kind is exhibited in giving amusement, the other in all the circumstances of life. We must therefore speak of these too, that we may the better see that in all things the mean is praiseworthy, and the extremes neither praiseworthy nor right, but worthy of blame. Now most of these states also have no names, but we must try, as in the other cases, to invent names ourselves so that we may be clear and easy to follow. With regard to truth, then, the intermediate is a truthful sort of person and the mean may be called truthfulness, while the pretence which exaggerates is boastfulness and the person characterized by it a boaster, and that which understates is mock modesty and the person characterized by it mock-modest. With regard to pleasantness in the giving of amusement the intermediate person is ready-witted and the disposition ready wit, the excess is buffoonery and the person characterized by it a buffoon, while the man who falls short is a sort of boor and his state is boorishness. With regard to the remaining kind of pleasantness, that which is exhibited in life in general, the man who is pleasant in the right way is friendly and the mean is friendliness, while the man who exceeds is an obsequious person if he has no end in view, a flatterer if he is aiming at his own advantage, and the man who falls short and is unpleasant in all circumstances is a quarrelsome and surly sort of person.

There are also means in the passions and concerned with the passions; since shame is not a virtue, and yet praise is extended to the modest man. For even in these matters one man is said to be intermediate, and another to exceed, as for instance the bashful man who is ashamed of everything; while he who falls short or is not ashamed of anything at all is shameless, and the intermediate person is modest. Righteous indignation is a mean between envy and spite, and these states are concerned with the pain and pleasure that are felt at the fortunes of our neighbours; the man who is characterized by righteous indignation is pained at undeserved good fortune, the envious man, going beyond him, is pained at all good fortune, and the spiteful man falls so far short of being pained that he even rejoices.

77. Since virtue is concerned with passions and actions, and on voluntary passions and actions praise and blame are bestowed, on those that are involuntary pardon, and sometimes also pity, to distinguish the voluntary and the involuntary is presumably necessary for those who are studying the nature of virtue, and useful also for legislators with a view to the assigning both of honours and of punishments.

Those things, then, are thought involuntary, which take place under compulsion or owing to ignorance; and that is compulsory of which the moving principle is outside, being a principle in which nothing is contributed by the person who is acting or is feeling the passion, e.g. if he were to be carried somewhere by a wind, or by men who had him in their power.

But with regard to the things that are done from fear of greater evils or for some noble object (e.g. if a tyrant were to order one to do something base, having one's parents and children in his power, and if one did the action they were to be saved, but otherwise would be put to death), it may be debated whether such actions are involuntary or voluntary. Something of the sort happens also with regard to the throwing of goods overboard in a storm; for in the abstract no one throws goods away voluntarily, but on condition of its securing the safety of himself and his crew any sensible man does so. Such actions, then, are mixed, but are more like voluntary actions; for they are worthy of choice at the time when they are done, and the end of an action is relative to the occasion. Both the terms, then, 'voluntary' and 'involuntary', must be used with reference to the moment of action. Now the man acts voluntarily; for the principle that moves the instrumental parts of the body in such actions is in him, and the things of which the moving principle is in a man himself are in his power to do or not to do. Such actions, therefore, are voluntary, but in the abstract perhaps involuntary; for no one would choose any such act in itself.

For such actions men are sometimes even praised, when they endure something base or painful in return for great and noble objects gained; in the opposite case they are blamed, since to endure the greatest indignities for no noble end or for a trifling end is the mark of an inferior person. On some actions praise indeed is not bestowed, but pardon is, when one does what he ought not under pressure which overstrains human nature and which no one could withstand. But some acts, perhaps, we cannot be forced to do, but ought rather to face death after the most fearful sufferings; for the things that 'forced' Euripides' Alcmaeon to slay his mother seem absurd. It is difficult sometimes to determine what should be chosen at what cost, and what should be endured in return for what gain, and yet more difficult to abide by our decisions; for as a rule what is expected is painful, and what we are forced to do is base, whence praise and blame are bestowed on those who have been compelled or have not.

What sort of acts, then, should be called compulsory? We answer that without qualification actions are so when the cause is in the external circumstances and the agent contributes nothing. But the things that in themselves are involuntary, but now and in return for these gains are worthy of choice, and whose moving principle is in the agent, are in themselves involuntary, but now and in return for these gains voluntary. They are more like voluntary acts; for actions are in the class of particulars, and the particular acts here are voluntary. What sort of things are to be chosen, and in return for what, it is not easy to state; for there are many differences in the particular cases.

But if some one were to say that pleasant and noble objects have a compelling power, forcing us from without, all acts would be for him compulsory; for it is for these objects that all men do everything they do. And those who act under compulsion and unwillingly act with pain, but those who do acts for their pleasantness and nobility do them with pleasure; it is absurd to make external circumstances responsible, and not one-self, as being easily caught by such attractions, and to make oneself responsible for noble acts but the pleasant objects responsible for base acts. The compulsory, then, seems to be that whose moving principle is outside, the person compelled contributing nothing.

Everything that is done by reason of ignorance is *not* voluntary; it is only what produces pain and repentance that is *in*voluntary. For the man who has done something owing to ignorance, and feels not the least vexation at his action, has not acted voluntarily, since he did not know what he was doing, nor yet involuntarily, since he is not pained. Of people, then, who act by reason of ignorance he who repents is thought an involuntary agent, and the man who does not repent may, since he is different, be called a not voluntary agent; for, since he differs from the other, it is better that he should have a name of his own.

Acting by reason of ignorance seems also to be different from acting *in* ignorance; for the man who is drunk or in a rage is thought to act as a result not of ignorance but of one of the causes mentioned, yet not knowingly but in ignorance.

Now every wicked man is ignorant of what he ought to do and what he ought to abstain from, and it is by reason of error of this kind that men become unjust and in general bad; but the term 'involuntary' tends to be used not if a man is ignorant of what is to his advantage—for it is not mistaken purpose that causes involuntary action (it leads rather to wickedness), nor ignorance of the universal (for *that* men are *blamed*), but ignorance of particulars, i.e. of the circumstances of the action and the objects with which it is concerned. For it is on these that both pity and pardon depend, since the person who is ignorant of any of these acts involuntarily.

Perhaps it is just as well, therefore, to determine their nature and number. A man may be ignorant, then, of who he is, what he is doing, what or whom he is acting on, and sometimes also what (e.g. what instrument) he is doing it with, and to what end (e.g. he may think his act will conduce to some one's safety), and how he is doing it (e.g. whether gently or violently). Now of all of these no one could be ignorant unless he were mad, and evidently also he could not be ignorant of the agent; for how could he not know himself? But of what he is doing a man might be ignorant, as for instance people say 'it slipped out of their mouths as they were speaking', or 'they did not know it was a secret', as Aeschylus said of the mysteries, or a man might say he 'let it go off' when he merely wanted to show its working', as the man did with the catapult. Again, one might think one's son was an enemy, as Merope did, or that a pointed spear had a button on it, or that a stone was pumice-stone; or one might give a man a draught to save him, and really kill him; or one might want to touch a man, as people do in spar-ring, and really wound him. The ignorance may re-late, then, to any of these things, i.e. of the circum-stances of the action, and the man who was ignorant of any of these is thought to have acted involuntarily, and especially if he was ignorant on the most important points; and these are thought to be the circumstances of the action and its end. Further, the doing of an act that is called involuntary in virtue of ignorance of this sort must be painful and involve repentance.

Since that which is done under compulsion or by reason of ignorance is involuntary, the voluntary would seem to be that of which the moving principle is in the agent himself, he being aware of the particular circumstances of the action. Presumably acts done by reason of anger or appetite are not rightly called involuntary. For in the first place, on that showing none of the other animals will act voluntarily, nor will children; and secondly, is it meant that we do not do voluntarily *any* of the acts that are due to appetite or anger, or that we do the noble acts voluntarily and the base acts involuntarily? Is not this absurd, when one and the same thing is the cause? But it would surely be odd to describe as involuntary the things one ought to desire; and we ought both to be angry at certain things and to have an appetite for certain things, e.g. for health and for learning. Also what is involuntary is thought to be painful, but what is in accordance with appetite is thought to be pleasant. Again, what is the difference in respect of involuntariness between errors committed upon calculation and those committed in anger? Both are to be avoided, but the irrational passions are thought not less human than reason is, and therefore also the actions which proceed from anger or appetite are the man's actions. It would be odd, then, to treat them as involuntary.

Both the voluntary and the involuntary having been delimited, we must next discuss choice; for it is thought to be most closely bound up with virtue and to discriminate characters better than actions do.

Choice, then, seems to be voluntary, but not the same thing as the voluntary; the latter extends more widely. For both children and the lower animals share in voluntary action, but not in choice, and acts done on the spur of the moment we describe as voluntary, but not as chosen.

Those who say it is appetite or anger or wish or a kind of opinion do not seem to be right. For choice is not common to irrational creatures as well, but appetite and anger are. Again, the incontinent man acts with appetite, but not with choice; while the continent man on the contrary acts with choice, but not with appetite. Again, appetite is contrary to choice, but not appetite to appetite. Again, appetite relates to the pleasant and the painful, choice neither to the painful nor to the pleasant.

Still less is it anger; for acts due to anger are thought to be less than any others objects of choice.

But neither is it wish, though it seems near to it; for choice cannot relate to impossibles, and if any one said he chose them he would be thought silly; but there may be a wish even for impossibles, e.g. for immortality. And wish may relate to things that could in no way be brought about by one's own efforts, e.g. that a particular actor or athlete should win in a competition; but no one chooses such things, but only the things that he thinks could be brought about by his own efforts. Again, wish relates rather to the end, choice to the means; for instance, we wish to be healthy, but we choose the acts which will make us healthy, and we wish to be happy and say we do, but we cannot well say we choose to be so; for, in general, choice seems to relate to the things that are in our own power.

For this reason, too, it cannot be opinion; for opinion is thought to relate to all kinds of things, no less to eternal things and impossible things than to things in our own power; and it is distinguished by its falsity or truth, not by its badness or goodness, while choice is distinguished rather by these.

Now with opinion in general perhaps no one even says it is identical. But it is not identical even with any kind of opinion; for by choosing what is good or bad we are men of a certain character, which we are not by holding certain opinions. And we choose to get or avoid something good or bad, but we have opinions about what a thing is or whom it is good for or how it is good for him; we can hardly be said to opine to get or avoid anything. And choice is praised for being related to the right object rather than for being rightly related to it, opinion for being truly related to its object. And we choose what we best know to be good, but we opine what we do not quite know; and it is not the same people that are thought to make the best choices and to have the best opinions, but some are thought to have fairly good opinions, but by reason of vice to choose what they should not. If opinion precedes choice or accompanies it, that makes no difference; for it is not this that we are considering, but whether it is *identical* with some kind of opinion.

What, then, or what kind of thing is it, since it is none of the things we have mentioned? It seems to be voluntary, but not all that is voluntary to be an object of choice. Is it, then, what has been decided on by previous deliberation? At any rate choice involves a rational principle and thought. Even the name seems to suggest that it is what is chosen before other things.

Do we deliberate about everything, and is everything a possible subject of deliberation, or is deliberation impossible about some things? We ought presumably to call not what a fool or a madman would deliberate about, but what a sensible man would deliberate about, a subject of deliberation. Now about eternal things no one deliberates, e.g. about the material universe or the incommensurability of the diagonal and the side of a square. But no more do we deliberate about the things that involve movement but always happen in the same way, whether of necessity or by nature or from any other cause, e.g. the solstices and the risings of the stars; nor about things that happen now in one way, now in another, e.g. droughts and rains; nor about chance events, like the finding of treasure. But we do not deliberate even about all human affairs; for instance, no Spartan deliberates about the best constitution for the Scythians. For none of these things can be brought about by our own efforts.

We deliberate about things that are in our power and can be done; and these are in fact what is left. For nature, necessity, and chance are thought to be causes, and also reason and everything that depends on man. Now every class of men deliberates about the things that can be done by their own efforts. And in the case of exact and self-contained sciences there is no deliberation, e.g. about the letters of the alphabet (for we have no doubt how they should be written); but the things that are brought about by our own efforts, but not always in the same way, are the things about which we deliberate, e.g. questions of medical treatment or of money-making. And we do so more in the case of the art of navigation than in that of gymnastics, inasmuch as it has been less exactly worked out, and again about other things in the same ratio, and more also in the case of the arts than in that of the sciences; for we have more doubt about the former. Deliberation is concerned with things that happen in a certain way for the most part, but in which the event is obscure, and with things in which it is indeterminate. We call in others to aid us in deliberation on important questions, distrusting ourselves as not being equal to deciding.

We deliberate not about ends but about means. For a doctor does not deliberate whether he shall heal, nor an orator whether he shall persuade, nor a statesman whether he shall produce law and order, nor does any

one else deliberate about his end. They assume the
end and consider how and by what means it is to be
attained; and if it seems to be produced by several
means they consider by which it is most easily and
best produced, while if it is achieved by one only they
consider how it will be achieved by this and by what
means *this* will be achieved, till they come to the first
cause, which in the order of discovery is last. For
the person who deliberates seems to investigate and
analyze in the way described as though he were analyz-
ing a geometrical construction (not all investigation
appears to be deliberation—for instance mathematical
investigations—but all deliberation is investigation),
and what is last in the order of analysis seems to be
first in the order of becoming. And if we come on an
impossibility, we give up the search, e.g. if we need
money and this cannot be got; but if a thing appears
possible we try to do it. By 'possible' things I mean
things that might be brought about by our own efforts;
and these in a sense include things that can be brought
about by the efforts of our friends, since the moving
principle is in ourselves. The subject of investigation
is sometimes the instruments, sometimes the use of
them; and similarly in the other cases—sometimes the
means, sometimes the mode of using it or the means of
bringing it about. It seems, then, as has been said,
that man is a moving principle of actions; now deliberation is about the things to be done by the agent himself,
and actions are for the sake of things other than themselves. For the end cannot be a subject of deliberation, but only the means; nor indeed can the particular
facts be a subject of it, as whether this is bread or
has been baked as it should; for these are matters of
perception. If we are to be always deliberating, we
shall have to go on to infinity.

The same thing is deliberated upon and is chosen, except that the object of choice is already determinate, since it is that which has been decided upon as a result of deliberation that is the object of choice. For every one ceases to inquire how he is to act when he has brought the moving principle back to himself and to the ruling part of himself; for this is what chooses. This is plain also from the ancient constitutions, which Homer represented; for the kings announced their choices to the people. The object of choice being one of the things in our own power which is desired after deliberation, choice will be deliberate desire of things in our own power; for when we have decided as a result of deliberation, we desire in accordance with our deliberation.

78. First let us speak of courage.

That it is a mean with regard to feelings of fear and confidence has already been made evident; and plainly the things we fear are terrible things, and these are, to speak without qualification, evils; for which reason people even define fear as expectation of evil. Now we fear all evil, e.g. disgrace, poverty, disease, friendlessness, death, but the brave man is not thought to be concerned with all; for to fear some things is even right and noble, and it is base not to fear them—e.g. disgrace; he who fears this is good and modest, and he who does not is shameless. He is, however, by some people called brave, by a transference of the word to a new meaning; for he has in him something which is like the brave man, since the brave man also is a fearless person. Poverty and disease we perhaps ought not to fear, nor in general the things that do not proceed from vice and are not due to a man himself. But not even the man who is fearless of these is brave. Yet we apply the word to him also in virtue of a similarity; for some who in the dangers of war are cowards are liberal and are confident in face of the loss of money. Nor is a man a coward if he fears insult to his wife and children or envy or anything of the kind; nor brave if he is confident when he is about to be flogged. With what sort of terrible things, then, is the brave man concerned? Surely with the greatest; for no one is more likely than he to stand his ground against what is awe-inspiring. Now death is the most terrible of all things; for it is the end, and nothing is thought to be any longer either good or bad for the dead. But the brave man would not seem to be concerned even with death in *all* circumstances, e.g. at sea or in disease. In what circumstances, then? Surely in the noblest. Now such deaths are those in battle; for these take place in the greatest and noblest danger. And these are correspondingly honoured in city-states and at the courts of monarchs. Properly, then, he will be called brave who is fearless in face of a noble death, and of all emergencies that involve death; and the emergencies of war are in the highest degree of this kind. Yet at sea also, and in disease, the brave man is fearless, but not in the same way as the seamen; for he has given up hope of safety, and is disliking the thought of death in this shape, while they are hopeful because of their experience. At the same time, we show courage in situations where there is the opportunity of showing prowess or where death is noble; but in these forms of death neither of these conditions is fulfilled.

What is terrible is not the same for all men; but we say there are things terrible even beyond human strength. These, then, are terrible to every one—at least to every sensible man; but the terrible things that are *not* beyond human strength differ in magnitude and degree, and so too do the things that inspire confidence. Now the brave man is as dauntless as man may be. Therefore, while he will fear even the things that are not beyond human strength, he will face them as he ought and as the rule directs, for honour's sake; for this is the end of virtue. But it is possible to fear these more, or less, and again to fear things that are not terrible as if they were. Of the faults that are committed one consists in fearing what one should not, another in fearing as we should not, another in fearing when we should not, and so on; and so too with respect to the things that inspire confidence. The man, then, who faces and who fears the right things and from the right motive, in the right way and at the right time, and who feels confidence under the corresponding conditions, is brave; for the brave man feels and acts according to the merits of the case and in whatever way the rule directs. Now the end of every activity is conformity to the corresponding state of character. This is true, therefore, of the brave man as well as of others. But courage is noble. Therefore the end also is noble; for each thing is defined by its end. Therefore it is for a noble end that the brave man endures and acts as courage directs.

Of those who go to excess he who exceeds in fearlessness has no name (we have said previously that many states of character have no names), but he would be a sort of madman or insensible person if he feared nothing, neither earthquakes nor the waves, as they say the Celts do not; while the man who exceeds in confidence about what really is terrible is rash. The rash man, however, is also thought to be boastful and only a pretender to courage; at all events, as the brave man *is* with regard to what is terrible, so the rash man wishes to *appear;* and so he imitates him in situations where he can. Hence also most of them are a mixture of rashness and cowardice; for, while in these situations they display confidence, they do not hold their ground against what is really terrible. The man who exceeds in fear is a coward; for he fears both what he ought not and as he ought not, and all the similar characterizations attach to him. He is lacking also in confidence; but he is more conspicuous for his excess of fear in painful situations. The coward, then, is a despairing sort of person; for he fears everything. The brave man, on the other hand, has the opposite disposition; for confidence is the mark of a hopeful disposition. The coward, the rash man, and the brave man, then, are concerned with the same objects but are differently disposed towards them; for the first two exceed and fall short, while the third holds the middle, which is the right, position; and rash men are precipitate; and wish for dangers beforehand but draw back when they are in them, while brave men are keen in the moment of action, but quiet beforehand.

As we have said, then, courage is a mean with respect to things that inspire confidence or fear, in the circumstances that have been stated; and it chooses or endures things because it is noble to do so, or because it is base not to do so. But to die to escape from poverty or love or anything painful is not the mark of a brave man, but rather of a coward; for it is softness to fly from what is troublesome, and such a man endures death not because it is noble but to fly from evil. . . .

Though courage is concerned with feelings of confidence and of fear, it is not concerned with both alike, but more with the things that inspire fear; for he who is undisturbed in face of these and bears himself as he should towards these is more truly brave than the man who does so towards the things that inspire confidence. It is for facing what is painful, then, as has been said, that men are called brave. Hence also courage involves pain, and is justly praised; for it is harder to face what is painful than to abstain from what is pleasant. Yet the end which courage sets before it would seem to be pleasant, but to be concealed by the attending circumstances, as happens also in athletic contests; for the end at which boxers aim is pleasant—the crown and the honours—but the blows they take are distressing to flesh and blood, and painful, and so is their whole exertion; and because the blows and the exertions are many the end, which is but small, appears to have nothing pleasant in it. And so, if the case of courage is similar, death and wounds will be painful to the brave man and against his will, but he will face them because it is noble to do so or because it is base not to do so. And the more he is possessed of virtue in its entirety and the happier he is, the more he will be pained at the thought of death; for life is best worth living for such a man, and he is knowingly losing the greatest goods, and this is painful. But he is none the less brave, and perhaps all the more so, because he chooses noble deeds of war at that cost. It is not the case, then, with all the virtues that the exercise of them is pleasant, except in so far as it reaches its end. But it is quite possible that the best soldiers may be not men of this sort but those who are less brave but have no other good; for these are ready to face danger, and they sell their life for trifling gains.

79. Since the lawless man was seen to be unjust and the law-abiding man just, evidently all lawful acts are in a sense just acts; for the acts laid down by the

legislative art are lawful, and each of these, we say, is just. Now the laws in their enactments on all subjects aim at the common advantage either of all or of the best or of those who hold power, or something of the sort; so that in one sense we call those acts just that tend to produce and preserve happiness and its components for the political society. And the law bids us do both the acts of a brave man (e.g. not to desert our post nor take to flight nor throw away our arms), and those of a temperate man (e.g. not to commit adultery nor to gratify one's lust), and those of a good-tempered man (e.g. not to strike another nor to speak evil), and similarly with regard to the other virtues and forms of wickedness, commanding some acts and forbidding others; and the rightly-framed law does this rightly, and the hastily conceived one less well.

This form of justice, then, is complete virtue, but not absolutely, but in relation to our neighbour. And therefore justice is often thought to be the greatest of virtues, and 'neither evening nor morning star' is so wonderful; and proverbially 'in justice is every virtue comprehended'. And it is complete virtue in its fullest sense, because it is the actual exercise of complete virtue. It is complete because he who possesses it can exercise his virtue not only in himself but towards his neighbour also; for many men can exercise virtue in their own affairs, but not in their relations to their neighbour. This is why the saying of Bias is thought to be true, that 'rule will show the man'; for a ruler is necessarily in relation to other men and a member of a society. For this same reason justice, alone of the virtues, is thought to be 'another's good', because it is related to our neighbour; for it does what is advantageous to another, either a ruler or a copartner. Now the worst man is he who exercises his wickedness both towards himself and towards his friends, and the best man is not he who exercises his virtue towards himself but he who exercises it towards another; for this is a difficult task. Justice in this sense, then, is not part of virtue but virtue entire, nor is the contrary injustice a part of vice but vice entire. What the difference is between virtue and justice in this sense is plain from what we have said; they are the same but their essence is not the same; what, as a relation to one's neighbour, is justice is, as a certain kind of state without qualification, virtue.

But at all events what we are investigating is the justice which is a *part* of virtue; for there is a justice of this kind, as we maintain. Similarly it is with injustice in the particular sense that we are concerned.

That there is such a thing is indicated by the fact that while the man who exhibits in action the other forms of wickedness acts wrongly indeed, but not graspingly (e.g. the man who throws away his shield through cowardice or speaks harshly through bad temper or fails to help a friend with money through meanness), when a man acts graspingly he often exhibits none of these vices,—no, nor all together, but certainly wickedness of some kind (for we blame him) and injustice. There is, then, another kind of injustice which is a part of injustice in the wide sense, and a use of the word 'unjust' which answers to a part of what is unjust in the wide sense of 'contrary to the law'. Again, if one man commits adultery for the sake of gain and makes money by it, while another does so at the bidding of appetite though he loses money and is penalized for it, the latter would be held to be self-indulgent rather than grasping, but the former is unjust, but not self-indulgent; evidently, therefore, he is unjust by reason of his making gain by his act. Again, all other unjust acts are ascribed invariably to some particular kind of wickedness, e.g. adultery to self-indulgence, the desertion of a comrade in battle to cowardice, physical violence to anger; but if a man makes gain, his action is ascribed to no form of wickedness but injustice. Evidently, therefore, there is apart from injustice in the wide sense another, 'particular', injustice which shares the name and nature of the first, because its definition falls within the same genus; for the significance of both consists in a relation to one's neighbour, but the one is concerned with honour or money or safety—or that which includes all these, if we had a single name for it—and its motive is the pleasure that arises from gain; while the other is concerned with all the objects with which the good man is concerned.

It is clear, then, that there is more than one kind of justice, and that there is one which is distinct from virtue entire; we must try to grasp its genus and differentia.

The unjust has been divided into the unlawful and the unfair, and the just into the lawful and the fair. To the unlawful answers the afore-mentioned sense of injustice. But since the unfair and the unlawful are not the same, but are different as a part is from its whole (for all that is unfair is unlawful, but not all that is unlawful is unfair), the unjust and injustice in the sense of the unfair are not the same as but different from the former kind, as part from whole; for injustice in this sense is a part of injustice in the wide sense, and similarly justice in the one sense of justice in the other. Therefore we must speak also about particular justice and particular injustice, and similarly about the just and the unjust. The justice, then, which answers to the whole of virtue, and the corresponding injustice, one being the exercise of virtue as a whole,

and the other that of vice as a whole, towards one's
neighbour, we may leave on one side. And how the
meanings of 'just' and 'unjust' which answer to these
are to be distinguished is evident; for practically the
majority of the acts commanded by the law are those
which are prescribed from the point of view of virtue
taken as a whole; for the law bids us practise every
virtue and forbids us to practise any vice. And the
things that tend to produce virtue taken as a whole are
those of the acts prescribed by the law which have been
prescribed with a view to education for the common
good. But with regard to the education of the individual as such, which makes him without qualification
a good *man,* we must determine later whether this
is the function of the political art or of another; for
perhaps it is not the same to be a good man and a
good citizen of any state taken at random.

Of particular justice and that which is just in the
corresponding sense, (A) one kind is that which is manifested in distributions of honour or money or the other
things that fall to be divided among those who have a
share in the constitution (for in these it is possible for
one man to have a share either unequal or equal to
that of another), and (B) one is that which plays a
rectifying part in transactions between man and man.
Of this there are two divisions; of transactions (1)
some are voluntary and (2) others involuntary—voluntary such transactions as sale, purchase, loan for consumption, pledging, loan for use, depositing, letting
(they are called voluntary because the origin of these
transactions is voluntary), while of the involuntary (*a*)
some are clandestine, such as theft, adultery, poisoning,
procuring, enticement of slaves, assassination, false witness, and (*b*) others are violent, such as assault, im-

prisonment, murder, robbery with violence, mutilation, abuse, insult.

(A) We have shown that both the unjust man and the unjust act are unfair or unequal; now it is clear that there is also an intermediate between the two unequals involved in either case. And this is the equal; for in any kind of action in which there is a more and a less there is also what is equal. If, then, the unjust is unequal, the just is equal, as all men suppose it to be, even apart from argument. And since the equal is intermediate, the just will be an intermediate. Now equality implies at least two things. The just, then, must be both intermediate and equal and relative (i.e. for certain persons). And *qua* intermediate it must be between certain things (which are respectively greater and less); *qua* equal, it involves *two* things; *qua* just, it is for certain people. The just, therefore, involves at least four terms; for the persons for whom it is in fact just are two, and the things in which it is manifested, the objects distributed, are two. And the same equality will exist between the persons and between the things concerned; for as the latter—the things concerned—are related, so are the former; if they are not equal, they will not have what is equal, but this is the origin of quarrels and complaints—when either equals have and are awarded unequal shares, or unequals equal shares. Further, this is plain from the fact that awards should be 'according to merit'; for all men agree that what is just in distribution must be according to merit in some sense, though they do not all specify the same sort of merit, but democrats identify it with the status of freeman, supporters of oligarchy with wealth (or with noble birth), and supporters of aristocracy with excellence.

The just, then, is a species of the proportionate (proportion being not a property only of the kind of number which consists of abstract units, but of number in general). For proportion is equality of ratios, and involves four terms at least (that discrete proportion involves four terms is plain, but so does continuous proportion, for it uses one term as two and mentions it twice; e.g. 'as the line A is to the line B, so is the line B to the line C'; the line B, then, has been mentioned twice, so that if the line B be assumed twice, the proportional terms will be four); and the just, too, involves at least four terms, and the ratio between one pair is the same as that between the other pair; for there is a similar distinction between the persons and between the things. As the term A, then, is to B, so will C be to D, and therefore, *alternando,* as A is to C, B will be to D. Therefore also the whole is in the same ratio to the whole; and this coupling the distribution effects, and, if the terms are so combined, effects justly. The conjunction, then, of the term A with C and of B with D is what is just in distribution, and this species of the just is intermediate, and the unjust is what violates the proportion; for the proportional is intermediate, and the just is proportional. (Mathematicians call this kind of proportion geometrical; for it is in geometrical proportion that it follows that the whole is to the whole as either part is to the corresponding part.) This proportion is not continuous; for we cannot get a single term standing for a person and a thing.

This, then, is what the just is—the proportional; the unjust is what violates the proportion. Hence one term becomes too great, the other too small, as indeed happens in practice; for the man who acts unjustly has too much, and the man who is unjustly treated too little, of what is good. In the case of evil the reverse is true; for the lesser evil is reckoned a good in comparison with the greater evil, since the lesser evil is rather to be chosen than the greater, and what is worthy of choice is good, and what is worthier of choice a greater good.

This, then, is one species of the just.

(B) The remaining one is the rectificatory, which arises in connexion with transactions both voluntary and involuntary. This form of the just has a different specific character from the former. For the justice which distributes common possessions is always in accordance with the kind of proportion mentioned above (for in the case also in which the distribution is made from the common funds of a partnership it will be according to the same ratio which the funds put into the business by the partners bear to one another); and the injustice opposed to this kind of justice is that which violates the proportion. But the justice in transactions between man and man is a sort of equality indeed, and the injustice a sort of inequality; not according to that kind of proportion, however, but according to arithmetical proportion. For it makes no difference whether a good man has defrauded a bad man or a bad man a good one, nor whether it is a good or a bad man that has committed adultery; the law looks only to the distinctive character of the injury, and treats the parties as equal, if one is in the wrong and the other is being wronged, and if one inflicted injury and the other has received it.

80. Our next subject is equity and the equitable ($\tau o\ \dot{\epsilon}\pi\iota\epsilon\iota\kappa\dot{\epsilon}s$), and their respective relations to justice and the just. For on examination they appear to be neither absolutely the same nor generically different; and while we sometimes praise what is equitable and the equitable man (so that we apply the name by way of praise even

to instances of the other virtues, instead of 'good', meaning by ἐπιεικέστερον that a thing is better), at other times, when we reason it out, it seems strange if the equitable, being something different from the just, is yet praiseworthy; for either the just or the equitable is not good, if they are different; or, if both are good, they are the same.

These, then, are pretty much the considerations that give rise to the problem about the equitable; they are all in a sense correct and not opposed to one another; for the equitable, though it is better than one kind of justice, yet is just, and it is not as being a different class of thing that it is better than the just. The same thing, then, is just and equitable, and while both are good the equitable is superior. What creates the problem is that the equitable is just, but not the legally just but a correction of legal justice. The reason is that all law is universal but about some things it is not possible to make a universal statement which shall be correct. In those cases, then, in which it is necessary to speak universally, but not possible to do so correctly, the law takes the usual case, though it is not ignorant of the possibility of error. And it is none the less correct; for the error is not in the law nor in the legislator but in the nature of the thing, since the matter of practical affairs is of this kind from the start. When the law speaks universally, then, and a case arises on it which is not covered by the universal statement, then it is right, where the legislator fails us and has erred by over-simplicity, to correct the omission—to say what the legislator himself would have said had he been present, and would have put into his law if he had known. Hence the equitable is just, and better than one kind of justice—not better than absolute justice but better than the error that arises from

the absoluteness of the statement. And this is the
nature of the equitable, a correction of law where it
is defective owing to its universality.

81. We divided the virtues of the soul and said that
some are virtues of character and others of intellect.
Now we have discussed in detail the moral virtues; with
regard to the others let us express our view as follows,
beginning with some remarks about the soul. We said
before that there are two parts of the soul—that which
grasps a rule or rational principle, and the irrational;
let us now draw a similar distinction within the part
which grasps a rational principle. And let it be assumed that there are two parts which grasp a rational
principle—one by which we contemplate the kind of
things whose originative causes are invariable, and one
by which we contemplate variable things; for where
objects differ in kind the part of the soul answering
to each of the two is different in kind, since it is in
virtue of a certain likeness and kinship with their objects that they have the knowledge they have. Let one
of these parts be called the scientific and the other
the calculative; for to deliberate and to calculate are
the same thing, but no one deliberates about the invariable. Therefore the calculative is one part of the faculty
which grasps a rational principle. We must, then,
learn what is the best state of each of these two parts;
for this is the virtue of each.

82. Regarding *practical wisdom* we shall get at the
truth by considering who are the persons we credit with
it. Now it is thought to be the mark of a man of practical wisdom to be able to deliberate well about what is
good and expedient for himself, not in some particular
respect, e.g. about what sorts of thing conduce to health

or to strength, but about what sorts of thing conduce
to the good life in general. . . . . .

Wisdom (1) in the arts we ascribe to their most
finished exponents, e.g. to Phidias as a sculptor and to
Polyclitus as a maker of portrait-statues, and here we
mean nothing by wisdom except excellence in art; but
(2) we think that some people are wise in general, not
in some particular field or in any other limited respect,
as Homer says in the *Margites,*

Him did the gods make neither a digger nor yet a
    ploughman
Nor wise in anything else.

Therefore wisdom must plainly be the most finished of
the forms of knowledge. It follows that the wise man
must not only know what follows from the first principles, but must also possess truth about the first principles. Therefore wisdom must be intuitive reason combined with scientific knowledge—scientific knowledge
of the highest objects which has received as it were
its proper completion.

83. Difficulties might be raised as to the utility of
these qualities of mind. For (1) philosophic wisdom will
contemplate none of the things that will make a man
happy (for it is not concerned with any coming into
being), and though practical wisdom has *this* merit,
for what purpose do we need it? Practical wisdom
is the quality of mind concerned with things just and
noble and good for man, but these are the things which
it is the mark of a *good* man to do, and we are none
the more able to act for *knowing* them if the virtues
are states of *character,* just as we are none the better
able to act for knowing the things that are healthy and

sound, in the sense not of producing but of issuing from the state of health; for we are none the more able to act for having the art of medicine or of gymnastics. But (2) if we are to say that a man should have practical wisdom not for the sake of knowing moral truths but for the sake of becoming good, practical wisdom will be of no use to those who *are* good; but again it is of no use to those who have *not* virtue; for it will make no difference whether they have practical wisdom themselves or obey others who have it, and it would be enough for us to do what we do in the case of health; though we wish to become healthy, yet we do not learn the art of medicine. (3) Besides this, it would be thought strange if practical wisdom, being inferior to philosophic wisdom, is to be put in authority over it, as seems to be implied by the fact that the art which produces anything rules and issues commands about that thing.

These, then, are the questions we must discuss; so far we have only stated the difficulties.

(1) Now first let us say that in themselves these states must be worthy of choice because they are the virtues of the two parts of the soul respectively, even if neither of them produce anything.

(2) Secondly, they do produce something, not as the art of medicine produces health, however, but as health produces health; so does philosophic wisdom produce happiness; for, being a part of virtue entire, by being possessed and by actualizing itself it makes a man happy.

(3) Again, the work of man is achieved only in accordance with practical wisdom as well as with moral virtue; for virtue makes us aim at the right mark, and practical wisdom makes us take the right means. . . .

We must therefore consider virtue also once more;

for virtue too is similarly related; as practical wisdom is to cleverness—not the same, but like it—so is natural virtue to virtue in the strict sense. For all men think that each type of character belongs to its possessors in some sense by nature; for from the very moment of birth we are just or fitted for self-control or brave or have the other moral qualities; but yet we seek something else as that which is good in the strict sense—we seek for the presence of such qualities in another way. For both children and brutes have the natural dispositions to these qualities, but without reason these are evidently hurtful. Only we seem to see this much, that, while one may be led astray by them, as a strong body which moves without sight may stumble badly because of its lack of sight, still, if a man once acquires reason, that makes a difference in action; and his state, while still like what it was, will then be virtue in the strict sense. Therefore, as in the part of us which forms opinions there are two types, cleverness and practical wisdom, so too in the moral part there are two types, natural virtue and virtue in the strict sense, and of these the latter involves practical wisdom. This is why some say that all the virtues are forms of practical wisdom, and why Socrates in one respect was on the right track while in another he went astray; in thinking that all the virtues were forms of practical wisdom he was wrong, but in saying they implied practical wisdom he was right. This is confirmed by the fact that even now all men, when they define virtue, after naming the state of character and its objects add 'that (state) which is in accordance with the right rule'; now the right rule is that which is in accordance with practical wisdom. All men, then, seem somehow to divine that this kind of state is virtue, viz. that which is in accordance with practical wisdom. But we must go a little further.

For it is not merely the state in accordance with the right rule, but the state that implies the *presence* of the right rule, that is virtue; and practical wisdom is a right rule about such matters. Socrates, then, thought the virtues were rules or rational principles (for he thought they were, all of them, forms of scientific knowledge), while we think they *involve* a rational principle.

It is clear, then, from what has been said, that it is not possible to be good in the strict sense without practical wisdom, nor practically wise without moral virtue.

STOP

84. We must consider first whether incontinent people act knowingly or not, and in what sense knowingly; then with what sorts of object the incontinent and the continent man may be said to be concerned (i.e. whether with any and every pleasure and pain or with certain determinate kinds), and whether the continent man and the man of endurance are the same or different; and similarly with regard to the other matters germane to this inquiry. The starting-point of our investigation is (a) the question whether the continent man and the incontinent are differentiated by their objects or by their attitude, i.e. whether the incontinent man is incontinent simply by being concerned with such and such objects, or, instead, by his attitude, or, instead of that, by both these things; (b) the second question is whether incontinence and continence are concerned with any and every object or not. The man who is incontinent in the unqualified sense is neither concerned with any and every object, but with precisely those with which the self-indulgent man is concerned, nor is he characterized by being simply related to these (for then his state would be the same as self-indulgence),

but by being related to them in a certain way. For
the one is led on in accordance with his own choice,
thinking that he ought always to pursue the present
pleasure; while the other does not think so, but yet
pursues it.

As for the suggestion that it is true opinion and
not knowledge against which we act incontinently, that
makes no difference to the argument; for some people
when in a state of opinion do not hesitate but think
they know exactly. If, then, the notion is that owing
to their weak conviction those who have opinion are
more likely to act against their judgement than those
who know, we answer that there need be no difference
between knowledge and opinion in this respect; for
some men are no less convinced of what they think
than others of what they know; as is shown by the
case of Heraclitus. But (*a*), since we use the word
'know' in two senses (for both the man who has knowledge but is not using it and he who is using it are
said to know), it *will* make a difference whether, when
a man does what he should not, he has the knowledge
but is not exercising it, or *is* exercising it; for the latter
seems strange, but not the former.

(*b*) Further, since there are two kinds of premisses,
there is nothing to prevent a man's having both premisses
and acting against his knowledge, provided that he
is using only the universal premiss and not the particular; for it is particular acts that have to be done.
And there are also two kinds of universal term; one
is predicable of the agent, the other of the object; e.g.
'dry food is good for every man', and 'I am a man',
or 'such and such food is dry'; but whether 'this food
is such and such', of this the incontinent man either
has not or is not exercising the knowledge. There will,
then, be, firstly, an enormous difference between these

manners of knowing, so that to know in one way when we act incontinently would not seem anything strange, while to know in the other way would be extraordinary.

And further (c) the possession of knowledge in another sense than those just named is something that happens to men; for within the case of having knowledge but not using it we see a difference of state, admitting of the possibility of having knowledge in a sense and yet not having it, as in the instance of a man asleep, mad, or drunk. But now this is just the condition of men under the influence of passions; for outbursts of anger and sexual appetites and some other such passions, it is evident, actually alter our bodily condition, and in some men even produce fits of madness. It is plain, then, that incontinent people must be said to be in a similar condition to men asleep, mad, or drunk. The fact that men use the language that flows from knowledge proves nothing; for even men under the influence of these passions utter scientific proofs and verses of Empedocles, and those who have just begun to learn a science can string together its phrases, but do not yet know it; for it has to become part of themselves, and that takes time; so that we must suppose that the use of language by men in an incontinent state means no more than its utterance by actors on the stage.

(d) Again, we may also view the cause as follows with reference to the facts of human nature. The one opinion is universal, the other is concerned with the particular facts, and here we come to something within the sphere of perception; when a single opinion results from the two, the soul must in one type of case affirm the conclusion, while in the case of opinions concerned with production it must immediately act (e.g. if 'everything sweet ought to be tasted', and 'this is sweet', in the sense of being one of the particular sweet things, the man who can act and is not prevented must at the same time actually act accordingly). When, then, the universal opinion is present in us forbidding us to taste, and there is also the opinion that 'everything sweet is pleasant', and that 'this is sweet' (now this is the opinion that is active), and when appetite happens to be present in us, the one opinion bids us avoid the object, but appetite leads us towards it (for it can move each of our bodily parts); so that it turns out that a man behaves incontinently under the influence (in a sense) of a rule and an opinion, and of one not contrary in itself, but only incidentally—for the appetite is contrary, not the opinion—to the right rule. It also follows that this is the reason why the lower animals are not incontinent, viz. because they have no universal judgement but only imagination and memory of particulars.

The explanation of how the ignorance is dissolved and the incontinent man regains his knowledge, is the same as in the case of the man drunk or asleep and is not peculiar to this condition; we must go to the students of natural science for it. Now, the last premiss both being an opinion about a perceptible object, and being what determines our actions, this a man either has not when he is in the state of passion, or has it in the sense in which having knowledge did not mean knowing but only talking, as a drunken man may mutter the verses of Empedocles. And because the last term is not universal nor equally an object of scientific knowledge with the universal term, the position that Socrates sought to establish actually seems to result; for it is not in the presence of what is thought to be knowledge proper that the affection of incontinence arises (nor is it this that is 'dragged about' as a result of the state of passion), but in that of perceptual knowledge.

85. If certain pleasures are bad, that does not prevent the chief good from being some pleasure, just as the chief good may be some form of knowledge though certain kinds of knowledge are bad. Perhaps it is even necessary, if each disposition has unimpeded activities, that, whether the activity (if unimpeded) of all our dispositions or that of some one of them is happiness, this should be the thing most worthy of our choice; and this activity is pleasure. Thus the chief good would be some pleasure, though most pleasures might perhaps be bad without qualification. And for this reason all men think that the happy life is pleasant and weave pleasure into their ideal of happiness—and reasonably too; for no activity is perfect when it is impeded, and happiness is a perfect thing; this is why the happy man needs the goods of the body and external goods, i.e. those of fortune, viz. in order that he may not be impeded in these ways. Those who say that the victim on the rack or the man who falls into great misfortunes is happy if he is good, are, whether they mean to or not, talking nonsense. . . .

What pleasure is, or what kind of thing it is, will become plainer if we take up the question again from the beginning. Seeing seems to be at any moment complete, for it does not lack anything which coming into being later will complete its form; and pleasure also seems to be of this nature. For it is a whole, and at no time can one find a pleasure whose form will be completed if the pleasure lasts longer. For this reason, too, it is not a movement. For every movement (e.g. that of building) takes time and is for the sake of an end, and is complete when it has made what it aims at.

It is complete, therefore, only in the whole time or at that final moment. In their parts and during the time they occupy, all movements are incomplete, and are different in kind from the whole movement and from each other. For the fitting together of the stones is different from the fluting of the column, and these are both different from the making of the temple; and the making of the temple is complete (for it lacks nothing with a view to the end proposed), but the making of the base or of the triglyph is incomplete; for each is the making of only a part. They differ in kind, then, and it is not possible to find at any and every time a movement complete in form, but if at all, only in the whole time. So, too, in the case of walking and all other movements. For if locomotion is a movement from here to there, it, too, has differences in kind— flying, walking, leaping, and so on. And not only so, but in walking itself there are such differences; for the whence and whither are not the same in the whole racecourse and in a part of it, nor in one part and in another, nor is it the same thing to traverse this line and that; for one traverses not only a line but one which is in a place, and this one is in a different place from that. We have discussed movement with precision in another work, but it seems that it is not complete at any and every time, but that the many movements are incomplete and different in kind, since the whence and whither give them their form. But of pleasure the form is complete at any and every time. Plainly, then, pleasure and movement must be different from each other, and pleasure must be one of the things that are whole and complete. This would seem to be the case, too, from the fact that it is not possible to move otherwise than in time, but it *is* possible to be pleased; for that which takes place in a moment is a whole.

From these considerations it is clear, too, that these thinkers are not right in saying there is a movement or a coming into being *of* pleasure. For these cannot be ascribed to all things, but only to those that are divisible and not wholes; there is no coming into being of seeing nor of a point nor of a unit, nor is any of these a movement or coming into being; therefore there is no movement or coming into being of pleasure either; for it is a whole.

Since every sense is active in relation to its object, and a sense which is in good condition acts perfectly in relation to the most beautiful of its objects (for perfect activity seems to be ideally of this nature; whether we say that *it* is active, or the organ in which it resides, may be assumed to be immaterial), it follows that in the case of each sense the best activity is that of the best-conditioned organ in relation to the finest of its objects. And this activity will be the most complete and pleasant. For, while there is pleasure in respect of any sense, and in respect of thought and contemplation no less, the most complete is pleasantest, and that of a well-conditioned organ in relation to the worthiest of its objects is the most complete; and the pleasure completes the activity. But the pleasure does not complete it in the same way as the combination of object and sense, both good, just as health and the doctor are not in the same way the cause of a man's being healthy. (That pleasure is produced in respect to each sense is plain; for we speak of sights and sounds as pleasant. It is also plain that it arises most of all when both the sense is at its best and it is active in reference to an object which corresponds; when both object and perceiver are of the best there will always be pleasure, since the requisite agent and patient are both present.) Pleasure completes the activity not as the corresponding permanent state does, by its immanence, but as an end which supervenes as the bloom of youth does on those in the flower of their age. So long, then, as both the intelligible or sensible object and the discriminating or contemplative faculty are as they should be, the pleasure will be involved in the activity; for when both the passive and the active factor are unchanged and are related to each other in the same way, the same result naturally follows.

How, then, is it that no one is continuously pleased? Is it that we grow weary? Certainly all human things are incapable of continuous activity. Therefore pleasure also is not continuous; for it accompanies activity. Some things delight us when they are new, but later do so less, for the same reason; for at first the mind is in a state of stimulation and intensely active about them, as people are with respect to their vision when they look hard at a thing, but afterwards our activity is not of this kind, but has grown relaxed; for which reason the pleasure also is dulled.

One might think that all men desire pleasure because they all aim at life; life is an activity, and each man is active about those things and with those faculties that he loves most; e.g. the musician is active with his hearing in reference to tunes, the student with his mind in reference to theoretical questions, and so on in each case; now pleasure completes the activities, and therefore life, which they desire. It is with good reason, then, that they aim at pleasure too, since for every one it completes life, which is desirable. But whether we choose life for the sake of pleasure or pleasure for the sake of life is a question we may dismiss for the present. For they seem to be bound up together and not to admit of separation, since without activity pleasure does not arise, and every activity is completed by the attendant pleasure.

For this reason pleasures seem, too, to differ in kind. For things different in kind are, we think, completed by different things (we see this to be true both of natural objects and of things produced by art, e.g. animals, trees, a painting, a sculpture, a house, an implement); and, similarly, we think that activities differing in kind are completed by things differing in kind. Now the activities of thought differ from those of the senses, and both differ among themselves, in kind; so, therefore, do the pleasures that complete them.

This may be seen, too, from the fact that each of the pleasures is bound up with the activity it completes. For an activity is intensified by its proper pleasure, since each class of things is better judged of and brought to precision by those who engage in the activity with pleasure; e. g. it is those who enjoy geometrical thinking that become geometers and grasp the various propositions better, and, similarly, those who are fond of music or of building, and so on, make progress in their proper function by enjoying it; so the pleasures intensify the activities, and what intensifies a thing is proper to it, but things different in kind have properties different in kind.

This will be even more apparent from the fact that activities are hindered by pleasures arising from other sources. For people who are fond of playing the flute are incapable of attending to arguments if they overhear some one playing the flute, since they enjoy flute-playing more than the activity in hand; so the pleasure connected with flute-playing destroys the activity concerned with argument. This happens, similarly, in all other cases, when one is active about two things at once; the more pleasant activity drives out the other, and if it is much more pleasant does so all the more, so that one even ceases from the other. This is why when we enjoy anything very much we do not throw ourselves into anything else, and do one thing only when we are not much pleased by another; e.g. in the theatre the people who eat sweets do so most when the actors are poor. Now since activities are made precise and more enduring and better by their proper pleasure, and injured by alien pleasures, evidently the two kinds of pleasure are far apart. For alien pleasures do pretty much what proper pains do, since activities are destroyed by their proper pains; e.g. if a man finds writing or doing sums unpleasant and painful, he does not write, or does not do sums, because the activity is painful. So an activity suffers contrary effects from its proper pleasures and pains, i.e. from those that supervene on it in virtue of its own nature. And alien pleasures have been stated to do much the same as pain; they destroy the activity, only not to the same degree.

Now since activities differ in respect of goodness and badness, and some are worthy to be chosen, others to be avoided, and others neutral, so, too, are the pleasures; for to each activity there is a proper pleasure. The pleasure proper to a worthy activity is good and that proper to an unworthy activity bad; just as the appetites for noble objects are laudable, those for base objects culpable. But the pleasures involved in activities are more proper to them than the desires; for the latter are separated both in time and in nature, while the former are close to the activities, and so hard to distinguish from them that it admits of dispute whether the activity is not the same as the pleasure. (Still, pleasure does not seem to *be* thought or perception—that would be strange; but because they are not found apart they appear to some people the same.) As activities are different, then, so are the corresponding pleasures. Now sight is superior to touch in purity, and hearing and smell to taste; the pleasures, therefore, are similarly superior, and those of thought superior to these, and within each of the two kinds some are superior to others.

Each animal is thought to have a proper pleasure, as it has a proper function; viz. that which corresponds to its activity. If we survey them species by species, too, this will be evident; horse, dog, and man have different pleasures, as Heraclitus says 'asses would prefer sweepings to gold'; for food is pleasanter than gold to asses. So the pleasures of creatures different in kind differ in kind, and it is plausible to suppose that those of a single species do not differ. But they vary to no small extent, in the case of men at least; the same things delight some people and pain others, and are painful and odious to some, and pleasant to and liked by others. This happens, too, in the case of sweet things; the same things do not seem sweet to a man in a fever and a healthy man—nor hot to a weak man and one in good condition. The same happens in other cases. But in all such matters that which appears to the good man is thought to be really so. If this is correct, as it seems to be, and virtue and the good man as such are the measure of each thing, those also will be pleasures which appear so to him, and those things pleasant which he enjoys. If the things he finds tiresome seem pleasant to some one, that is nothing surprising; for men may be ruined and spoilt in many ways; but the things are not pleasant, but only pleasant to these people and to people in this condition. Those which are admittedly disgraceful plainly should not be said to be pleasures, except to a perverted taste; but of those that are thought to be good what kind of pleasure or what pleasure should be said to be that proper to man? Is it not plain from the corresponding activities? The pleasures follow these. Whether, then, the perfect and supremely happy man has one or more activities, the pleasures that perfect these will be said in the strict sense to be pleasures proper to man, and the rest will be so in a secondary and fractional way, as are the activities.

86. After what we have said, a discussion of friendship would naturally follow, since it is a virtue or implies virtue, and is besides most necessary with a view to living. For without friends no one would choose to live, though he had all other goods; even rich men and those in possession of office and of dominating power are thought to need friends most of all; for what is the use of such prosperity without the opportunity of beneficence, which is exercised chiefly and in its most laudable form towards friends? Or how can prosperity be guarded and preserved without friends? The greater it is, the more exposed is it to risk. And in poverty and in other misfortunes men think friends are the only refuge. It helps the young, too, to keep from error; it aids older people by ministering to their needs and supplementing the activities that are failing from weakness; those in the prime of life it stimulates to noble actions—'two going together'—for with friends men are more able both to think and to act. Again, parent seems by nature to feel it for offspring and offspring for parent, not only among men but among birds and among most animals; it is felt mutually by members of the same race, and especially by men, whence we praise lovers of their fellow-men. We may

see even in our travels how near and dear every man is to every other. Friendship seems too to hold states together, and lawgivers to care more for it than for justice; for unanimity seems to be something like friendship, and this they aim at most of all, and expel faction as their worst enemy; and when men are friends they have no need of justice, while when they are just they need friendship as well, and the truest form of justice is thought to be a friendly quality.

But it is not only necessary but also noble; for we praise those who love their friends, and it is thought to be a fine thing to have many friends; and again we think it is the same people that are good men and are friends.

87. Friendly relations with one's neighbours, and the marks by which friendships are defined, seem to have proceeded from a man's relations to himself. For (1) we define a friend as one who wishes and does what is good, or seems so, for the sake of his friend, or (2) as one who wishes his friend to exist and live, for his sake; which mothers do to their children, and friends do who have come into conflict. And (3) others define him as one who lives with and (4) has the same tastes as another, or (5) one who grieves and rejoices with his friend; and this too is found in mothers most of all. It is by some one of these characteristics that friendship too is defined.

Now each of these is true of the good man's relation to himself (and of all other men in so far as they think themselves good; virtue and the good man seem, as has been said, to be the measure of every class of things). For his opinions are harmonious, and he desires the same things with all his soul; and therefore he wishes for himself what is good and what seems so, and does it (for it is characteristic of the good man to work out the good), and does so for his own sake (for he does it for the sake of the intellectual element in him, which is thought to be the man himself); and he wishes himself to live and be preserved, and especially the element by virtue of which he thinks. For existence is good to the virtuous man, and each man wishes himself what is good, while no one chooses to possess the whole world if he has first to become some one else (for that matter, even now God possesses the good); he wishes for this only on condition of being whatever he is; and the element that thinks would seem to be the individual man, or to be so more than any other element in him. And such a man wishes to live with himself; for he does so with pleasure, since the memories of his past acts are delightful and his hopes for the future are good, and therefore pleasant. His mind is well stored too with subjects of contemplation. And he grieves and rejoices, more than any other, with himself; for the same thing is always painful, and the same thing always pleasant, and not one thing at one time and another at another; he has, so to speak, nothing to repent of.

Therefore, since each of these characteristics belongs to the good man in relation to himself, and he is related to his friend as to himself (for his friend is another self), friendship too is thought to be one of these attributes, and those who have these attributes to be friends. Whether there is or is not friendship between a man and himself is a question we may dismiss for the present; there would seem to be friendship in so far as he is two or more, to judge from the aforementioned attributes of friendship, and from the fact that the extreme of friendship is likened to one's love for oneself.

But the attributes named seem to belong even to the

majority of men, poor creatures though they may be. Are we to say then that in so far as they are satisfied with themselves and think they are good, they share in these attributes? Certainly no one who is thoroughly bad and impious has these attributes, or even seems to do so. They hardly belong even to inferior people; for they are at variance with themselves, and have appetites for some things and rational desires for others. This is true, for instance, of incontinent people; for they choose, instead of the things they themselves think good, things that are pleasant but hurtful; while others again, through cowardice and laziness, shrink from doing what they think best for themselves. And those who have done many terrible deeds and are hated for their wickedness even shrink from life and destroy themselves. And wicked men seek for people with whom to spend their days, and shun themselves; for they remember many a grievous deed, and anticipate others like them, when they are by themselves, but when they are with others they forget. And having nothing lovable in them they have no feeling of love to themselves. Therefore also such men do not rejoice or grieve with themselves; for their soul is rent by faction, and one element in it by reason of its wickedness grieves when it abstains from certain acts, while the other part is pleased, and one draws them this way and the other that, as if they were pulling them in pieces. If a man cannot at the same time be pained and pleased, at all events after a short time he is pained *because* he was pleased, and he could have wished that these things had not been pleasant to him; for bad men are laden with repentance.

Therefore the bad man does not seem to be amicably disposed even to himself, because there is nothing in him to love; so that if to be thus is the height of wretchedness, we should strain every nerve to avoid wickedness and should endeavour to be good; for so and only so can one be either friendly to oneself or a friend to another.

88. If happiness is activity in accordance with virtue, it is reasonable that it should be in accordance with the highest virtue; and this will be that of the best thing in us. Whether it be reason or something else that is this element which is thought to be our natural ruler and guide and to take thought of things noble and divine, whether it be itself also divine or only the most divine element in us, the activity of this in accordance with its proper virtue will be perfect happiness. That this activity is contemplative we have already said.

Now this would seem to be in agreement both with what we said before and with the truth. For, firstly, this activity is the best (since not only is reason the best thing in us, but the objects of reason are the best of knowable objects); and, secondly, it is the most continuous, since we can contemplate truth more continuously than we can *do* anything. And we think happiness has pleasure mingled with it, but the activity of philosophic wisdom is admittedly the pleasantest of virtuous activities; at all events the pursuit of it is thought to offer pleasures marvellous for their purity and their enduringness, and it is to be expected that those who know will pass their time more pleasantly than those who inquire. And the self-sufficiency that is spoken of must belong most to the contemplative activity. For while a philosopher, as well as a just man or one possessing any other virtue, needs the necessaries of life, when they are sufficiently equipped with things of that sort the just man needs people towards whom and with whom he shall act justly, and the temperate man, the brave man, and each of the others is in the same case, but the philosopher, even when by himself, can contemplate truth, and the better the wiser he is; he can perhaps do so better if he has fellow-workers, but still he is the most self-sufficient. And this activity alone would seem to be loved for its own sake; for nothing arises from it apart from the contemplating, while from practical activities we gain more or less apart from the action. And happiness is thought to depend on leisure; for we are busy that we may have leisure, and make war that we may live in peace. Now the activity of the practical virtues is exhibited in political or military affairs, but the actions concerned with these seem to be unleisurely. Warlike actions are completely so (for no one chooses to be at war, or provokes war, for the sake of being at war; any one would seem absolutely murderous if he were to make enemies of his friends in order to bring about battle and slaughter); but the action of the statesman is also unleisurely, and—apart from the political action itself—aims at despotic power and honours, or at all events happiness, for him and his fellow-citizens— a happiness different from political action, and evidently sought as being different. So if among virtuous actions political and military actions are distinguished by nobility and greatness, and these are unleisurely and aim at an end and are not desirable for their own sake, but the activity of reason, which is contemplative, seems both to be superior in serious worth and to aim at no end beyond itself, and to have its pleasure proper to itself (and this augments the activity), and the self-sufficiency, leisureliness, unweariedness (so far as this is possible for man), and all the other attributes ascribed to the supremely happy man are evidently those connected with this activity, it follows that this will be the complete happiness of man, if it be allowed a complete term of life (for none of the attributes of happiness is *in*complete).

But such a life would be too high for man; for it is not in so far as he is man that he will live so, but in so far as something divine is present in him; and by so much as this is superior to our composite nature is its activity superior to that which is the exercise of the other kind of virtue. If reason is divine, then, in comparison with man, the life according to it is divine in comparison with human life. But we must not follow those who advise us, being men, to think of human things, and, being mortal, of mortal things, but must, so far as we can, make ourselves immortal, and strain every nerve to live in accordance with the best thing in us; for even if it be small in bulk, much more does it in power and worth surpass everything. This would seem, too, to be each man himself, since it is the authoritative and better part of him. It would be strange, then, if he were to choose not the life of his self but that of something else. And what we said before will apply now; that which is proper to each thing is by nature best and most pleasant for each thing; for man, therefore, the life according to reason is best and pleasantest, since reason more than anything else *is* man. This life therefore is also the happiest.

But in a secondary degree the life in accordance with the other kind of virtue is happy; for the activities in accordance with this befit our human estate. Just and brave acts, and other virtuous acts, we do in relation to each other, observing our respective duties with regard to contracts and services and all manner of actions and with regard to passions; and all of these seem to be typically human. Some of them seem even to arise from the body, and virtue of character to be in many ways bound up with the passions. Practical wisdom, too, is linked to virtue of character, and this to practical wisdom, since the principles of practical wisdom are in accordance with the moral virtues and rightness in morals is in accordance with practical wisdom. Being connected with the passions also, the moral virtues must belong to our composite nature; and the virtues of our composite nature are human; so, therefore, are the life and the happiness which correspond to these. The excellence of the reason is a thing apart; we must be content to say this much about it, for to describe it precisely is a task greater than our purpose requires. It would seem, however, also to need external equipment but little, or less than moral virtue does. Grant that both need the necessaries, and do so equally, even if the statesman's work is the more concerned with the body and things of that sort; for there will be little difference there; but in what they need for the exercise of their activities there will be much difference. . . .

But, being a man, one will also need external prosperity; for our nature is not self-sufficient for the purpose of contemplation, but our body also must be healthy and must have food and other attention. Still, we must not think that the man who is to be happy will need many things or great things, merely because he cannot be supremely happy without external goods; for self-sufficiency and action do not involve excess, and we can do noble acts without ruling earth and sea; for even with moderate advantages one can act virtuously.

89. Now some think that we are made good by nature, others by habituation, others by teaching. Nature's

part evidently does not depend on us, but as a result of some divine causes is present in those who are truly fortunate; while argument and teaching, we may suspect, are not powerful with all men, but the soul of the student must first have been cultivated by means of habits for noble joy and noble hatred, like earth which is to nourish the seed. For he who lives as passion directs will not hear argument that dissuades him, nor understand it if he does; and how can we persuade one in such a state to change his ways? And in general passion seems to yield not to argument but to force. The character, then, must somehow be there already with a kinship to virtue, loving what is noble and hating what is base.

But it is difficult to get from youth up a right training for virtue if one has not been brought up under right laws; for to live temperately and hardily is not pleasant to most people, especially when they are young. For this reason their nurture and occupations should be fixed by law; for they will not be painful when they have become customary. But it is surely not enough that when they are young they should get the right nurture and attention; since they must, even when they are grown up, practise and be habituated to them, we shall need laws for this as well, and generally speaking to cover the whole of life; for most people obey necessity rather than argument, and punishments rather than the sense of what is noble.

This is why some think that legislators ought to stimulate men to virtue and urge them forward by the motive of the noble, on the assumption that those who have been well advanced by the formation of habits will attend to such influences; and that punishments and penalties should be imposed on those who disobey and are of inferior nature, while the incurably bad should be completely banished. A god man (they think), since he lives with his mind fixed on what is noble, will submit to argument, while a bad man, whose desire is for pleasure, is corrected by pain like a beast of burden. This is, too, why they say the pains inflicted should be those that are most opposed to the pleasures such men love.

However that may be, if (as we have said) the man who is to be good must be well trained and habituated, and go on to spend his time in worthy occupations and neither willingly nor unwillingly do bad actions, and if this can be brought about if men live in accordance with a sort of reason and right order, provided this has force,—if this be so, the paternal command indeed has not the required force or compulsive power (nor in general has the command of one man, unless he be a king or something similar), but the law *has* compulsive power, while it is at the same time a rule proceeding from a sort of practical wisdom and reason. . . .

Now our predecessors have left the subject of legislation to us unexamined; it is perhaps best, therefore, that we should ourselves study it, and in general study the question of the constitution, in order to complete to the best of our ability our philosophy of human nature.

90. Every state is a community of some kind, and every community is established with a view to some good; for mankind always act in order to obtain that which they think good. But, if all communities aim at some good, the state or political community, which is the highest of all, and which embraces all the rest, aims at good in a greater degree than any other, and at the highest good.

Some people think that the qualifications of a statesman, king, householder, and master are the same, and that they differ, not in kind, but only in the number of their subjects. For example, the ruler over a few is called a master; over more, the manager of a household; over a still larger number, a statesman or king, as if there were no difference between a great household and a small state. The distinction which is made between the king and the statesman is as follows: When the government is personal, the ruler is a king; when, according to the rules of the political science, the citizens rule and are ruled in turn, then he is called a statesman.

But all this is a mistake; for governments differ in kind, as will be evident to any one who considers the matter according to the method which has hitherto guided us. As in other departments of science, so in politics, the compound should always be resolved into the simple elements or least parts of the whole. We must therefore look at the elements of which the state is composed, in order that we may see in what the different kinds of rule differ from one another, and whether any scientific result can be attained about each one of them.

He who thus considers things in their first growth and origin, whether a state or anything else, will obtain the clearest view of them. In the first place there must be a union of those who cannot exist without each other; namely, of male and female, that the race may continue (and this is a union which is formed, not of deliberate purpose, but because, in common with other animals and with plants, mankind have a natural desire to leave behind them an image of themselves), and of natural ruler and subject, that both may be preserved. For that which can foresee by the exercise of mind is by nature intended to be lord and master, and that which can with its body give effect to such foresight is a subject, and by nature a slave; hence master and slave have the same interest. Now nature has distinguished between the female and the slave. For she is not niggardly, like the smith who fashions the Delphian knife for many uses; she makes each thing for a single use, and every instrument is best made when intended for one and not for many uses. But among barbarians no distinction is made between women and slaves, because there is no natural ruler among them: they are a community of slaves, male and female. Wherefore the poets say:

'It is meet that Hellenes should rule over barbarians';

as if they thought that the barbarian and the slave were by nature one.

Out of these two relationships between man and woman, master and slave, the first thing to arise is the family, and Hesiod is right when he says:

'First house and wife and an ox for the plough',

for the ox is the poor man's slave. The family is the association established by nature for the supply of men's everyday wants, and the members of it are called by Charondas 'companions of the cupboard', and by Epimenides the Cretan, 'companions of the manger'. But when several families are united, and the association aims at something more than the supply of daily needs, the first society to be formed is the village. And the most natural form of the village appears to be that of a colony from the family, composed of the children and grandchildren, who are said to be 'suckled with the same milk'. And this is the reason why Hellenic states were originally governed by kings; because the Hellenes were under royal rule before they came together, as the barbarians still are. Every family is ruled by the eldest, and therefore in the colonies of the family the kingly form of government prevailed because they were of the same blood. As Homer says,

'Each one gives law to his children and to his wives.'

For they lived dispersedly, as was the manner in ancient times. Wherefore men say that the Gods have a king, because they themselves either are or were in ancient times under the rule of a king. For they imagine, not only the forms of the Gods, but their ways of life to be like their own.

When several villages are united in a single complete community, large enough to be nearly or quite self-sufficing, the state comes into existence, originating in the bare needs of life, and continuing in existence for the sake of a good life. And therefore, if the earlier forms of society are natural, so is the state, for it is the end of them, and the nature of a thing is its end. For what each thing is when fully developed, we call its nature, whether we are speaking of a man, a horse, or a family. Besides, the final cause and end of a thing is the best, and to be self-sufficing is the end and the best.

Hence it is evident that the state is a creation of nature, and that man is by nature a political animal. And he who by nature and not by mere accident is without a state, is either a bad man or above humanity; he is like the

'Tribeless, lawless, hearthless one,'

whom Homer denounces—the natural outcast is forthwith a lover of war; he may be compared to an isolated piece at draughts.

Now, that man is more of a political animal than bees or any other gregarious animals is evident. Nature, as we often say, makes nothing in vain, and man is the only animal whom she has endowed with the gift of speech. And whereas mere voice is but an indication of pleasure or pain, and is therefore found in other animals (for their nature attains to the perception of pleasure and pain and the intimation of them to one another, and no further), the power of speech is intended to set forth the expedient and inexpedient, and therefore likewise the just and the unjust. And it is a characteristic of man that he alone has any sense of good and evil, of just and unjust, and the like, and the association of living beings who have this sense makes a family and a state.

Further, the state is by nature clearly prior to the family and to the individual, since the whole is of necessity prior to the part; for example, if the whole body be destroyed, there will be no foot or hand, except in an equivocal sense, as we might speak of a stone hand; for when destroyed the hand will be no better than that. But things are defined by their working and power; and we ought not to say that they are the same when they no longer have their proper quality, but only that they have the same name. The proof that the state is a creation of nature and prior to the individual is that the individual, when isolated, is not self-sufficing; and therefore he is like a part in relation to the whole. But he who is unable to live in society, or who has no need because he is sufficient for himself, must be either a beast or a god: he is no part of a state. A social instinct is implanted in all men by nature, and yet he who first founded the state was the greatest of benefactors. For man, when perfected, is the best of animals, but, when separated from law and justice, he is the worst of all; since armed injustice is the more dangerous, and he is equipped at birth with arms, meant to be used by intelligence and virtue, which he may use for the worst ends. Wherefore, if he have not virtue, he is the most unholy and the most savage of animals, and the most full of lust and gluttony. But justice is the bond of men in states, for the administration of justice, which is the determination of what is just, is the principle of order in political society.

91. Let us first speak of master and slave, looking to the needs of practical life and also seeking to attain some better theory of their relation than exists at present. For some are of opinion that the rule of a master is a science, and that the management of a household, and the mastership of slaves, and the political and royal rule, as I was saying at the outset, are all the same. Others affirm that the rule of a master over slaves is contrary to nature, and that the distinction between slave and freeman exists by law only, and not by nature; and being an interference with nature is therefore unjust.

Property is a part of the household, and the art of acquiring property is a part of the art of managing the household; for no man can live well, or indeed live at all, unless he be provided with necessaries. And as in the arts which have a definite sphere the workers must have their own proper instruments for the accomplishment of their work, so it is in the management of a household. Now instruments are of various sorts; some are living, others lifeless; in the rudder, the pilot of a ship has a lifeless, in the look-out man, a living instrument; for in the arts the servant is a kind of instrument. Thus, too, a possession is an instrument for maintaining life. And so, in the arrangement of the family, a slave is a living possession, and property a number of such instruments; and the servant is himself an instrument which takes precedence of all other instruments. For if every instrument could accomplish its own work, obeying or anticipating the will of others, like the statues of Daedalus, or the tripods of Hephaestus, which, says the poet,

'of their own accord entered the assembly of the Gods';

if, in like manner, the shuttle would weave and the plectrum touch the lyre without a hand to guide them, chief workmen would not want servants, nor masters slaves. Here, however, another distinction must be drawn: the instruments commonly so called are instruments of production, whilst a possession is an instrument of action. The shuttle, for example, is not only of use; but something else is made by it, whereas of a garment or of a bed there is only the use. Further, as production and action are different in kind, and both require instruments, the instruments which they employ must likewise differ in kind. But life is action and not production, and therefore the slave is the minister of action. Again, a possession is spoken of as a part is spoken of; for the part is not only a part of something else, but wholly belongs to it; and this is also true of a possession. The master is only the master of the slave; he does not belong to him, whereas the slave is not only the slave of his master, but wholly belongs to him. Hence we see what is the nature and office of a slave; he who is by nature not his own but another's man, is by nature a slave; and he may be said to be another's man who, being a human being, is also a possession. And a possession may be defined as an instrument of action, separable from the possessor.

But is there any one thus intended by nature to be a slave, and for whom such a condition is expedient and right, or rather is not all slavery a violation of nature?

There is no difficulty in answering this question, on grounds both of reason and of fact. For that some should rule and others be ruled is a thing not only necessary, but expedient; from the hour of their birth, some are marked out for subjection, others for rule.

And there are many kinds both of rulers and subjects (and that rule is the better which is exercised over better subjects—for example, to rule over men is better than to rule over wild beasts; for the work is better which is executed by better workmen, and where one man rules and another is ruled, they may be said to have a work); for in all things which form a composite whole and which are made up of parts, whether continuous or discrete, a distinction between the ruling and the subject element comes to light. Such a duality exists in living creatures, but not in them only; it originates in the constitution of the universe; even in things which have no life there is a ruling principle, as in a musical mode. But we are wandering from the subject. We will therefore restrict ourselves to the living creature, which, in the first place, consists of soul and body: and of these two, the one is by nature the ruler, and the other the subject. But then we must look for the intentions of nature in things which retain their nature, and not in things which are corrupted. And therefore we must study the man who is in the most perfect state both of body and soul, for in him we shall see the true relation of the two; although in

bad or corrupted natures the body will often appear to
rule over the soul, because they are in an evil and unnatural condition.   At all events we may firstly observe in living creatures both a despotical and a constitutional rule; for the soul rules the body with a
despotical rule, whereas the intellect rules the appetites
with a constitutional and royal rule.   And it is clear
that the rule of the soul over the body, and of the mind
and the rational element over the passionate, is natural
and expedient; whereas the equality of the two or the
rule of the inferior is always hurtful.   The same holds
good of animals in relation to men; for tame animals
have a better nature than wild, and all tame animals
are better off when they are ruled by man; for then
they are preserved.   Again, the male is by nature superior, and the female inferior; and the one rules, and
the other is ruled; this principle, of necessity, extends
to all mankind.

Where then there is such a difference as that between
soul and body, or between men and animals (as in the
case of those whose business is to use their body, and
who can do nothing better), the lower sort are by nature
slaves, and it is better for them as for all inferiors that
they should be under the rule of a master.   For he who
can be, and therefore is, another's, and he who partici-
pates in rational principle enough to apprehend, but not
to have, such a principle, is a slave by nature.   Whereas
the lower animals cannot even apprehend a principle;
they obey their instincts.   And indeed the use made of
slaves and of tame animals is not very different; for both
with their bodies minister to the needs of life.   Nature
would like to distinguish between the bodies of freemen
and slaves, making the one strong for servile labour, the
other upright, and although useless for such services,
useful for political life in the arts both of war and

peace. But the opposite often happens—that some
have the souls and others have the bodies of freemen.
And doubtless if men differed from one another in the
mere forms of their bodies as much as the statues of
the Gods do from men, all would acknowledge that
the inferior class should be slaves of the superior.
And if this is true of the body, how much more just
that a similar distinction should exist in the soul? but
the beauty of the body is seen, whereas the beauty of
the soul is not seen. It is clear, then, that some men
are by nature free, and others slaves, and that for
these latter slavery is both expedient and right.

But that those who take the opposite view have in
a certain way right on their side, may be easily seen.
For the words slavery and slave are used in two senses.
There is a slave or slavery by law as well as by nature.
The law of which I speak is a sort of convention—the
law by which whatever is taken in war is supposed to
belong to the victors. But this right many jurists im-
peach, as they would an orator who brought forward an
unconstitutional measure: they detest the notion that,
because one man has the power of doing violence and is
superior in brute strength, another shall be his slave
and subject. Even among philosophers there is a difference of opinion. The origin of the dispute, and
what makes the views invade each other's territory, is
as follows: in some sense virtue, when furnished with
means, has actually the greatest power of exercising
force: and as superior power is only found where there
is superior excellence of some kind, power seems to
imply virtue, and the dispute to be simply one about
justice (for it is due to one party identifying justice
with goodwill, while the other identifies it with the
mere rule of the stronger). If these views are thus
set out separately, the other views have no force or

plausibility against the view that the superior in virtue ought to rule, or be master.

Others, clinging, as they think, simply to a principle of justice (for law and custom are a sort of justice), assume that slavery in accordance with the custom of war is justified by law, but at the same moment they deny this. For what if the cause of the war be unjust? And again, no one would ever say that he is a slave who is unworthy to be a slave. Were this the case, men of the highest rank would be slaves and the children of slaves if they or their parents chance to have been taken captive and sold. Wherefore Hellenes do not like to call Hellenes slaves, but confine the term to barbarians. Yet, in using this language, they really mean the natural slave of whom we spoke at first; for it must be admitted that some are slaves everywhere, others nowhere. The same principle applies to nobility. Hellenes regard themselves as noble everywhere, and not only in their own country, but they deem the barbarians noble only when at home, thereby implying that there are two sorts of nobility and freedom, the one absolute, the other relative. The Helen of Theodectes says:

'Who would presume to call me servant who am on both sides sprung from the stem of the Gods?'

What does this mean but that they distinguish freedom and slavery, noble and humble birth, by the two principles of good and evil? They think that as men and animals beget men and animals, so from good men a good man springs. But this is what nature, though she may intend it, cannot always accomplish.

We see then that there is some foundation for this difference of opinion, and that all are not either slaves by nature or freemen by nature, and also that there is in some cases a marked distinction between the two classes, rendering it expedient and right for the one to be slaves and the others to be masters: the one practising obedience, the others exercising the authority and lordship which nature intended them to have.

92. Next let us consider what should be our arrangements about property: should the citizens of the perfect state have their possessions in common or not? This question may be discussed separately from the enactments about women and children. Even supposing that the women and children belong to individuals, according to the custom which is at present universal, may there not be an advantage in having and using possessions in common? Three cases are possible: (1) the soil may be appropriated, but the produce may be thrown for consumption into the common stock; and this is the practice of some nations. Or (2), the soil may be common, and may be cultivated in common, but the produce divided among individuals for their private use; this is a form of common property which is said to exist among certain barbarians. Or (3), the soil and the produce may be alike common.

When the husbandmen are not the owners, the case will be different and easier to deal with; but when they till the ground for themselves the question of ownership will give a world of trouble. If they do not share equally in enjoyments and toils, those who labour much and get little will necessarily complain of those who labour little and receive or consume much. But indeed there is always a difficulty in men living together and having all human relations in common, but especially in their having common property. The partnerships of fellow-travellers are an example to the point; for they generally fall out over everyday matters and quarrel about any trifle which turns up. So with ser-

vants: we are most liable to take offence at those with
whom we most frequently come into contact in daily life.

These are only some of the disadvantages which attend the community of property; the present arrangement, if improved as it might be by good customs and
laws, would be far better, and would have the advantages of both systems. Property should be in a certain sense common, but, as a general rule, private;
for, when every one has a distinct interest, men will
not complain of one another, and they will make more
progress, because every one will be attending to his
own business. And yet by reason of goodness, and in
respect of use, 'Friends', as the proverb says, 'will
have all things common.' Even now there are traces of
such a principle, showing that it is not impracticable,
but, in well-ordered states, exists already to a certain
extent and may be carried further. For, although
every man has his own property, some things he will
place at the disposal of his friends, while of others he
shares the use with them. The Lacedaemonians, for
example, use one another's slaves, and horses, and
dogs, as if they were their own; and when they lack
provisions on a journey, they appropriate what they
find in the fields throughout the country. It is clearly
better that property should be private, but the use of
it common; and the special business of the legislator
is to create in men this benevolent disposition. Again,
how immeasurably greater is the pleasure, when a man
feels a thing to be his own; for surely the love of self
is a feeling implanted by nature and not given in vain,
although selfishness is rightly censured; this, however,
is not the mere love of self, but the love of self in
excess, like the miser's love of money; for all, or almost
all, men love money and other such objects in a measure.
And further, there is the greatest pleasure in doing

a kindness or service to friends or guests or companions, which can only be rendered when a man has private property. These advantages are lost by excessive unification of the state. The exhibition of two virtues, besides, is visibly annihilated in such a state: first, temperance towards women (for it is an honourable action to abstain from another's wife for temperance sake; secondly, liberality in the matter of property. No one, when men have all things in common, will any longer set an example of liberality or do any liberal action; for liberality consists in the use which is made of property.

Such legislation may have a specious appearance of benevolence; men readily listen to it, and are easily induced to believe that in some wonderful manner everybody will become everybody's friend, especially when some one is heard denouncing the evils now existing in states, suits about contracts, convictions for perjury, flatteries of rich men and the like, which are said to arise out of the possession of private property. These evils, however, are due to a very different cause —the wickedness of human nature. Indeed, we see that there is much more quarrelling among those who have all things in common, though there are not many of them when compared with the vast numbers who have private property.

Again, we ought to reckon, not only the evils from which the citizens will be saved, but also the advantages which they will lose. The life which they are to lead appears to be quite impracticable. The error of Socrates must be attributed to the false notion of unity from which he starts. Unity there should be, both of the family and of the state, but in some respects only. For there is a point at which a state may attain such a degree of unity as to be no longer a state,

or at which, without actually ceasing to exist, it will
become an inferior state, like harmony passing into
unison, or rhythm which has been reduced to a single
foot. The state, as I was saying, is a plurality, which
should be united and made into a community by education; and it is strange that the author of a system of
education which he thinks will make the state virtuous,
should expect to improve his citizens by regulations
of this sort, and not by philosophy or by customs and
laws, like those which prevail at Sparta and Crete
respecting common meals, whereby the legislator has
made property common. Let us remember that we
should not disregard the experience of ages; in the
multitude of years these things, if they were good,
would certainly not have been unknown; for almost
everything has been found out, although sometimes
they are not put together; in other cases men do not
use the knowledge which they have.

93. In the opinion of some, the regulation of property
is the chief point of all, that being the question upon
which all revolutions turn. This danger was recognized by Phaleas of Chalcedon, who was the first to
affirm that the citizens of a state ought to have equal
possessions. He thought that in a new colony the
equalization might be accomplished without difficulty,
not so easily when a state was already established;
and that then the shortest way of compassing the desired end would be for the rich to give and not to
receive marriage portions, and for the poor not to
give but to receive them.

Plato in the *Laws* was of opinion that, to a certain
extent, accumulation should be allowed, forbidding, as
I have already observed, any citizen to possess more
than five times the minimum qualification. But those

who make such laws should remember what they are apt to forget,—that the legislator who fixes the amount of property should also fix the number of children; for if the children are too many for the property, the law must be broken. And, besides the violation of the law, it is a bad thing that many from being rich should become poor; for men of ruined fortunes are sure to stir up revolutions. That the equalization of property exercises an influence on political society was clearly understood even by some of the old legislators. Laws were made by Solon and others prohibiting an individual from possessing as much land as he pleased; and there are other laws in states which forbid the sale of property: among the Locrians, for example, there is a law that a man is not to sell his property unless he can prove unmistakably that some misfortune has befallen him. Again, there have been laws which enjoin the preservation of the original lots. Such a law existed in the island of Leucas, and the abrogation of it made the constitution too democratic, for the rulers no longer had the prescribed qualification. Again, where there is equality of property, the amount may be either too large or too small, and the possessor may be living either in luxury or penury. Clearly, then, the legislator ought not only to aim at the equalization of properties, but at moderation in their amount. Further, if he prescribe this moderate amount equally to all, he will be no nearer the mark; for it is not the possessions but the desires of mankind which require to be equalized, and this is impossible, unless a sufficient education is provided by the laws. But Phaleas will probably reply that this is precisely what he means; and that, in his opinion, there ought to be in states, not only equal property, but equal education. Still he should tell us what will be the character of his

education; there is no use in having one and the same
for all, if it is of a sort that predisposes men to avarice,
or ambition, or both. Moreover, civil troubles arise, not
only out of the inequality of property, but out of the
inequality of honour, though in opposite ways. For
the common people quarrel about the inequality of
property, the higher class about the equality of honour;
as the poet says,—

'The bad and good alike in honour share.'

There are crimes of which the motive is want; and
for these Phaleas expects to find a cure in the equalization of property, which will take away from a man the
temptation to be a highwayman, because he is hungry or
cold. But want is not the sole incentive to crime; men
also wish to enjoy themselves and not to be in a state
of desire—they wish to cure some desire, going beyond
the necessities of life, which preys upon them; nay, this
is not the only reason—they may desire superfluities
in order to enjoy pleasures unaccompanied with pain,
and therefore they commit crimes.

Now what is the cure of these three disorders? Of
the first, moderate possessions and occupation; of the
second, habits of temperance; as to the third, if any
desire pleasures which depend on themselves, they will
find the satisfaction of their desires nowhere but in
philosophy; for all other pleasures we are dependent
on others. The fact is that the greatest crimes are
caused by excess and not by necessity. Men do not
become tyrants in order that they may not suffer cold;
and hence great is the honour bestowed, not on him
who kills a thief, but on him who kills a tyrant. Thus
we see that the institutions of Phaleas avail only against
petty crimes.

There is another objection to them. They are chiefly
designed to promote the internal welfare of the state.

But the legislator should consider also its relation to neighbouring nations, and to all who are outside of it. The government must be organized with a view to military strength; and of this he has said not a word. And so with respect to property: there should not only be enough to supply the internal wants of the state, but also to meet dangers coming from without. The property of the state should not be so large that more powerful neighbours may be tempted by it, while the owners are unable to repel the invaders; nor yet so small that the state is unable to maintain a war even against states of equal power, and of the same character. Phaleas has not laid down any rule; but we should bear in mind that abundance of wealth is an advantage. The best limit will probably be, that a more powerful neighbour must have no inducement to go to war with you by reason of the excess of your wealth, but only such as he would have had if you had possessed less. There is a story that Eubulus, when Autophradates was going to besiege Atarneus, told him to consider how long the operation would take, and then reckon up the cost which would be incurred in the time. 'For', said he, 'I am willing for a smaller sum than that to leave Atarneus at once.' These words of Eubulus made an impression on Autophradates, and he desisted from the siege.

The equalization of property is one of the things that tend to prevent the citizens from quarrelling. Not that the gain in this direction is very great. For the nobles will be dissatisfied because they think themselves worthy of more than an equal share of honours; and this is often found to be a cause of sedition and revolution. And the avarice of mankind is insatiable; at one time two obols was pay enough; but now, when this sum has become customary, men always want more

and more without end; for it is of the nature of desire
not to be satisfied, and most men live only for the grati-
fication of it.   The beginning of reform is not so much
to equalize property as to train the nobler sort of natures not to desire more, and to prevent the lower from
getting more; that is to say, they must be kept down,
but not ill-treated.

94. The conclusion is evident: that governments which
have a regard to the common interest are constituted
in accordance with strict principles of justice, and are
therefore true forms; but those which regard only the
interest of the rulers are all defective and perverted
forms, for they are despotic, whereas a state is a community of freemen.

Having determined these points, we have next to
consider how many forms of government there are, and
what they are; and in the first place what are the
true forms, for when they are determined the perversions of them will at once be apparent.   The words
constitution and government have the same meaning,
and the government, which is the supreme authority
in states, must be in the hands of one, or of a few, or
of the many.   The true forms of government, therefore,
are those in which the one, or the few, or the many,
govern with a view to the common interest; but governments which rule with a view to the private interest,
whether of the one, or of the few, or of the many, are
perversions.   For the members of a state, if they are
truly citizens, ought to participate in its advantages.
Of forms of government in which one rules, we call that
which regards the common interests, kingship or royalty; that in which more than one, but not many, rule,
aristocracy; and it is so called, either because the rulers
are the best men, or because they have at heart the

best interests of the state and of the citizens. But when the citizens at large administer the state for the common interest, the government is called by the generic name,—a constitution. And there is a reason for this use of language. One man or a few may excel in virtue; but as the number increases it becomes more difficult for them to attain perfection in every kind of virtue, though they may in military virtue, for this is found in the masses. Hence in a constitutional government the fighting-men have the supreme power, and those who possess arms are the citizens.

Of the above-mentioned forms, the perversions are as follows:—of royalty, tyranny; of aristocracy, oligarchy; of constitutional government, democracy. For tyranny is a kind of monarchy which has in view the interest of the monarch only; oligarchy has in view the interest of the wealthy; democracy, of the needy: none of them the common good of all.

95. Let us begin by considering the common definitions of oligarchy and democracy, and what is justice oligarchical and democratical. For all men cling to justice of some kind, but their conceptions are imperfect and they do not express the whole idea. For example, justice is thought by them to be, and is, equality, not, however, for all, but only for equals. And inequality is thought to be, and is, justice; neither is this for all, but only for unequals. When the persons are omitted, then men judge erroneously. The reason is that they are passing judgment on themselves, and most people are bad judges in their own case. And whereas justice implies a relation to persons as well as to things, and a just distribution, as I have already said in the *Ethics,* implies the same ratio between the persons and between the things, they agree about the equality of the things,

but dispute about the equality of the persons, chiefly for the reason which I have just given,—because they are bad judges in their own affairs; and secondly, because both the parties to the argument are speaking of a limited and partial justice, but imagine themselves to be speaking of absolute justice. For the one party, if they are unequal in one respect, for example wealth, consider themselves to be unequal in all; and the other party, if they are equal in one respect, for example free birth, consider themselves to be equal in all. But they leave out the capital point. For if men met and associated out of regard to wealth only, their share in the state would be proportioned to their property, and the oligarchical doctrine would then seem to carry the day. It would not be just that he who paid one mina should have the same share of a hundred minae, whether of the principal or of the profits, as he who paid the remaining ninety-nine. But a state exists for the sake of a good life, and not for the sake of life only: if life only were the object, slaves and brute animals might form a state, but they cannot, for they have no share in happiness or in a life of free choice. Nor does a state exist for the sake of alliance and security from injustice, nor yet for the sake of exchange and mutual intercourse; for then the Tyrrhenians and the Carthaginians, and all who have commercial treaties with one another, would be the citizens of one state. True, they have agreements about imports, and engagements that they will do no wrong to one another, and written articles of alliance. But there are no magistracies common to the contracting parties who will enforce their engagements; different states have each their own magistracies. Nor does one state take care that the citizens of the other are such as they ought to be, nor see that those who come under the terms

of the treaty do no wrong or wickedness at all, but
only that they do no injustice to one another. Whereas,
those who care for good government take into consideration virtue and vice in states. Whence it may be
further inferred that virtue must be the care of a state
which is truly so called, and not merely enjoys the
name: for without this end the community becomes a
mere alliance which differs only in place from alliances
of which the members live apart; and law is only a convention, 'a surety to one another of justice', as the
sophist Lycophron says, and has no real power to make
the citizens good and just.

This is obvious; for suppose distinct places, such
as Corinth and Megara, to be brought together so that
their walls touched, still they would not be one city,
not even if the citizens had the right to intermarry,
which is one of the rights peculiarly characteristic of
states. Again, if men dwelt at a distance from one
another, but not so far off as to have no intercourse,
and there were laws among them that they should not
wrong each other in their exchanges, neither would this
be a state. Let us suppose that one man is a carpenter,
another a husbandman, another a shoemaker, and so on,
and that their number is ten thousand: nevertheless,
if they have nothing in common but exchange, alliance,
and the like, that would not constitute a state. Why
is this? Surely not because they are at a distance
from one another: for even supposing that such a community were to meet in one place, but that each man
had a house of his own, which was in a manner his
state, and that they made alliance with one another,
but only against evil-doers; still an accurate thinker
would not deem this to be a state, if their intercourse
with one another was of the same character after as
before their union. It is clear then that a state is not

a mere society, having a common place, established for the prevention of mutual crime and for the sake of exchange. These are conditions without which a state cannot exist; but all of them together do not constitute a state, which is a community of families and aggregations of families in well-being, for the sake of a perfect and self-sufficing life. Such a community can only be established among those who live in the same place and intermarry. Hence arise in cities family connexions, brotherhoods, common sacrifices, amusements which draw men together. But these are created by friendship, for the will to live together is friendship. The end of the state is the good life, and these are the means towards it. And the state is the union of families and villages in a perfect and self-sufficing life, by which we mean a happy and honourable life.

Our conclusion, then, is that political society exists for the sake of noble actions, and not of mere companionship. Hence they who contribute most to such a society have a greater share in it than those who have the same or a greater freedom or nobility of birth but are inferior to them in political virtue; or than those who exceed them in wealth but are surpassed by them in virtue.

From what has been said it will be clearly seen that all the partisans of different forms of government speak of a part of justice only.

96. We have now to inquire what is the best constitution for most states, and the best life for most men, neither assuming a standard of virtue which is above ordinary persons, nor an education which is exceptionally favoured by nature and circumstances, nor yet an ideal state which is an aspiration only, but having regard to the life in which the majority are able to share, and

to the form of government which states in general can
attain. As to those aristocracies, as they are called, of
which we were just now speaking, they either lie beyond the possibilities of the greater number of states,
or they approximate to the so-called constitutional government, and therefore need no separate discussion.
And in fact the conclusion at which we arrive respecting all these forms rests upon the same grounds. For
if what was said in the *Ethics* is true, that the happy life
is the life according to virtue lived without impediment,
and that virtue is a mean, then the life which is in a
mean, and in a mean attainable by every one, must be
the best. And the same principles of virtue and vice
are characteristic of cities and of constitutions; for the
constitution is in a figure the life of the city.

Now in all states there are three elements: one class
is very rich, another very poor, and a third in a mean.
It is admitted that moderation and the mean are best,
and therefore it will clearly be best to possess the gifts
of fortune in moderation; for in that condition of life
men are most ready to follow rational principle. But
he who greatly excels in beauty, strength, birth, or
wealth, or on the other hand who is very poor, or very
weak, or very much disgraced, finds it difficult to follow
rational principle. Of these two the one sort grow into
violent and great criminals, the others into rogues and
petty rascals. And two sorts of offences correspond
to them, the one committed from violence, the other from
roguery. Again, the middle class is least likely to
shrink from rule, or to be over-ambitious for it; both
of which are injuries to the state. Again, those who
have too much of the goods of fortune, strength, wealth,
friends, and the like, are neither willing nor able to
submit to authority. The evil begins at home; for
when they are boys, by reason of the luxury in which

they are brought up, they never learn, even at school, the habit of obedience. On the other hand, the very poor, who are in the opposite extreme, are too degraded. So that the one class cannot obey, and can only rule despotically; the other knows not how to command and must be ruled like slaves. Thus arises a city, not of freemen, but of masters and slaves, the one despising, the other envying; and nothing can be more fatal to friendship and good fellowship in states than this: for good fellowship springs from friendship; when men are at enmity with one another, they would rather not even share the same path. But a city ought to be composed, as far as possible, of equals and similars; and these are generally the middle classes. Wherefore the city which is composed of middle-class citizens is necessarily best constituted in respect of the elements of which we say the fabric of the state naturally consists. And this is the class of citizens which is most secure in a state, for they do not, like the poor, covet their neighbours' goods; nor do others covet theirs, as the poor covet the goods of the rich; and as they neither plot against others, nor are themselves plotted against, they pass through life safely. Wisely then did Phocylides pray,—'Many things are best in the mean; I desire to be of a middle condition in my city.'

Thus it is manifest that the best political community is formed by citizens of the middle class, and that those states are likely to be well-administered, in which the middle class is large, and stronger if possible than both the other classes, or at any rate than either singly; for the addition of the middle class turns the scale, and prevents either of the extremes from being dominant. . . .

The portion of the state which desires the permanence of the constitution ought to be stronger than that which desires the reverse. Now every city is composed of quality and quantity. By quality I mean freedom, wealth, education, good birth, and by quantity, superiority of numbers. Quality may exist in one of the classes which make up the state, and quantity in the other. For example, the meanly-born may be more in number than the well-born, or the poor than the rich, yet they may not so much exceed in quantity as they fall short in quality; and therefore there must be a comparison of quantity and quality. Where the number of the poor is more than proportioned to the wealth of the rich, there will naturally be a democracy, varying in form with the sort of people who compose it in each case. If, for example, the husbandmen exceed in number, the first form of democracy will then arise; if the artisans and labouring class the last; and so with the intermediate forms. But where the rich and the notables exceed in quality more than they fall short in quantity, there oligarchy arises, similarly assuming various forms according to the kind of superiority possessed by the oligarchs.

The legislators should always include the middle class in his government; if he makes his laws oligarchical, to the middle class let him look; if he makes them democratical, he should equally by his laws try to attach this class to the state. There only can the government ever be stable where the middle class exceeds one or both of the others, and in that case there will be no fear that the rich will unite with the poor against the rulers. For neither of them will ever be willing to serve the other, and if they look for some form of government more suitable to both, they will find none better than this, for the rich and the poor will never consent to rule in turn, because they mistrust one another. The arbiter is always the one trusted, and he who is in the middle is an arbiter. The more perfect the admixture of the political elements, the more lasting will be the constitution.

97. If we are right in our view, and happiness is assumed to be virtuous activity, the active life will be the best, both for every city collectively, and for individuals. Not that a life of action must necessarily have relation to others, as some persons think, nor are those ideas only to be regarded as practical which are pursued for the sake of practical results, but much more the thoughts and contemplations which are independent and complete in themselves; since virtuous activity, and therefore a certain kind of action, is an end, and even in the case of external actions the directing mind is most truly said to act. Neither, again, is it necessary that states which are cut off from others and choose to live alone should be inactive; for activity, as well as other things, may take place by sections; there are many ways in which the sections of a state act upon one another. The same thing is equally true of every individual. If this were otherwise, God and the universe, who have no external actions over and above their own energies, would be far enough from perfection. Hence it is evident that the same life is best for each individual, and for states and for mankind collectively.

Thus far by way of introduction. In what has preceded I have discussed other forms of government; in what remains the first point to be considered is what should be the conditions of the ideal or perfect state; for the perfect state cannot exist without a due supply of the means of life. And therefore we must presuppose many purely imaginary conditions, but nothing impossible. There will be a certain number of citizens,

a country in which to place them, and the like. As
the weaver or shipbuilder or any other artisan must
have the material proper for his work (and in proportion as this is better prepared, so will the result of
his art be nobler), so the statesman or legislator must
also have the materials suited to him.

First among the materials required by the statesman
is population: he will consider what should be the
number and character of the citizens, and then what
should be the size and character of the country. Most
persons think that a state in order to be happy ought
to be large; but even if they are right, they have no
idea what is a large and what a small state. For they
judge of the size of the city by the number of the
inhabitants; whereas they ought to regard, not their
number, but their power. A city too, like an individual,
has a work to do; and that city which is best adapted
to the fulfilment of its work is to be deemed greatest,
in the same sense of the word great in which Hippocrates might be called greater, not as a man, but as
a physician, than some one else who was taller. And
even if we reckon greatness by numbers, we ought
not to include everybody, for there must always be
in cities a multitude of slaves and sojourners and foreigners; but we should include those only who are
members of the state, and who form an essential part
of it. The number of the latter is a proof of the
greatness of a city; but a city which produces numerous
artisans and comparatively few soldiers cannot be great,
for a great city is not to be confounded with a populous
one. Moreover, experience shows that a very populous
city can rarely, if ever, be well governed; since all
cities which have a reputation for good government
have a limit of population. We may argue on grounds
of reason, and the same result will follow. For law

is order, and good law is good order; but a very great multitude cannot be orderly: to introduce order into the unlimited is the work of a divine power—of such a power as holds together the universe. Beauty is realized in number and magnitude, and the state which combines magnitude with good order must necessarily be the most beautiful. To the size of states there is a limit, as there is to other things, plants, animals, implements; for none of these retain their natural power when they are too large or too small, but they either wholly lose their nature, or are spoiled. For example, a ship which is only a span long will not be a ship at all, nor a ship a quarter of a mile long; yet there may be a ship of a certain size, either too large or too small, which will still be a ship, but bad for sailing. In like manner a state when composed of too few is not, as a state ought to be, self-sufficing; when of too many, though self-sufficing in all mere necessaries, as a nation may be, it is not a state, being almost incapable of constitutional government. For who can be the general of such a vast multitude, or who the herald, unless he have the voice of a Stentor?

A state, then, only begins to exist when it has attained a population sufficient for a good life in the political community: it may indeed, if it somewhat exceed this number, be a greater state. But, as I was saying, there must be a limit. What should be the limit will be easily ascertained by experience. For both governors and governed have duties to perform; the special functions of a governor are to command and to judge. But if the citizens of a state are to judge and to distribute offices according to merit, then they must know each other's characters; where they do not possess this knowledge, both the election to offices and the decision of lawsuits will go wrong. When the population is very large they are manifestly settled at haphazard, which clearly ought not to be. Besides, in an over-populous state foreigners and metics will readily acquire the rights of citizens, for who will find them out? Clearly then the best limit of the population of a state is the largest number which suffices for the purposes of life, and can be taken in at a single view.

98. Since we are here speaking of the best form of government, i.e. that under which the state will be most happy (and happiness, as has been already said, cannot exist without virtue), it clearly follows that in the state which is best governed and possesses men who are just absolutely, and not merely relatively to the principle of the constitution, the citizens must not lead the life of mechanics or tradesmen, for such a life is ignoble and inimical to virtue. Neither must they be husbandmen, since leisure is necessary both for the development of virtue and for the performance of political duties.

Again, there is in a state a class of warriors, and another of councillors, who advise about the expedient and determine matters of law, and these seem in an especial manner parts of a state. Now, should these two classes be distinguished, or are both functions to be assigned to the same persons? Here again there is no difficulty in seeing that both functions will in one way belong to the same, in another, to different persons. To different persons in so far as these employments are suited to different primes of life, for the one requires wisdom and the other strength. But on the other hand, since it is an impossible thing that those who are able to use or to resist force should be willing to remain always in subjection, from this point of view the persons are the same; for those who carry arms can always determine the fate of the constitution. It remains therefore that both functions should be entrusted by the ideal constitution to the same persons, not, however, at the same time, but in the order prescribed by nature, who has given to young men strength and to older men wisdom. Such a distribution of duties will be expedient and also just, and is founded upon a principle of conformity to merit. Besides, the ruling class should be the owners of property, for they are citizens, and as citizens of a state should be in good circumstances; whereas mechanics or any other class which is not a producer of virtue have no share in the state. This follows from our first principle, for happiness cannot exist without virtue, and a city is not to be termed happy in regard to a portion of the citizens, but in regard to them all. And clearly property should be in their hands, since the husbandmen will of necessity be slaves or barbarian Perioeci.

Of the classes enumerated there remain only the priests, and the manner in which their office is to be regulated is obvious. No husbandman or mechanic should be appointed to it; for the Gods should receive honour from the citizens only. Now since the body of the citizens is divided into two classes, the warriors and the councillors, and it is beseeming that the worship of the Gods should be duly performed, and also a rest provided in their service for those who from age have given up active life, to the old men of these two classes should be assigned the duties of the priesthood.

We have shown what are the necessary conditions, and what the parts of a state: husbandmen, craftsmen, and labourers of all kinds are necessary to the existence of states, but the parts of the state are the warriors and councillors. And these are distinguished severally from one another, the distinction being in some cases permanent, in others not.

99. We have already said that the city should be open to the land and to the sea, and to the whole country as far as possible. In respect of the place itself our wish would be that its situation should be fortunate in four things. The first, health—this is a necessity: cities which lie towards the east, and are blown upon by winds coming from the east, are the healthiest; next in healthfulness are those which are sheltered from the north wind, for they have a milder winter. The site of the city should likewise be convenient both for political administration and for war. With a view to the latter it should afford easy egress to the citizens, and at the same time be inaccessible and difficult of capture to enemies. There should be a natural abundance of springs and fountains in the town, or, if there is a deficiency of them, great reservoirs may be established for the collection of rain-water, such as will not fail when the inhabitants are cut off from the country by war. Special care should be taken of the health of the inhabitants, which will depend chiefly on the healthiness of the locality and of the quarter to which they are exposed, and secondly, on the use of pure water; this latter point is by no means a secondary consideration. For the elements which we use most and oftenest for the support of the body contribute most to health, and among these are water and air. Wherefore, in all wise states, if there is a want of pure water, and the supply is not all equally good, the drinking water ought to be separated from that which is used for other purposes.

As to strongholds, what is suitable to different forms of government varies: thus an acropolis is suited to an oligarchy or a monarchy, but a plain to a democracy;

neither to an aristocracy, but rather a number of strong places. The arrangement of private houses is considered to be more agreeable and generally more convenient, if the streets are regularly laid out after the modern fashion which Hippodamus introduced, but for security in war the antiquated mode of building, which made it difficult for strangers to get out of a town and for assailants to find their way in, is preferable. A city should therefore adopt both plans of building: it is possible to arrange the houses irregularly, as husbandmen plant their vines in what are called 'clumps'. The whole town should not be laid out in straight lines, but only certain quarters and regions; thus security and beauty will be combined.

As to walls, those who say that cities making any pretension to military virtue should not have them, are quite out of date in their notions; and they may see the cities which prided themselves on this fancy confuted by facts. True, there is little courage shown in seeking for safety behind a rampart when an enemy is similar in character and not much superior in number; but the superiority of the besiegers may be and often is too much both for ordinary human valour and for that which is found only in a few; and if they are to be saved and to escape defeat and outrage, the strongest wall will be the truest soldierly precaution, more especially now that missiles and siege engines have been brought to such perfection. To have no walls would be as foolish as to choose a site for a town in an exposed country, and to level the heights; or as if an individual were to leave his house unwalled, lest the inmates should become cowards. Nor must we forget that those who have their cities surrounded by walls may either take advantage of them or not, but cities which are unwalled have no choice.

If our conclusions are just, not only should cities have walls, but care should be taken to make them ornamental, as well as useful for warlike purposes, and adapted to resist modern inventions. For as the assailants of a city do all they can to gain an advantage, so the defenders should make use of any means of defence which have been already discovered, and should devise and invent others, for when men are well prepared no enemy even thinks of attacking them.

As the walls are to be divided by guard-houses and towers built at suitable intervals, and the body of citizens must be distributed at common tables, the idea will naturally occur that we should establish some of the common tables in the guard-houses. These might be arranged as has been suggested; while the principal common tables of the magistrates will occupy a suitable place, and there also will be the buildings appropriated to religious worship except in the case of those rites which the law or the Pythian oracle has restricted to a special locality. The site should be a spot seen far and wide, which gives due elevation to virtue and towers over the neighbourhood. Below this spot should be established an agora, such as that which the Thessalians call the 'freemen's agora'; from this all trade should be excluded, and no mechanic, husbandman, or any such person allowed to enter, unless he be summoned by the magistrates. It would be a charming use of the place, if the gymnastic exercises of the elder men were performed there. For in this noble practice different ages should be separated, and some of the magistrates should stay with the boys, while the grown-up men remain with the magistrates; for the presence of the magistrates is the best mode of inspiring true modesty and ingenuous fear. There should also be a traders' agora, distinct and apart from the other, in a situation which is convenient for the reception of goods both by sea and land.

But in speaking of the magistrates we must not forget another section of the citizens, viz. the priests, for whom public tables should likewise be provided in their proper place near the temples. The magistrates who deal with contracts, indictments, summonses, and the like, and those who have the care of the agora and of the city respectively, ought to be established near an agora and some public place of meeting; the neighbourhood of the traders' agora will be a suitable spot; the upper agora we devote to the life of leisure, the other is intended for the necessities of trade.

The same order should prevail in the country, for there too the magistrates, called by some 'Inspectors of Forests' and by others 'Wardens of the Country', must have guard-houses and common tables while they are on duty; temples should also be scattered throughout the country, dedicated, some to Gods, and some to heroes.

But it would be a waste of time for us to linger over details like these. The difficulty is not in imagining but in carrying them out. We may talk about them as much as we like, but the execution of them will depend upon fortune. Wherefore let us say no more about these matters for the present.

100. No one will doubt that the legislator should direct his attention above all to the education of youth; for the neglect of education does harm to the constitution. The citizen should be moulded to suit the form of government under which he lives. For each government has a peculiar character which originally formed and which continues to preserve it. The character of democracy creates democracy, and the character of oli-

garchy creates oligarchy; and always the better the character, the better the government.

Again, for the exercise of any faculty or art a previous training and habituation are required; clearly therefore for the practice of virtue. And since the whole city has one end, it is manifest that education should be one and the same for all, and that it should be public, and not private,—not as at present, when every one looks after his own children separately, and gives them separate instruction of the sort which he thinks best; the training in things which are of common interest should be the same for all. Neither must we suppose that any one of the citizens belongs to himself, for they all belong to the state, and are each of them a part of the state, and the care of each part is inseparable from the care of the whole. In this particular as in some others the Lacedaemonians are to be praised, for they take the greatest pains about their children, and make education the business of the state.

That education should be regulated by law and should be an affair of state is not to be denied, but what should be the character of this public education, and how young persons should be educated, are questions which remain to be considered. As things are, there is disagreement about the subjects. For mankind are by no means agreed about the things to be taught, whether we look to virtue or the best life. Neither is it clear whether education is more concerned with intellectual or with moral virtue. The existing practice is perplexing; no one knows on what principle we should proceed—should the useful in life, or should virtue, or should the higher knowledge, be the aim of our training; all three opinions have been entertained. Again, about the means there is no agreement; for different persons, starting with different ideas about the nature of virtue, naturally disagree about the practice of it. There can be no doubt that children should be taught those useful things which are really necessary, but not all useful things; for occupations are divided into liberal and illiberal; and to young children should be imparted only such kinds of knowledge as will be useful to them without vulgarizing them. And any occupation, art, or science, which makes the body or soul or mind of the freeman less fit for the practice or exercise of virtue, is vulgar; wherefore we call those arts vulgar which tend to deform the body, and likewise all paid employments, for they absorb and degrade the mind. There are also some liberal arts quite proper for a freeman to acquire, but only in a certain degree, and if he attend to them too closely, in order to attain perfection in them, the same evil effects will follow. The object also which a man sets before him makes a great difference; if he does or learns anything for his own sake or for the sake of his friends, or with a view to excellence, the action will not appear illiberal; but if done for the sake of others, the very same action will be thought menial and servile. The received subjects of instruction, as I have already remarked, are partly of a liberal and partly of an illiberal character.

The customary branches of education are in number four; they are—(1) reading and writing, (2) gymnastic exercises, (3) music, to which is sometimes added (4) drawing. Of these, reading and writing and drawing are regarded as useful for the purposes of life in a variety of ways, and gymnastic exercises are thought to infuse courage. Concerning music a doubt may be raised—in our own day most men cultivate it for the sake of pleasure, but originally it was included in education, because nature herself, as has been often said, requires that we should be able, not only to work well, but to use leisure well; for, as I must repeat once again, the first principle of all action is leisure. Both are required, but leisure is better than occupation and is its end; and therefore the question must be asked, what ought we to do when at leisure? Clearly we ought not to be amusing ourselves, for then amusement would be the end of life. But if this is inconceivable, and amusement is needed more amid serious occupations than at other times (for he who is hard at work has need of relaxation, and amusement gives relaxation, whereas occupation is always accompanied with exertion and effort), we should introduce amusements only at suitable times, and they should be our medicines, for the emotion which they create in the soul is a relaxation, and from the pleasure we obtain rest. But leisure of itself gives pleasure and happiness and enjoyment of life, which are experienced, not by the busy man, but by those who have leisure. For he who is occupied has in view some end which he has not attained; but happiness is an end, since all men deem it to be accompanied with pleasure and not with pain. This pleasure, however, is regarded differently by different persons, and varies according to the habit of individuals; the pleasure of the best man is the best, and springs from the noblest sources.

It is clear then that there are branches of learning and education which we must study merely with a view to leisure spent in intellectual activity, and these are to be valued for their own sake; whereas those kinds of knowledge which are useful in business are to be deemed necessary, and exist for the sake of other things. And therefore our fathers admitted music into education, not on the ground either of its necessity or utility, for it is not necessary, nor indeed useful in the same manner as reading and writing, which are useful in money-making, in the management of a household, in the acquisition of knowledge and in political life, nor like drawing, useful for a more correct judgement of the works of artists, nor again like gymnastic, which gives health and strength; for neither of these is to be gained from music. There remains, then, the use of music for intellectual enjoyment in leisure; which is in fact evidently the reason of its introduction, this being one of the ways in which it is thought that a freeman should pass his leisure; as Homer says—

'But he who alone should be called to the pleasant feast',

and afterwards he speaks of others whom he describes as inviting

'The bard who would delight them all'.

And in another place Odysseus says there is no better way of passing life than when men's hearts are merry and

'The banqueters in the hall, sitting in order, hear the voice of the minstrel'.

It is evident, then, that there is a sort of education in which parents should train their sons, not as being useful or necessary, but because it is liberal or noble. Whether this is of one kind only, or of more than one, and if so, what they are, and how they are to be imparted, must hereafter be determined. Thus much we are now in a position to say, that the ancients witness to us; for their opinion may be gathered from the fact that music is one of the received and traditional branches of education. Further, it is clear that children should be instructed in some useful things,—for example, in reading and writing,—not only for their usefulness, but also because many other sorts of knowledge are acquired through them. With a like view they may be taught drawing, not to prevent their making mistakes in their own purchases, or in order that they may not be imposed upon in the buying or selling of articles, but perhaps rather because it makes them judges of the beauty of the human form. To be always seeking after the useful does not become free and exalted souls.

101. Young men have strong passions, and tend to gratify them indiscriminately. Of the bodily desires, it is the sexual by which they are most swayed and in which they show absence of self-control. They are changeable and fickle in their desires, which are violent while they last, but quickly over: their impulses are keen but not deep-rooted, and are like sick people's attacks of hunger and thirst. They are hot-tempered and quick-tempered, and apt to give way to their anger; bad temper often gets the better of them, for owing to their love of honour they cannot bear being slighted, and are indignant if they imagine themselves unfairly treated. While they love honour, they love victory still more; for youth is eager for superiority over others, and victory is one form of this. They love both more than they love money, which indeed they love very little, not having yet learnt what it means to be without it—this is the point of Pittacus' remark about Amphiaraus. They look at the good side rather than the bad, not having yet witnessed many instances of wickedness. They trust others readily, because they

have not yet often been cheated. They are sanguine; nature warms their blood as though with excess of wine; and besides that, they have as yet met with few disappointments. Their lives are mainly spent not in memory but in expectation; for expectation refers to the future, memory to the past, and youth has a long future before it and a short past behind it: on the first day of one's life one has nothing at all to remember, and can only look forward. They are easily cheated, owing to the sanguine disposition just mentioned. Their hot tempers and hopeful dispositions make them more courageous than older men are; the hot temper prevents fear, and the hopeful disposition creates confidence; we cannot feel fear so long as we are feeling angry, and any expectation of good makes us confident. They are shy, accepting the rules of society in which they have been trained, and not yet believing in any other standard of honour. They have exalted notions, because they have not yet been humbled by life or learnt its necessary limitations; moreover, their hopeful disposition makes them think themselves equal to great things —and that means having exalted notions. They would always rather do noble deeds than useful ones: their lives are regulated more by moral feeling than by reasoning; and whereas reasoning leads us to choose what is useful, moral goodness leads us to choose what is noble. They are fonder of their friends, intimates, and companions than older men are, because they like spending their days in the company of others, and have not yet come to value either their friends or anything else by their usefulness to themselves. All their mistakes are in the direction of doing things excessively and vehemently. They disobey Chilon's precept by overdoing everything; they love too much and hate too much, and the same with everything else. They think they know everything, and are always quite sure about it; this, in fact, is why they overdo everything. If they do wrong to others, it is because they mean to insult them, not to do them actual harm. They are ready to pity others, because they think every one an honest man, or anyhow better than he is: they judge their neighbour by their own harmless natures, and so cannot think he deserves to be treated in that way. They are fond of fun and therefore witty, wit being well-bred insolence.

Such, then, is the character of the Young. The character of Elderly Men—men who are past their prime—may be said to be formed for the most part of elements that are the contrary of all these. They have lived many years; they have often been taken in, and often made mistakes; and life on the whole is a bad business. The result is that they are sure about nothing and *under-do* everything. They 'think', but they never 'know'; and because of their hesitation they always add a 'possibly' or a 'perhaps', putting everything this way and nothing .positively. They are cynical; that is, they tend to put the worse construction on everything. Further, their experience makes them distrustful and therefore suspicious of evil. Consequently they neither love warmly nor hate bitterly, but following the hint of Bias they love as though they will some day hate and hate as though they will some day love. They are small-minded, because they have been humbled by life; their desires are set upon nothing more exalted or unusual than what will help them to keep alive. They are not generous, because money is one of the things they must have, and at the same time their experience has taught them how hard it is to get and how easy to lose. They are cowardly, and are always anticipating danger; unlike that of the young,

who are warm-blooded, their temperament is chilly; old
age has paved the way for cowardice; fear is, in fact,
a form of chill. They love life; and all the more when
their last day has come, because the object of all desire is something we have not got, and also because we
desire most strongly that which we need most urgently.
They are too fond of themselves; this is one form
that small-mindedness takes. Because of this, they
guide their lives too much by considerations of what
is useful and too little by what is noble—for the useful is what is good for oneself, and the noble what
is good absolutely. They are not shy, but shameless
rather; caring less for what is noble than for what
is useful, they feel contempt for what people may think
of them. They lack confidence in the future; partly
through experience—for most things go wrong, or anyhow turn out worse than one expects; and partly because of their cowardice. They live by memory rather
than by hope; for what is left to them of life is but
little as compared with the long past; and hope is of
the future, memory of the past. This, again, is the
cause of their loquacity; they are continually talking
of the past, because they enjoy remembering it. Their
fits of anger are sudden but feeble. Their sensual
passions have either altogether gone or have lost their
vigour: consequently they do not feel their passions
much, and their actions are inspired less by what they
do feel than by the love of gain. Hence men at this
time of life are often supposed to have a self-controlled
character; the fact is that their passions have slackened,
and they are slaves to the love of gain. They guide
their lives by reasoning more than by moral feeling;
reasoning being directed to utility and moral feeling
to moral goodness. If they wrong others, they mean

to injure them, not to insult them. Old men may feel
pity, as well as young men, but not for the same reason. Young men feel it out of kindness; old men out
of weakness, imagining that anything that befalls any
one else might easily happen to them, which, as we
saw, is a thought that excites pity. Hence they are
querulous, and not disposed to jesting or laughter—the
love of laughter being the very opposite of querulous-
ness.

Such are the characters of Young Men and Elderly
Men. People always think well of speeches adapted
to, and reflecting, their own character: and we can now
see how to compose our speeches so as to adapt both
them and ourselves to our audiences.

As for Men in their Prime, clearly we shall find that
they have a character between that of the young and
that of the old, free from the extremes of either. They
have neither that excess of confidence which amounts
to rashness, nor too much timidity, but the right amount
of each. They neither trust everybody nor distrust
everybody, but judge people correctly. Their lives
will be guided not by the sole consideration either of
what is noble or of what is useful, but by both; neither
by parsimony nor by prodigality, but by what is fit
and proper. So, too, in regard to anger and desire; they
will be brave as well as temperate, and temperate as
well as brave; these virtues are divided between the
young and the old; the young are brave but intemperate,
the old temperate but cowardly. To put it generally,
all the valuable qualities that youth and age divide
between them are united in the prime of life, while
all their excesses or defects are replaced by moderation and fitness. The body is in its prime from thirty
to five-and-thirty; the mind about forty-nine.

102. It is clear that the general origin of poetry was due to two causes, each of them part of human nature. Imitation is natural to man from childhood, one of his advantages over the lower animals being this, that he is the most imitative creature in the world, and learns at first by imitation. And it is also natural for all to delight in works of imitation. The truth of this second point is shown by experience: though the objects themselves may be painful to see, we delight to view the most realistic representations of them in art, the forms for example of the lowest animals and of dead bodies. The explanation is to be found in a further fact: to be learning something is the greatest of pleasures not only to the philosopher but also to the rest of mankind, however small their capacity for it; the reason of the delight in seeing the picture is that one is at the same time learning—gathering the meaning of things, e.g. that the man there is so-and-so; for if one has not seen the thing before, one's pleasure will not be in the picture as an imitation of it, but will be due to the execution or colouring or some similar cause. Imitation, then, being natural to us—as also the sense of harmony and rhythm, the metres being obviously species of rhythms—it was through their original aptitude, and by a series of improvements for the most part gradual on their first efforts, that they created poetry out of their improvisations.

Poetry, however, soon broke up into two kinds according to the differences of character in the individual poets; for the graver among them would represent noble actions, and those of noble personages; and the meaner sort the actions of the ignoble. The latter class produced invectives at first, just as others did hymns and panegyrics. We know of no such poem by any of the pre-Homeric poets, though there were probably many such writers among them; instances, however, may be found from Homer downwards, e.g. his *Margites,* and the similar poems of others. In this poetry of invective its natural fitness brought an iambic metre into use; hence our present term 'iambic', because it was the metre of their 'iambs' or invectives against one another. The result was that the old poets became some of them writers of heroic and others of iambic verse. Homer's position, however, is peculiar: just as he was in the serious style the poet of poets, standing alone not only through the literary excellence, but also through the dramatic character of his imitations, so too he was the first to outline for us the general forms of Comedy by producing not a dramatic invective, but a dramatic picture of the Ridiculous; his *Margites* in fact stands in the same relation to our comedies as the *Iliad* and *Odyssey* to our tragedies. As soon, however, as Tragedy and Comedy appeared in the field, those naturally drawn to the one line of poetry became writers of comedies instead of iambs, and those naturally drawn to the other, writers of tragedies instead of epics, because these new modes of art were grander and of more esteem than the old.

If it be asked whether Tragedy is now all that it need be in its formative elements, to consider that, and decide it theoretically and in relation to the theatres, is a matter for another inquiry.

It certainly began in improvisations—as did also Comedy; the one originating with the authors of the Dithyramb, the other with those of the phallic songs, which still survive as institutions in many of our cities. And its advance after that was little by little, through their improving on whatever they had before them at each stage. It was in fact only after a long series of changes that the movement of Tragedy stopped on its attaining to its natural form. (1) The number of actors was first increased to two by Aeschylus, who curtailed the business of the Chorus, and made the dialogue, or spoken portion, take the leading part in the play. (2) A third actor and scenery were due to Sophocles. (3) Tragedy acquired also its magnitude. Discarding short stories and a ludicrous diction, through its passing out of its satyric stage, it assumed, though only at a late point in its progress, a tone of dignity; and its metre changed then from trochaic to iambic. The reason for their original use of the trochaic tetrameter was that their poetry was satyric and more connected with dancing than it now is. As soon, however, as a spoken part came in, nature herself found the appropriate metre. The iambic, we know, is the most speakable of metres, as is shown by the fact that we very often fall into it in conversation, whereas we rarely talk hexameters, and only when we depart from the speaking tone of voice. (4) Another change was a plurality of episodes or acts. As for the remaining matters, the superadded embellishments and the account of their introduction, these must be taken as said, as it would probably be a long piece of work to go through the details.

As for Comedy, it is (as has been observed) an imitation of men worse than the average; worse, however, not as regards any and every sort of fault, but only as regards one particular kind, the Ridiculous, which is a species of the Ugly. The Ridiculous may be defined as a mistake or deformity not productive of pain or harm to others; the mask, for instance, that excites laughter, is something ugly and distorted without causing pain.

Though the successive changes in Tragedy and their authors are not unknown, we cannot say the same of Comedy; its early stages passed unnoticed, because it was not as yet taken up in a serious way. It was only at a late point in its progress that a chorus of comedians was officially granted by the archon; they used to be mere volunteers. It had also already certain definite forms at the time when the record of those termed comic poets begins. Who it was who supplied it with masks, or prologues, or a plurality of actors and the like, has remained unknown. The invented Fable, or Plot, however, originated in Sicily, with Epicharmus and Phormis; of Athenian poets Crates was the first to drop the Comedy of invective and frame stories of a general non-personal nature, in other words, Fables or Plots.

Epic poetry, then, has been seen to agree with Tragedy to this extent, that of being an imitation of serious subjects in a grand kind of verse. It differs from it, however, (1) in that it is in one kind of verse and in narrative form; and (2) in its length—which is due to its action having no fixed limit of time, whereas Tragedy endeavours to keep as far as possible within a single circuit of the sun, or something near that. This, I say, is another point of difference between them, though at first the practice in this respect was just the same in tragedies as in epic poems. They differ also (3) in their constituents, some being common to both and others peculiar to Tragedy—hence a judge of good and bad in Tragedy is a judge of that in epic poetry also. All the parts of an epic are included in Tragedy; but those of Tragedy are not all of them to be found in the Epic.

103. Let us proceed now to the discussion of Tragedy; before doing so, however, we must gather up the definition resulting from what has been said. A tragedy, then, is the imitation of an action that is serious and also, as having magnitude, complete in itself; in lan-

guage with pleasurable accessories, each kind brought in separately in the parts of the work; in a dramatic, not in a narrative form; with incidents arousing pity and fear, wherewith to accomplish its catharsis of such emotions. Here by 'language with pleasurable accessories' I mean that with rhythm and harmony or song superadded; and by 'the kinds separately' I mean that some portions are worked out with verse only, and others in turn with song.

I. As they act the stories, it follows that in the first place the Spectacle (or stage-appearance of the actors) must be some part of the whole; and in the second Melody and Diction, these two being the means of their imitation. Here by 'Diction' I mean merely this, the composition of the verses; and by 'Melody', what is too completely understood to require explanation. But further: the subject represented also is an action; and the action involves agents, who must necessarily have their distinctive qualities both of character and thought, since it is from these that we ascribe certain qualities to their actions. There are in the natural order of things, therefore, two causes, Thought and Character, of their actions, and consequently of their success or failure in their lives. Now the action (that which was done) is represented in the play by the Fable or Plot. The Fable, in our present sense of the term, is simply this, the combination of the incidents, or things done in the story; whereas Character is what makes us ascribe certain moral qualities to the agents; and Thought is shown in all they say when proving a particular point or, it may be, enunciating a general truth. There are six parts consequently of every tragedy, as a whole (that is) of such or such quality, viz. a Fable or Plot, Characters, Diction, Thought, Spectacle, and Melody; two of them arising from the means, one from the manner, and three from the objects of the dramatic imitation; and there is nothing else besides these six. Of these, its formative elements, then, not a few of the dramatists have made due use, as every play, one may say, admits of Spectacle, Character, Fable, Diction, Melody, and Thought.

II. The most important of the six is the combination of the incidents of the story. Tragedy is essentially an imitation not of persons but of action and life, of happiness and misery. All human happiness or misery takes the form of action; the end for which we live is a certain kind of activity, not a quality. Character gives us qualities, but it is in our actions —what we do—that we are happy or the reverse. In a play accordingly they do not act in order to portray the Characters; they include the Characters for the sake of the action. So that it is the action in it, i.e. its Fable or Plot, that is the end and purpose of the tragedy; and the end is everywhere the chief thing. Besides this, a tragedy is impossible without action, but there may be one without Character. The tragedies of most of the moderns are characterless—a defect common among poets of all kinds, and with its counterpart in painting in Zeuxis as compared with Polygnotus; for whereas the latter is strong in character, the work of Zeuxis is devoid of it. And again: one may string together a series of characteristic speeches of the utmost finish as regards Diction and Thought, and yet fail to produce the true tragic effect; but one will have much better success with a tragedy which, however inferior in these respects, has a Plot, a combination of incidents, in it. And again: the most powerful elements of attraction in Tragedy, the Peripeties and Discoveries, are parts of the Plot. A further proof is in the fact that beginners succeed earlier with the Diction and Characters than with the construction of a story; and the same may be said of nearly all the early dramatists. We maintain, therefore, that the first essential, the life and soul, so to speak, of Tragedy is the Plot; and that the Characters come second—compare the parallel in painting, where the most beautiful colours laid on without order will not give one the same pleasure as a simple black-and-white sketch of a portrait. We maintain that Tragedy is primarily an imitation of action, and that it is mainly for the sake of the action that it imitates the personal agents. Third comes the element of Thought, i.e. the power of saying whatever can be said, or what is appropriate to the occasion. This is what, in the speeches in Tragedy, falls under the arts of Politics and Rhetoric; for the older poets make their personages discourse like statesmen, and the moderns like rhetoricians. One must not confuse it with Character. Character in a play is that which reveals the moral purpose of the agents, i.e. the sort of thing they seek or avoid, where that is not obvious—hence there is no room for Character in a speech on a purely indifferent subject. Thought, on the other hand, is shown in all they say when proving or disproving some particular point, or enunciating some universal proposition. Fourth among the literary elements is the Diction of the personages, i.e., as before explained, the expression of their thoughts in words, which is practically the same thing with verse as with prose. As for the two remaining parts, the Melody is the greatest of the pleasurable accessories of Tragedy. The Spectacle, though an attraction, is the least artistic of all the parts, and has least to do with the art of poetry. The tragic effect is quite possible without a public performance and actors; and besides, the getting-up of the Spectacle is more a matter for the costumier than the poet.

Having thus distinguished the parts, let us now consider the proper construction of the Fable or Plot, as that is at once the first and the most important thing in Tragedy. We have laid it down that a tragedy is an imitation of an action that is complete in itself, as a whole of some magnitude; for a whole may be of no magnitude to speak of. Now a whole is that which has beginning, middle, and end. A beginning is that which is not itself necessarily after anything else, and which has naturally something else after it; an end is that which is naturally after something itself, either as its necessary or usual consequent, and with nothing else after it; and a middle, that which is by nature after one thing and has also another after it. A well-constructed Plot, therefore, cannot either begin or end at any point one likes; beginning and end in it must be of the forms just described. Again: to be beautiful, a living creature, and every whole made up of parts, must not only present a certain order in its arrangement of parts, but also be of certain definite magnitude. Beauty is a matter of size and order, and therefore impossible either (1) in a very minute creature, since our perception becomes indistinct as it approaches instantaneity; or (2) in a creature of vast size—one, say, 1,000 miles long—as in that case, instead of the object being seen all at once, the unity and wholeness of it is lost to the beholder. Just in the same way, then, as a beautiful whole made up of parts, or a beautiful living creature, must be of some size, but a size to be taken in by the eye, so a story or Plot must be of some length, but of a length to be taken in by the memory. As for the limit of its length, so far as that is relative to public performances and spectators, it does not fall within the theory of poetry. If they had to perform a hundred tragedies, they would be timed by water-clocks, as they are said to have been at one period. The limit, however, set by the actual nature of the thing is this: the longer the story, consistently with its being comprehensible as a whole, the finer it is by reason of its magnitude. As a rough general formula, 'a length which allows of the hero passing by a series of probable or necessary stages from misfortune to happiness, or from happiness to misfortune', may suffice as a limit for the magnitude of the story.

The Unity of a Plot does not consist, as some suppose, in its having one man as its subject. An infinity of things befall that one man, some of which it is impossible to reduce to unity; and in like manner there are many actions of one man which cannot be made to form one action. One sees, therefore, the mistake of all the poets who have written a *Heracleid,* a *Theseid,* or similar poems; they suppose that, because Heracles was one man, the story also of Heracles must be one story. Homer, however, evidently understood this point quite well, whether by art or instinct, just in the same way as he excels the rest in every other respect. In writing an *Odyssey,* he did not make the poem cover all that ever befell his hero—it befell him, for instance, to get wounded on Parnassus and also to feign madness at the time of the call to arms, but the two incidents had no necessary or probable connexion with one another—instead of doing that, he took as the subject of the *Odyssey,* as also of the *Iliad,* an action with a Unity of the kind we are describing. The truth is that, just as in the other imitative arts one imitation is always of one thing, so in poetry the story, as an imitation of action, must represent one action, a com-

plete whole, with its several incidents so closely connected that the transposal or withdrawal of any one
of them will disjoin and dislocate the whole. For
that which makes no perceptible difference by its presence or absence is no real part of the whole.

From what we have said it will be seen that the poet's
function is to describe, not the thing that has happened,
but a kind of thing that might happen, i.e. what is possible as being probable or necessary. The distinction
between historian and poet is not in the one writing
prose and the other verse—you might put the work of
Herodotus into verse, and it would still be a species
of history; it consists really in this, that the one describes the thing that has been, and the other a kind
of thing that might be. Hence poetry is something more
philosophic and of graver import than history, since
its statements are of the nature rather of universals,
whereas those of history are singulars. By a universal
statement I mean one as to what such or such a kind
of man will probably or necessarily say or do—which
is the aim of poetry, though it affixes proper names
to the characters; by a singular statement, one as to
what, say, Alcibiades did or had done to him. In
Comedy this has become clear by this time; it is only
when their plot is already made up of probable incidents that they give it a basis of proper names, choosing for the purpose any names that may occur to them,
instead of writing like the old iambic poets about particular persons. In Tragedy, however, they still adhere to the historic names; and for this reason: what
convinces is the possible; now whereas we are not yet
sure as to the possibility of that which has not happened, that which has happened is manifestly possible,
else it would not have come to pass. Nevertheless even
in Tragedy there are some plays with but one or two

known names in them, the rest being inventions; and there are some without a single known name, e.g. Agathon's *Antheus,* in which both incidents and names are of the poet's invention; and it is no less delightful on that account. So that one must not aim at a rigid adherence to the traditional stories on which tragedies are based. It would be absurd, in fact, to do so, as even the known stories are only known to a few, though they are a delight none the less to all.

It is evident from the above that the poet must be more the poet of his stories or Plots than of his verses, inasmuch as he is a poet by virtue of the imitative element in his work, and it is actions that he imitates. And if he should come to take a subject from actual history, he is none the less a poet for that; since some historic occurrences may very well be in the probable and possible order of things; and it is in that aspect of them that he is their poet.

Of simple Plots and actions the episodic are the worst. I call a Plot episodic when there is neither probability nor necessity in the sequence of its episodes. Actions of this sort bad poets construct through their own fault, and good ones on account of the players. His work being for public performance, a good poet often stretches out a Plot beyond its capabilities, and is thus obliged to twist the sequence of incident.

Tragedy, however, is an imitation not only of a complete action, but also of incidents arousing pity and fear. Such incidents have the very greatest effect on the mind when they occur unexpectedly and at the same time in consequence of one another; there is more of the marvellous in them then than if they happened of themselves or by mere chance. Even matters of chance seem most marvellous if there is an appearance of design as it were in them; as for instance the statue

of Mitys at Argos killed the author of Mitys' death
by falling down on him when a looker-on at a public
spectacle; for incidents like that we think to be not
without a meaning. A plot, therefore, of this sort is
necessarily finer than others.

Plots are either simple or complex, since the actions
they represent are naturally of this twofold description.
The action, proceeding in the way defined, as one continuous whole, I call simple, when the change in the
hero's fortunes takes place without Peripety or Discovery; and complex, when it involves one or the other,
or both. These should each of them arise out of the
structure of the Plot itself, so as to be the consequence,
necessary or probable, of the antecedents. There is
a great difference between a thing happening *propter
hoc* and *post hoc*.

A Peripety is the change of the kind described from
one state of things within the play to its opposite, and
that too in the way we are saying, in the probable or
necessary sequence of events; as it is for instance in
Oedipus: here the opposite state of things is produced
by the Messenger, who, coming to gladden Oedipus
and to remove his fears as to his mother, reveals the
secret of his birth. And in *Lynceus:* just as he is being
led off for execution, with Danaus at his side to put
him to death, the incidents preceding this bring it
about that he is saved and Danaus put to death. A
Discovery is, as the very word implies, a change from
ignorance to knowledge, and thus to either love or hate,
in the personages marked for good or evil fortune.
The finest form of Discovery is one attended by Peripeties, like that which goes with the Discovery in *Oedipus*.
There are no doubt other forms of it; what we have
said may happen in a way in reference to inanimate
things, even things of a very casual kind; and it is also

possible to discover whether some one has done or not
done something. But the form most directly connected
with the Plot and the action of the piece is the first-
mentioned. This, with a Peripety, will arouse either
pity or fear—actions of that nature being what Tragedy
is assumed to represent; and it will also serve to bring
about the happy or unhappy ending. The Discovery,
then, being of persons, it may be that of one party
only to the other, the latter being already known; or
both the parties may have to discover themselves.
Iphigenia, for instance, was discovered to Orestes by
sending the letter; and another Discovery was required
to reveal him to Iphigenia.

Two parts of the Plot, then, Peripety and Discovery, are on matters of this sort. A third part is Suffer-
ing; which we may define as an action of a destructive
or painful nature, such as murders on the stage, tor-
tures, woundings, and the like. The other two have
been already explained. . . .

The next points after what we have said above will
be these: (1) What is the poet to aim at, and what is
he to avoid, in constructing his Plots? and (2) What
are the conditions on which the tragic effect depends?

We assume that, for the finest form of Tragedy, the
Plot must be not simple but complex; and further, that
it must imitate actions arousing fear and pity, since
that is the distinctive function of this kind of imitation. It follows, therefore, that there are three forms
of Plot to be avoided. (1) A good man must not be
seen passing from happiness to misery, or (2) a bad
man from misery to happiness. The first situation is
not fear-inspiring or piteous, but simply odious to us.
The second is the most untragic that can be; it has no
one of the requisites of Tragedy; it does not appeal
either to the human feeling in us, or to our pity, or

to our fears. Nor, on the other hand, should (3) an extremely bad man be seen falling from happiness into misery. Such a story may arouse the human feeling in us, but it will not move us to either pity or fear; pity is occasioned by undeserved misfortune, and fear by that of one like ourselves; so that there will be nothing either piteous or fear-inspiring in the situation. There remains, then, the intermediate kind of personage, a man not pre-eminently virtuous and just, whose misfortune, however, is brought upon him not by vice and depravity but by some error of judgment, of the number of those in the enjoyment of great reputation and prosperity; e.g. Oedipus, Thyestes, and the men of note of similar families. The perfect Plot, accordingly, must have a single, and not (as some tell us) a double issue; the change in the hero's fortunes must be not from misery to happiness, but on the contrary from happiness to misery; and the cause of it must lie not in any depravity, but in some great error on his part; the man himself being either such as we have described, or better, not worse, than that.

Fact also confirms our theory. Though the poets began by accepting any tragic story that came to hand, in these days the finest tragedies are always on the story of some few houses, on that of Alcmeon, Oedipus, Orestes, Meleager, Thyestes, Telephus, or any others that may have been involved, as either agents or sufferers, in some deed of horror. The theoretically best tragedy, then, has a Plot of this description. The critics, therefore, are wrong who blame Euripides for taking this line in his tragedies, and giving many of them an unhappy ending. It is, as we have said, the right line to take. The best proof is this: on the stage, and in the public performances, such plays, properly worked out, are seen to be the most truly tragic; and Euripides, even if his execution be faulty in every other point, is seen to be nevertheless the most tragic certainly of the dramatists. After this comes the construction of Plot which some rank first, one with a double story (like the *Odyssey*) and an opposite issue for the good and the bad personages. It is ranked as first only through the weakness of the audiences; the poets merely follow their public, writing as its wishes dictates. But the pleasure here is not that of Tragedy. It belongs rather to Comedy, where the bitterest enemies in the piece (e.g. Orestes and Aegisthus) walk off good friends at the end, with no slaying of any one by any one.

The tragic fear and pity may be aroused by the Spectacle; but they may also be aroused by the very structure and incidents of the play—which is the better way and shows the better poet. The Plot in fact should be so framed that, even without seeing the things take place, he who simply hears the account of them shall be filled with horror and pity at the incidents; which is just the effect that the mere recital of the story in *Oedipus* would have on one. . . .

The Dénouement should arise out of the plot itself, and not depend on a stage-artifice, as in *Medea,* or in the story of the (arrested) departure of the Greeks in the *Iliad.* The artifice must be reserved for matters outside the play—for past events beyond human knowledge, or events yet to come, which require to be foretold or announced; since it is the privilege of the Gods to know everything. There should be nothing improbable among the actual incidents. If it be unavoidable, however, it should be outside the tragedy, like the improbability in the *Oedipus* of Sophocles. But to return to the Characters. As Tragedy is an imitation of personages better than the ordinary man, we in our way should follow the example of good portrait-painters, who reproduce the distinctive features of a man, and at the same time, without losing the likeness, make him handsomer than he is. The poet in like manner, in portraying men quick or slow to anger, or with similar infirmities of character, must know how to represent them as such, and at the same time as good men, as Agathon and Homer have represented Achilles.

GLOSSARY OF CHIEF TERMS

GREEK-ENGLISH

'Αγαθόν (*agathon*) good.

'Αδιόριστος (*adioristos*), indefinite (used of judgment).

Αἴσθησις (*aisthesis*), perception, sensation.

Αἰτία, Αἴτιον (*aitia, aition*), cause.

'Ακίνητος (*akinetos*), unmovable, unchangeable.

Ἄκρον (*akron*), extreme, term (in syllogism).

'Αλλοίωσις (*alloiōsis*), change of quality, alteration.

Ἄμεσος (*amesos*), immediate.

'Ανάγκη (*ananke*), necessity.

'Αναλογία (*analogia*), proportion.

'Αντίθεσις (*antithesis*), opposition.

'Αντικείμενον (*antikeimenon*), opposite.

'Αντίφασις (*antiphasis*), contradiction.

'Αόριστος (*aoristos*), infinite (used of noun or verb).

Ἄπειρος (*apeiros*), infinite.

'Απλῶς (*haplōs*), without qualification.

'Απόδειξις (*apodeixis*), demonstration.

'Απόφασις (*apophasis*), negation.

'Αρετή (*aretē*), virtue, excellence.

'Αρχή (*archē*), beginning, starting point, originative source,
first principle, basic truth.

Ἄτομος (*atomos*) indivisible.

Αὔξησις (*auxēsis*), increase of size.

Αὐτόματος (*automatos*), fortuitous, spontaneous.

'Αφαίρεσις (*aphairesis*), abstraction.

'Αχώριστος (*achōristos*), inseparable, incapable of existing
apart.

Βούλευσις (*bouleusis*), deliberation.

Βούλησις (*boulesis*), (rational) wish.

Γένεσις (*genesis*), coming to be, generation, production.

Γένος (*genos*), genus, class.

Διαίρεσις (*diairesis*), division.

Διάνοια (*dianoia*), understanding.

Διαφορά (*diaphora*), differentia.

Διότι, τό (*to dioti*), the why, the reason.

Δύναμις (*dunamis*), power, potency, potentiality.

Εἶδος (*eidos*), form, species.

Εἶναι (*einai*), to be. ὄν (*on*), being, τί ἐστι, τί ἦν εἶναι (*ti esti, ti ēn einai*), essence.

Ἐναντίος (*enantios*), contrary.

Ἐνδέχεσθαι (*endechesthai*), to be possible. Ἐνδεχόμενον ἄλλως ἔχειν (*endechomenon allōs echein*), contingent, variable.

Ἐνέργεια (*energeia*), activity, actuality.

Ἐντελέχεια (*entelecheia*), actuality, complete reality.

Ἕξις (*hexis*), (permanent) state, habit.

Ἐπαγωγή (*epagogē*), induction.

Ἐπιθυμία (*epithumia*), appetite.

Ἐπιστήμη (*epistēmē*), knowledge, science.

Ἔσχατος (*eschatos*), extreme, individual.

Ἧι (*he*), qua, in so far as.

Θεωρία (*theōria*), theory, contemplation, speculation.

Θρεπτικός (*threptikos*), nutritive.

Ἴδιον (*idion*), property

Καθ' αὑτό (*kath' hauto*), *per se,* essentially.

Καθ' ἕκαστον (*kath' hekaston*) individual.

Κάθαρσις (*katharsis*), purgation.

Καθόλου (*katholou*), universal.

Κακία (*kakia*), vice.

Κατάφασις (*kataphasis*), affirmation.

Κατηγορία (*katēgoria*), predicate, category.

Κίνησις (*kinēsis*), movement, change.

Λογικός (*logikos*), linguistic, verbal, abstract.

Λογιστικός (*logistikos*), calculative.

Λόγος (*logos*), word, account, definition, formula, rational principle, rule, ratio.

Ἐν μέρει, κατὰ μέρος (*en merei, kata meros*), particular.

Μέσον (*meson*), middle term.

Μεσότης (*mesotēs*), mean.

Μεταβολή (*metabolē*), change.

Μορφή (*morphē*), shape, form.

Νόησις (*noēsis*), (*intuitive*) thinking.

Νοῦς (*nous*), (intuitive) reason.

'Ομοιομερής (*homoiomerēs*), homogeneous.

'Ομώνυμος (*homōnumos*), ambiguous, equivocal。

"Ορεξις (*orexis*), desire (in general).

'Ορισμός (*horismos*), definition.

"Ορος (*horos*), term.

"Οτι, τὸ (*to hoti*), the "that", the fact.

Οὗ ἕνεκα (*hou heneka*), end, final cause.

Οὐσία (*ousia*) substance, essence.

Παθητικός (*pathetikos*), passive.

Παράδειγμα (*paradeigma*), example.

Ποίησις (*poiēsis*), making, production.

Ποιόν, ποιότης (*poion, poiotēs*), quality.

Ποσόν (*poson*), quantity.

Πρᾶξις (*prāxis*), doing, action, conduct.

Προαίρεσις (*proairesis*), choice, purpose.

Πρός τι (*pros ti*), relative, relation.

Πρότασις (*protasis*), premise.

Πρῶτος (*prōtos*), first, primary, immediate, direct.

Σημεῖον (*sēmeion*), sign.

Σοφία (*sophia*), (philosophic) wisdom, philosophy。

Στέρησις (*sterēsis*), privation.

Στοιχεῖον (*stoicheion*), element.

Συλλογισμός (*sullogismos*), syllogism.

Συμβεβηκός (*sumbebēkos*), accident, concomitant.

Συμπέρασμα (*sumperasma*), conclusion.

Συμπλοκή (*sumplokē*), connexion.

Συνεχής (*sunechēs*), continuous.

Συνώνυμος (*sunōnumos*), unambiguous, univocal.

Σχῆμα (*schēma*), figure (e.g. of syllogism).

Τέλος (*telos*), end.

Τέχνη (*technē*), art.

Τόδε τι (*tode ti*), a "this," an individual.

Τόπος (*topos*), place.

Τρόπος (*tropos*), mood (of syllogism).

Τύχη (*tuchē*), chance, luck.

Ὕλη (*hulē*), matter.
Ὑποκείμενον (*hupokeimenon*), substratum, subject.
Φαντασία (*phantasia*), imagination.
Φορά (*phora*), locomotion.
Φρόνησις (*phronēsis*), practical wisdom.
Φυσική (*phusikē*), natural philosophy.
Φύσις (*phusis*), nature.
Χρόνος (*chronos*), time.
Χωριστός (*chōristos*), separable, capable of existing apart.
Ψυχή (*psuchē*), soul, vital principle.

ENGLISH–GREEK

Abstract. v. *Linguistic.*
Abstraction, Ἀφαίρεσις (*aphairesis*).
Accident, Συμβεβηκός (*sumbebēkos*).
Account. v. *Word.*
Action. v. *Doing.*
Activity, Ἐνέργεια (*energeia*).
Actuality, Ἐντελέχεια (*entelecheia*). v. *Activity.*
Affirmation, Κατάφασις (*kataphasis*).
Alteration. v. *Change of quality.*
Ambiguous, Ὁμώνυμος (*homōnumos*).
Appetite, Ἐπιθυμία (*epithumia*).
Art, Τέχνη (*technē*).
Basic truth. v. *Beginning.*
Be, Εἶναι (*einai*); Being, ὄν (*on*).
Beginning, Ἀρχή (*archē*).
Calculative, Λογιστικός (*logistikos*).
Capable of existing apart. v. *Separable.*
Category. v. *Predicate.*
Cause, Αἰτία, Αἴτιον (*aitia, aition*).
Chance, Τύχη (*tuchē*).
Change, Μεταβολή (*metabolē*). v. *Movement.*
Change of quality, Ἀλλοίωσις (*alloiōsis*). v. *Alteration.*
Choice, Προαίρεσις (*proairesis*).
City, Πόλις (*polis*).
Class. v. *Genus.*

Coming to be, Γένεσις (*genesis*).
Conclusion, Συμπέρασμα (*sumperasma*).
Concomitant. v. *Accident*.
Conduct. v. *Doing*.
Connexion, Συμπλοκή (*sumplokē*).
Constitution, Πολιτεία (*politeia*).
Contemplation. v. *Theory*.
Contingent, 'Ενδεχόμενον ἄλλως ἔχειν (*endechomenon allōs echein*).
Continuous, Συνεχής (*sunechēs*).
Contradiction, 'Αντίφασις (*antiphasis*).
Contrary, 'Εναντίος (*enantios*).
Definition, 'Ορισμός (*horismos*). v. *Word*.
Deliberation, Βούλευσις (*bouleusis*).
Demonstration, 'Απόδειξις (*apodeixis*).
Desire (in general), "Ορεξις (*orexis*).
Differentia, Διαφορά (*diaphora*).
Direct. v. *First*.
Division, Διαίρεσις (*diairesis*).
Doing, Πρᾶξις (*prāxis*).
Element, Στοιχεῖον (*stoicheion*).
End, Τέλος, Οὗ ἕνεκα (*telos, hou heneka*).
Equivocal. v. *Ambiguous*.
Essence, Τί ἐστι, τί ἦν εἶναι (*ti esti, ti ēn einai*).
Essentially. v *Per se*.
Example, Παράδειγμα (*paradeigma*).
Excellence. v. *Virtue*.
Extreme, "Ακρον, "Εσχατος (*akron, eschatos*).
Fact. v. "*That*."
Figure (e.g. of syllogism), Σχῆμα (*schēma*).
Final cause. v. *End*.
First, Πρῶτος (*prōtos*).
First principle. v. *Beginning*.
Form, Εἶδος (*eidos*). v. *Shape*.
Formula. v. *Word*.
Fortuitous, Αὐτόματος (*automatos*).
Generation. v. *Coming to be*.
Genus, Γένος (*genos*).
Good, 'Αγαθόν (*agathon*).
Habit. v. *State*.

Homogeneous, 'Ομοιομερής (*homoiomerēs*).

Imagination, Φαντασία (*phantasia*).

Immediate, "Αμεσος (*amesos*).

In so far as. v. *Qua.*

Incapable of existing apart. v. *Inseparable.*

Increase of size, Αὔξησις (*auxēsis*).

Indefinite (used of judgment), 'Αδιόριστος (*adioristos*).

Individual, Καθ' ἕκαστον (*kath' hekaston*). v. *Extreme, "This."*

Indivisible, "Ατομος (*atomos*).

Induction, 'Επαγωγή (*epagogē*).

Infinite, "Απειρος (*apeiros*); (used of noun or verb) 'Αόριστος (*aoristos*).

Inseparable, 'Αχώριστος (*achōristos*).

Knowledge, 'Επιστήμη (*epistēmē*).

Law, νόμος (*nomos*).

Linguistic, Λογικός (*logikos*).

Locomotion, Φορά (*phora*).

Luck. v. *Chance.*

Making, Ποίησις (*poiēsis*).

Matter, "Υλη (*hulē*)

Mean, Μεσότης (*mesotēs*).

Middle term, Μέσον (*meson*).

Mood (of syllogism), Τρόπος (*tropos*).

Movement, Κίνησις (*kinēsis*).

Natural philosophy, Φυσική (*phusikē*).

Nature, Φύσις (*phusis*).

Necessity, 'Ανάγκη (*anankē*).

Negation, 'Απόφασις (*apophasis*).

Nutritive, Θρεπτικός (*threptikos*).

Opposite, 'Αντικείμενον (*antikeimenon*).

Opposition, 'Αντίθεσις (*antithesis*).

Originative source. v. *Beginning.*

Particular, 'Εν μέρει, κατὰ μέρος (*en merei, kata meros*).

Passive, Παθητικός (*pathētikos*).

Per se, Καθ' αὑτό (*kath' hauto*).

Perception, Αἴσθησις (*aisthēsis*).

Philosophy. v. *Wisdom.*

Place, Τόπος (*topos*).

Possible, to be, 'Ενδέχεσθαι (*endechesthai*).

Potency, potentiality, power, Δύναμις (dunamis).
Predicate, Κατηγορία (katēgoria).
Premiss, Πρότασις (protasis).
Pride, Μεγαλοψυχία (megalopsuchia).
Primary. v. First.
Privation, Στέρησις (sterēsis)
Production. v. Coming to be, Making.
Property, "Ιδιον (idion).
Proportion, 'Αναλογία (analogia).
Purgation, Κάθαρσις (katharsis).
Purpose. v. Choice.
Qua, 'Ηι (hē).
Qualification, without, 'Απλῶς (haplōs).
Quality, Ποιόν, ποιότης (poion, poiotēs).
Quantity, Ποσόν (poson).
Ratio, rational principle. v. Word.
Reality (complete). v. Actuality.
Reason, the. v. Why.
Reason (intuitive), Νοῦς (nous).
Relation, relative, Πρός τι (pros ti).
Rule. v. Word.
Science. v. Knowledge.
Sensation. v. Perception.
Separable, Χωριστός (chōristos).
Shape, Μορφή (morphē).
Sign, Σημεῖον (sēmeion).
Soul, Ψυχή (psuchē).
Species. v. Form.
Speculation. v. Theory.
Spontaneous. v. Fortuitous.
Starting point. v. Beginning.
State (permanent), "Εξις (hexis); (political) v. City.
Subject. v. Substratum.
Substance, Οὐσία (ousia).
Substratum, 'Υποκείμενον (hupokeimenon).
Syllogism, Συλλογισμός (sullogismos).
Term (in syllogism), "Ορος (horos). v. Extreme.
"That," the, "Οτι, τὸ (to hoti).
Theory, Θεωρία (theōria).

Thinking, Νόησις (*noēsis*).

"This," a, Τόδε τι (*tode ti*).

Time, Χρόνος (*chronos*).

Unambiguous, Συνώνυμος (*sunōnumos*).

Unchangeable. v. *Unmovable*.

Understanding, Διάνοια (*dianoia*).

Universal, Καθόλου (*katholou*).

Univocal. v. *Unambiguous*.

Unmovable, 'Ακίνητος (*akinētos*).

Variable. v. *Contingent*.

Verbal. v. *Linguistic*.

Vice, Κακία (*kakia*).

Virtue, 'Αρετή (*aretē*).

Vital principle. v. *Soul*.

Why, the, Διότι, τὸ (*to dioti*).

Wisdom (philosophic), Σοφία (*sophia*); (practical), Φρόνησις (*phro-nēsis*).

Wish (rational), Βούλησις (*boulēsis*).

Word, Λόγος (*logos*).

INDEX

Accident, 15, 17.

Achilles, 97–8, 343.

Actuality, ix, 61, 79, 80, 81–3, 106–7, 109, 137, 189, 200, 205, 213–4.

Aegisthus, 342.

Aeschylus, 241, 330.

Affirmation, 10–11.

Agathon, 338, 343.

Ages of Man, the Three, 323–8.

Alcmeon, 341.

All, the, 84–5, 121–2.

Ambition, 235–6.

Amphiaraus, 323.

Analogy, 82.

Anaxagoras, 48, 107, 132, 182, 212, 213.

Antheus, 338.

Appetite, 242–3.

Argos, 339.

Aristocracy, 303, 307.

Aristotle, comparison with Plato, vi–ix; knowledge of mathematics, vii–ix; of biology, ix–xi; failure in physics and chemistry, xii; "an orderly mind," xii–xiv; his works and development, xiv–xxvi.

Arrow, the Flying, 97–8.

Art, 39, 70–3, 118–9, 159–62, 166–7, 189–91, 233, 261, 319, 328–43.

Association of Ideas, 215–18.

Astronomy, xii, 105–18, 124–37, 175.

Atarneus, 301.

Atoms, 131.

Autophradates, 301.

Axiom, 27.

Basic Truth, 27–9, 29–31, 35–8.

Batrachus, 153.

Beauty, 110, 312, 335.

Becoming, vii, 70–74, 101, 137, 196. 270 (*and see* Generation).

Bees, 153–9.

Beginning of philosophy, 43.

Being, vii, 53–4, 59–61, 80–81, 137, 196, 222.

Bias, 325.

Biology, ix, x, xi, 175–8.

Body, 121, 124–6, 199–207 (*and see* Substance).

Calliphus, 113.

Case, T., xv.

Categories, vii, xiii, xxii, 3, 60, 64, 68, 70, 87.

Categories, xvii, xxii, xxiii, 1–7.

Catharsis, 332.

Cause, 25, 32–4, 40, 42, 44–5, 49–52, 56–9, 106–18, 178–80.

Celts, 249.

Chance, 119–20, 162, 167.

Change, ix, 86–7, 99–100, 118, 122 (*and see* Movement).

Chaos, 107.

Characters (of drama), 332–4, 342–3.

Charondas, 286.

353